FORUM BOOKS

*General Editor* Martin E. Marty

*Other Forum Books published by SCM Press*

CONTEMPORARY RELIGIOUS THINKERS
From Idealist Metaphysicians to Existential Theologians
*edited by John Macquarrie*

OLD TESTAMENT ISSUES
*edited by Samuel Sandmel*

ON BEING RESPONSIBLE
Issues in Personal Ethics
*edited by James M. Gustafson and James T. Laney*

PHENOMENOLOGY OF RELIGION
Eight Modern Descriptions of the Essence of Religion
*edited by Joseph Dabney Bettis*

SCIENCE AND RELIGION
New Perspectives on the Dialogue
*edited by Ian G. Barbour*

SOCIAL ETHICS
Issues in Ethics and Society
*edited by Gibson Winter*

THE THEOLOGIAN AT WORK
A Common Search for Religious Understanding
*edited by A. Roy Eckardt*

# Attitudes Toward Other Religions

## Some Christian Interpretations

*edited by*
*Owen C. Thomas*

**SCM PRESS LTD**
**LONDON**

*1. Christianity - and other religions*

SBN 334 00057 2

© Owen C. Thomas 1969

First published 1969
by SCM Press Ltd
56 Bloomsbury Street London WC1

Printed in Great Britain by
Richard Clay (The Chaucer Press) Ltd
Bungay, Suffolk

To
Frances Arnold Thomas (1885–1967)
who dedicated her life to world
peace and understanding

# CONTENTS

*Foreword by Martin E. Marty, General Editor*                     xi

INTRODUCTION

  1 The Problem of World Community                                1
  2 Factors Determining the Relations Among the
     Religions                                                     4
  3 The Encounter of the World Religions                          7
  4 The Christian Looks at Other Religions                       10
  5 Earlier Christian Attitudes and Interpretations             12
  6 The Variety of Christian Attitudes: A Summary               19
     (*a*) Truth–Falsehood                                       19
     (*b*) Relativity                                            20
     (*c*) Essence                                               21
     (*d*) Development–Fulfillment                               22
     (*e*) Salvation History                                     23
     (*f*) Revelation–Sin                                        24
     (*g*) New Departures                                        26

1 RATIONALISM   Herbert of Cherbury                               29
  Common Notions Concerning Religion                            32

2 ROMANTICISM   Friedrich Schleiermacher                          49
  Religion and the Religions                                    51

3 RELATIVISM   Ernst Troeltsch                                    71
  The Place of Christianity Among the World
    Religions                                                  73

4 EXCLUSIVISM   Karl Barth                                        93
  The Revelation of God as the Abolition of Religion           96

5  DIALECTIC   Emil Brunner                                    113
   Revelation and Religion                                   115

6  RECONCEPTION   William Ernest Hocking                      133
   The Way of Reconception                                   135

7  TOLERANCE   Arnold Toynbee                                 151
   What Should be the Christian Approach to the
   Contemporary Non-Christian Faiths?                        153

8  DIALOGUE   Paul Tillich                                    173
   A Christian–Buddhist Conversation                         175

9  CATHOLICISM   Hans Küng                                    191
   The Freedom of Religions                                  193

10 PRESENCE   M. A. C. Warren, John Taylor                    219
   Christian Presence Amid African Religion                  222

# FORUM BOOKS

The editors of this series recognize the need for books of a convenient size on religion and related topics. Laymen and clergymen, students and the interested general reader can use *Forum Books* for personal study, or as a basis for group discussion. At a time when religious institutions are experiencing dramatic change, when religious ideas are being debated with new intensity, and when religious elements in culture are being called into question, the books in the series gather together examples of important writings which reproduce both historical and contemporary reflections on these subjects. Each editor has taken pains to provide helpful background comment as a context for the readings, but for the most part the selections speak for themselves with clarity and force.

MARTIN E. MARTY, *General Editor*
*Divinity School*
*University of Chicago*

# INTRODUCTION

## *Owen C. Thomas*

### 1  THE PROBLEM OF WORLD COMMUNITY

THE MOST URGENT problem facing mankind today is that of
avoiding the catastrophe of nuclear war. Population and economic development constitute serious challenges only if there
is peace. Modern science and technology have created for the
first time in recorded history a pattern of civilization which is
effectively universal, a unitary global society based on industrial
production and rapid communication. But this interdependent
world society is threatened by political disunity and the resulting danger of atomic war. We live in a world society which des-
perately seeks some measure of world community in order to
survive.

A great deal of attention has been given to the technological,
economic, and political aspects of the problem of world community. But comparatively little concern and effort have been
directed to the cultural, ideological, and religious dimensions. If
differences in this area are at the root of political misunderstanding, tension, and conflict, then the cultural area requires much
greater attention by those concerned with world peace and community.

In this context the diversity of world religions is sometimes
considered to be only a minor nuisance. According to this view
religion is understood to be an epiphenomenon or by-product
of culture, a symbolic and poetic projection of the concerns and

values of a particular ethnic group. Thus the problem of the plurality of religions is not a serious one and will be taken care of as a measure of cultural unity or community emerges.

There is, however, another view of the relation of religion to culture which would make more sense to the average adherent of one of the world religions. According to this interpretation, religion is the foundation of culture and determines the forms of culture. It is a people's fundamental beliefs and values which inform their culture. It is a people's attitude toward nature, man, history, and the divine which determines their view of the family, the state, the economic order, art, and science.

To be sure, this view of the relation of religion and culture involves a different understanding of the nature of religion from that in the first interpretation mentioned above. Here religion is man's "ultimate concern", to use Tillich's phrase, namely, that interest, value, or concern (or group of them) which has first priority in life, to which all others are sacrificed when they come into conflict with it. Thus religion is the standard of moral decisions and the answer to the question about the meaning of life.

The interpretation of the nature of religion, however, is a perennial problem and will be dealt with implicitly throughout this volume, as in other volumes in this series. But if the latter view of religion is accepted, then the fact of religious diversity or pluralism becomes one of the most fundamental issues in the quest for world community.[1]

The same question can be approached in a somewhat different way. It is sometimes held that religion is merely a private affair, an optional department of life, which ought not to obtrude into more important matters. It is asserted that we can get on with the business of reducing international tensions, implementing economic development and technical advance without muddying the waters with such extraneous issues as religious faith and practice. But this is yet another example of that Western arrogance which Asians and Africans have come so to detest. It is the assumption that other peoples must understand and solve the

---

[1] See, for example, Arnold J. Toynbee, *Civilization on Trial* (New York and London: Oxford University Press, 1948), pp. 91, 94, 216, 234 f.

problems of world community in the same way that we Westerners do. We tend to divide life into two spheres, the religious and the secular, and we assume that other peoples do the same or ought to as they become more civilized.

But peoples in non-Western cultures view the relation of religion to the rest of culture in a way quite different from that suggested above. They see religion as integrally related to and inseparable from all the other areas of life and experience. As a matter of fact they generally look upon their religion as the basis of their culture, that which gives form and meaning to the whole. So the peoples of Asia and Africa are not willing to disregard their religious convictions and practices in order to get on with other matters. They see their growing independence as an opportunity to reaffirm and revitalize their religious traditions as the basis of their national and cultural integrity.[2]

But it may be objected that it is not religious diversity which is the cause of the tensions endangering world peace but rather ideological differences. It is the hostility and mistrust between the capitalist and communist blocs, the adversaries in the cold war, which threaten human survival, and not the religious divisions. There is obviously a great deal of validity in this objection. But if we define religion as we have done above, then it becomes clear that the communist ideology, and to a lesser extent the capitalist ideology, perform the function of a religion in the lives and society of their adherents. Thus Communism has often been described as a religion or a quasi-religion with the tendency to develop the traditional trappings of religion, such as a mythology, a dogma, a chosen people, and an eschatology.

There is some evidence, however, that the communist–capitalist or East–West ideological struggle is moving into the background. The cold war has thawed considerably since the days of Stalin. The communist bloc has been shattered into two main and many minor splinters, and the United States, Great Britain, and France have become increasingly isolated from each other

[2] I am indebted to Wilfred Cantwell Smith of Harvard University for many of the insights in the foregoing paragraphs. See his book *The Faith of Other Men* (New York: New American Library, 1963), pp. 101 ff.

and from their former allies. Daniel Bell has argued that the old ideologies with roots in the nineteenth century are dying rapidly and that new ideologies of race and nation are springing up in the new states of Asia and Africa.[3] Many commentators have warned that the dangerous hostilities and conflicts of the future will be between the Have and the Have-not nations, between the white and the colored nations. But it is in the new colored nations of the southern hemisphere where we see the revival of ancient religious traditions. Thus it seems clear that religious diversity will play an increasing part in the relations between the nations and that therefore the inter-religious issue cannot be over-looked.

The hope is often expressed today that the age of holy wars is long past, that the wars of Muslim expansion, the Crusades, and the religious wars of the seventeenth century are of only historical interest. But the twentieth century has seen too much bloodshed in wars in which religious difference has been a funda-mental factor: at the partition of India in 1947, in the Near East in 1948, 1956, and 1967. Even in Cyprus and Vietnam hostility between religious groups has been a continuing source of strife. In the light of these considerations it becomes clear that the problem of the relations between the religions of the world is decisive in the quest for world peace and community.

## 2  FACTORS DETERMINING THE RELATIONS AMONG THE RELIGIONS

Three pervasive developments in the current world situation have to be kept in mind in order to comprehend the complex problem of the relations among the religions. On the surface these developments seem to be contradictory. They are the wide-spread anti-Western feeling, the universal desire for Western technology, and the resurgence of the religions of Asia and Africa. The end of the colonial era has brought a revolt against Western imperialism in all its forms, including cultural aggres-sion or the sense of Western cultural and religious superiority.

[3] *The End of Ideology* (New York: The Free Press, 1960), pp. 393 ff.

Western Christian missionaries are no longer welcome in the nations of Asia and Africa. The bitterness and violent feelings harbored by colonial peoples against their former rulers and exploiters are manifest in such a book as Franz Fanon's *The Wretched of the Earth* (Grove Press, 1965).

But to this general rejection of Western culture there is obviously one outstanding exception, namely, Western science and technology. The revolution of rising human expectations in the under-developed nations has produced an insatiable desire among these peoples for the fruits of technological progress, in public health and agricultural production as well as industrial development. The rising self-confidence and self-assertiveness of the new nations demand the fruits of technological progress but reject any suggestion of Western paternalism, superiority, or cultural aggression.

But along with technological development go its social and cultural counterparts, namely, urbanization and secularization. The typical social unit of the industrial age is the metropolis. The rural areas of the world will become more and more dependent upon the urban centers even if they are not swallowed up in them. But more important for our concern here is the secularization of life which always accompanied scientific and technological progress. "Secularization" is a very slippery word and the process it denotes is praised or blamed depending upon one's definition and point of view. For our purposes it can be defined as the focussing of human concern upon the world as understood and capable of being transformed by empirical science, and a focussing of attention upon human life in this world especially in so far as its conditions can be changed by human effort. It is a turning away from the traditional religious concern with the immortal soul and the spiritual life in relation to the divine or the eternal which is beyond the world. As such, secularization runs directly counter to some of the traditional concerns of the great religions of Asia and Africa. A remarkable example of the clash of secularization with Asian religion occurred at the time of the eclipse of the sun and the alignment of the planets in India in 1962. The religious reaction to these "heavenly" events practically shut down the budding industries and transport of the Indian cities. But the growth of industrialization and thus of secularization seems inevitable in Asia, and it is doubtful if such an occurrence would be repeated in a generation.

In the light of the rapid spread of technology and secularization especially since World War II, it seems paradoxical that this same period has seen a surprising resurgence on the part of the religions of the world. Americans have been aware of the religious revival in the United States during the past twenty years, but probably very few have known of the renaissance of Buddhism, Hinduism, and Islam during this same period.

The Conference of the World Federation of Buddhists in Cambodia in 1961 manifested a vigor and missionary zeal which rivalled that of the great Christian missionary councils of this century. Muslim bodies in Africa are at present growing at ten times the rate of the Christian churches in that area. Many observers have reported on the remarkable renaissance of Hinduism in India and other parts of Asia and Africa. And the results of this revival of other religions have become visible in the Western world. The shaven heads and saffron robes of Buddhist monks are often seen in the universities of America. There are few large urban centers in the West today without Hindu swamis and temples, as well as Muslim preachers and mosques. This religious revival is closely related to the rise of the new nations of Asia and Africa which have turned to their traditional religions for a sense of national identity and cohesiveness.

A final complicating factor in the confusing pattern of the religious situation of the modern world is a new understanding of the relation between the Western religious tradition and the rise of modern science and its twin fruits of technology and secularization. First of all it is clear that these phenomena are the product of the Western cultural tradition and have very few, if any, counterparts in Eastern cultures. This in itself raises the question of whether or not such typically Western phenomena can be assimilated in Eastern cultures without disrupting them.

But beyond this an increasing number of historians are suggesting that the scientific, technological, secular attitude toward

life and the world is the historical product of the impact of the
biblical understanding of reality upon the Western mind.[4] To be
sure these offspring, if that is what they are, of the Western religious tradition are largely ignorant of, and independent of, their
parentage and now manifest a dynamic life of their own. The
important point for our discussion is that the nations of Asia and
Africa, while rejecting the Western religious tradition, have
eagerly accepted certain historical products of that same tradition.
The obvious problem which this poses is whether or not the
religions of the East can come to terms with these powerful
forces which derive from a quite different cultural and religious
tradition.

## 3 THE ENCOUNTER OF THE WORLD RELIGIONS

We live in a world society bound together by economic inter-
dependence, rapid communication and travel, and the common
threat of atomic war. For the first time mankind is united in one
world history. The spread of Western technology is "drawing
nations out of the pools of unhistorical existence and out of the
rivulets of tribal history into a single current of world history".[5]
It is less and less possible for us to isolate ourselves from the
encounter whith other cultures and religions. No longer are the
devotees of other religions the idle curiosities of travellers' tales.
There is increased meeting with persons of other faiths not only
through international business, governmental, and cultural affairs,
but also in daily life. We meet a neighbor who is studying Zen
Buddhism. Our local church sponsors a Black Muslim speaker.
A Hindu swami opens a study and meditation center in our city.
"It will become increasingly apparent, and is already essentially
true, that to be a Christian in the modern world, or a Jew or an

[4] See references in the following works: Ian G. Barbour, *Issues in
Science and Religion* (Englewood Cliffs, N.J.: Prentice-Hall, 1966 and
London: SCM Press Ltd, 1967), pp. 44 ff.; Langdon Gilkey, *Maker of
Heaven and Earth* (Garden City, N.Y.: Doubleday and Co., 1959), Ch. 5;
Harvey G. Cox, *The Secular City* (New York: The Macmillan Co. and
Lonlon: SCM Press Ltd, 1965), Ch. 1.

[5] J. E. Lesslie Newbigin, *A Faith for This One World?* (New York:
Harper and Row and London: SCM Press Ltd, 1961), p. 28.

agnostic, is to be so in a society in which other men, intelligent, devout, and righteous, are Buddhists, Muslims, Hindus."[6]

The ecumenical movement has been described as the "great new fact of our time". But the Christian ecumenical movement is beginning to seem increasingly parochial. The "great new fact" of the last third of this century may well be a true ecumenical movement in the sense of comprising the whole inhabited world (*oikoumene*) with its plurality of cultures and religions.

The real encounter of the world religions takes place primarily in the meeting of persons of different faiths, and this can be a profound and transforming experience. Deep affinities and deep divergences will be discovered. This meeting can raise radical questions about one's own faith, whether this be Christian, Jewish, humanist, or agnostic. It has been the experience of many that this kind of encounter can lead to a much deeper understanding of one's own religion. This has been the universal experience of Christians involved in the analogous situation of the Protestant–Roman Catholic dialogue. One author attests that it was the study of the Muslim mystical poets which led him for the first time to a real appreciation of the mystical element in his own Christian tradition.

But deeper understanding may involve significant changes in a person's interpretation of his faith. William Ernest Hocking coined the term "reconception" for what could and should happen when one religion meets another in real encounter. The impact of Western culture has led to profound modifications of Buddhism and Hinduism especially in regard to their attitude toward material goods, social justice, and the meaning of history. Arnold J. Toynbee has argued that the impact of Western culture upon Eastern societies will soon be followed by an equally profound influence of Eastern cultures upon the West.[7] So the Western religionist must approach his meeting with his Eastern counterpart not only with openness and sensitivity but also with a sense of adventure, risk, and expectancy.

For all these reasons it behooves Westerners to reflect seriously

[6] W. C. Smith, *op. cit.*, p. 12.
[7] *Op. cit.*, Ch. 11.

upon their attitude toward and understanding of other religions. And it is the purpose of this book to promote just this kind of reflection.

We have decided to limit the readings in this volume to authors writing from a Christian point of view. There are several reasons for this. In the first place Christians have addressed themselves to this question since the beginning of our era. The Christian Church first gained self-consciousness in reflection on the pressing issue of its relation to Judaism. And it was soon faced with the problem of its relation to the philosophical and mystery religions of the Hellenistic world.

Furthermore, most of the Western authors who have addressed themselves to the question of their attitude toward other religions have been Christians. Authors representing other Western viewpoints, such as idealism, naturalism, positivism, or communism, when they have been concerned with religious problems, have usually been preoccupied with their relation to the Judeo-Christian tradition rather than with non-Western religions. (Somewhat the same applies to Jewish authors, i.e. they have usually been preoccupied with their relation to Christianity.) When they have dealt with non-Western religions, their attitudes have covered the same spectrum of types which we will find among Christian authors. This latter point applies to anyone who addresses himself to this question, whatever his religious point of view. He will find in the types of attitude represented in this book the kind of options open to him in developing his own point of view on this problem. For example, if he believes that all religion is folly and projection, he will find in the attitude of Karl Barth, for example, a congenial counterpart to his own view.

There are, however, some important exceptions to the suggestion above that other authors have been preoccupied with the Judeo-Christian tradition. Many writers outside this religious tradition have manifested a fascination with Eastern religions. Kraemer mentions as examples Goethe, Schopenhauer, Jung, Huxley, Hesse, Stace, and Northrop.[8] Many explanations have

[8] *World Cultures and World Religions: The Coming Dialogue* (London: Lutterworth Press, 1960), Ch. 9, pp. 324 ff.

been given for this partiality for the religions of the East: cultural self-questioning in the West, a form of rebellion against the Western religious tradition, the attractiveness of Eastern attitudes of relativity and tolerance, the compatibility of Eastern monism with scientific naturalism, the theory that mysticism is the essence of all religion, etc. It is clear that there is in the West a growing interest in and openness toward Eastern religions. This, combined with the new missionary sense among these religions, makes the question of one's attitude toward other religions a live and pressing one.

## 4  THE CHRISTIAN LOOKS AT OTHER RELIGIONS

For the Christian the question of his attitude toward other religions is part of the larger question of his attitude toward all aspects of culture, both Western and Eastern, toward politics, economics, the family, science, and art, as well as religion. As the late H. R. Niebuhr has put it, the Christian's attitude toward other religions is but one aspect of his view of the relation of Christ to culture as a whole.[9] For this reason it can be understood as a problem in Christian philosophy or in particular a Christian philosophy of religion.[10] But since it involves attitudes and actions in relation to other persons, it can be interpreted also as a question in Christian ethics. Finally, this has perhaps most often been treated as a problem of missionary theology and strategy, and the adherent of another religion has been seen as one to whom the Christian is called to give testimony about God's revelation in Christ.

Thus the fact of the other great world religions is a pressing theoretical and practical issue for Christians. It is an urgent

[9] See his book *Christ and Culture* (New York: Harper and Brothers, 1951 and London: Faber & Faber Ltd, 1952). Niebuhr analyzes five typical solutions to this problem which correspond closely to the types of Christian attitude toward other religions which will be analyzed and illustrated in this book.

[10] For a further elaboration of this approach and its problems see my book *William Temple's Philosophy of Religion* (London: SPCK, 1961), Ch. XVI.

theoretical issue because it seems to challenge the Christian claim to uniqueness as a universal religion. Or at least, the fact of the existence of great living religions with ancient traditions, millions of adherents and claims to universality, cries out for interpretation from a Christian point of view. We have outlined the practical issue in terms of the emergence of one world society, the necessity of a measure of world community in the face of cultural and religious diversity, and the beginning of real encounter between adherents of the world religions.

We will find that theory and practice, interpretation and attitude, are involved in every type of Christian approach to other religions, because they are deeply interrelated here. Different attitudes will follow from different interpretations of the significance of other religions. If other religions are understood to be simply idolatry and the creation of human self-assertion, then one attitude may be appropriate. If, however, other religions are seen to be honest human attempts to respond to the manifestation of God in nature and conscience, then quite a different attitude will follow. Conversely, a strong conviction about the rightness of a particular attitude toward another religion will tend to lead to a particular interpretation of the significance of that religion.

The readings in this book will be limited to the modern period. Christians have been in contact with other religions from the beginning, but several factors make the situation of the last few centuries unique. Until the seventh century Christians knew only of Judaism and the pagan religions of the Hellenistic world. With the rise of Islam the Christian Church was faced for the first time with a new and powerful missionary religion. But contact with Muslims occurred more on the battlefield than in searching dialogue, and the distortions of Islamic beliefs by Christians made real encounter almost impossible.

The first real meeting with Asian religions came at the hands of the friar missionaries, beginning in the sixteenth century, but again this was hampered by inadequate knowledge of the history and beliefs of these religions. There are many important exceptions to these generalizations, but there is little doubt that widespread and genuine encounter between the religions did not occur until the eighteenth century. This was made possible by Western colonial and cultural expansion, by the rise of the worldwide missionary activity of the Christian Church, and by the emergence of the scientific historical study of the religions. This put Christians in extensive contact with the religions of Asia and Africa, and placed in their hands exact knowledge of these religions.

Because these factors have produced a new situation in the relations between the religions, the readings in this book have been taken with one exception from the last two centuries. It is clear, however, that these modern views are based on attitudes and interpretations which appeared in the Bible and the early centuries of the Christian era. Therefore, it is necessary at this point to take some account of these earlier views.

## 5  EARLIER CHRISTIAN ATTITUDES AND INTERPRETATIONS [11]

The early Christians looked to the Old Testament for clues on this question. In the Old Testament the attitude toward other religions is strongly condemnatory. Pagan religions are idolatry, the worship of the creature, and man's self-assertion. The prophets have nothing positive to say about the religion of the nations surrounding Israel. The pagan gods are at first treated as real but inferior to the God of Israel in power and righteousness. In the later prophets, however, the gods of the nations have no reality at all. "I am the first and I am the last; besides me there is no god. Who is like me? Let him proclaim it" (Isa. 44. 6 f.).

But there are other strands in the Old Testament tradition which indicate a more open and positive attitude toward the other nations and their religions. Throughout the Old Testament

---

[11] More extensive treatments of the history of Christian attitudes toward other religions can be found in the following works: E. L. Allen, *Christianity Among the Religions* (Boston: Beacon Press, 1961); Hendrik Kraemer, *Religion and the Christian Faith* (Philadelphia: The Westminster Press, 1957 and London: Lutterworth Press, 1956), Parts 3 and 4; Gerhard Rosenkranz, *Der christliche Glaube angesichts der Weltreligionen* (Bern: Francke Verlag, 1967).

it is affirmed that all men are the creatures of God. Moreover, all men are created "in the image of God", that is, in a special relationship of responsibility to God. All mankind also stands in a solidarity of sin, of having turned away from God in rebellion and disobedience. And this applies to Israel as well as to the other nations. Thus all nations stand under the grace and judgment of God who is the sovereign Lord of all mankind (see Amos 9. 7). So the pagan nations and their rulers often appear as fulfilling the divine will in the judgment of Israel (see Isa. 10. 5 f.).

Another element of the tradition sees Israel and the nations standing in a special relation to God, known as the covenant. In the ninth chapter of Genesis it is asserted that God enters into a covenant with Noah and his descendants, that is, with all mankind, a covenant involving the promise of God's favor as manifest in the order of nature. Then within this universal covenant God establishes his special covenant with Israel as his chosen people. But this covenant which begins with Abraham does not involve simply a favored position for Israel but rather a special responsibility, namely, to bring God's blessing to all mankind (see Gen. 12. 1–3; Isa. 49. 6). Thus the whole of human history becomes a history of salvation, a history of God's seeking out all his children to bring them to their fulfillment. Because of this all men stand in relation to God, and there are a few suggestions in the Old Testament that even pagan religion can be a proper response to him (see Mal. 1. 11). So outside of Israel there is not simply darkness and divine judgment, but even there God reigns and is graciously at work.

In the New Testament Jesus presents himself and is presented as the fulfillment of the covenant between God and Israel which is intended for all mankind. He is a Jew who is sent to herald the judgment and fulfillment of Judaism in the Kingdom of God, whose presence is manifest in his words and deeds. He knows little or nothing of pagan religion, but he continually rejects the nationalistic and exclusivistic attitude toward the Gentiles which he finds among some of his Jewish contemporaries. The Gentiles will share in the salvation of the Kingdom of God and will be judged on the same basis as the Jews. Jesus even threatens the

Jews that their place in the Kingdom will be taken by the Gentiles if they do not repent. He often points to the faith and love of Gentiles as putting the Jews to shame.[12]

Paul, as the apostle to the Gentiles, is directly concerned with their religion. He addresses himself to it in the first chapter of his letter to the Romans, which has always been a classic passage in the discussion of the Christian attitude toward other religions. Here he condemns pagan religion as idolatry, the worship of the creature instead of the creator. But his point is that the Gentiles are responsible for this, since they should have known better. "For what can be known about God is plain to them, because God has shown it to them. Ever since the creation of the world his invisible nature, namely, his eternal power and deity, has been clearly perceived in the things that have been made" (vv. 19 f.). The Gentiles should have known God through his revelation in the creation, but they refused to acknowledge and honor him as God and instead worshipped images of man and animals. God's judgment on the Gentiles is to "deliver" them into all kinds of immorality. But the Jews are no better off, because they, too, are under the power of sin. So Paul's purpose is to demonstrate that all men have fallen short and are saved only by God's grace.

A similar interpretation of pagan religion is put into the mouth of Paul by the author of the Book of Acts. In two sermons Paul asserts that God has not left himself without a witness among the Gentiles but has shown forth his goodness in the gifts of the creation and is not far from anyone. So even in their pagan worship the Gentiles have shown an obscure awareness of God. But now Paul declares to them the true God and calls them to turn from their idolatry (see Acts 14. 15–17, 17. 22–31).

A passage in the New Testament which bears only indirectly upon the attitude toward other religions but which was to play a larger part in later discussions is the prologue to the gospel of John (John 1. 1–14). Here the active word or reason (*logos*) of God which was his agent in the creation of the world (see Gen. 1. 3, 6,

---

[12] See the parable of the Good Samaritan, Luke 10. 29–37; also Luke 17. 11–19; Matt. 8. 5–13.

etc., Ps. 33. 6, 9) is seen as the "light of man" which "enlightens every man". And this word of God has become man in Jesus Christ and shown forth the glory and grace of God. Thus every human life is related to God through its creation and illumination by the word of God. We will see below how this idea was used to interpret pagan religion.

To sum up, the general attitude of the Bible toward other religions is on the surface strongly negative, but there are many themes in the Bible which indicate that on a deeper level its approach is more open and universal. God is the Lord of all men; he has not left himself without witness among any people, and wills to bring all mankind to salvation.

In its early years the Christian Church apparently understood itself primarily as a sect of Judaism which saw in Jesus the expected Messiah. But as more Gentiles came into the Church issues arose in regard to the applicability of the Jewish law which caused the Church more and more to distinguish itself from Judaism. In the letters of Paul we see a first-century Christian struggling with the question of the relation of the Church to Judaism (see especially Rom. 9–11; Gal. 3–4). By the second century the Church confronted Judaism as another religion, but its relation to Judaism was so unique that it can hardly be taken as a type of its relation to any other religion. It held in common with Judaism the Old Testament tradition of God as creator and Lord who had called Israel into being to be a light to the nations. In the eyes of the early Christians Judaism was the religion of those Jews who had not perceived that Jesus was the Messiah foreseen by the prophets and in fact the fulfillment of the whole Old Testament tradition. So the Christian interpretation of and attitude toward Judaism has been a very special problem which has vexed Christians from the beginning. But its very peculiarity has rendered it of not much use as a theological model for the Christian intepretation of other religions. Moreover, the terrible and shameful history of Christian treatment of the Jews has rendered it useless as a model in the moral sense.

Beginning in the second century pagan religion, through its spokesmen in pagan philosophy, began to attack Christianity as irrational, immoral, and subversive. The Christian thinkers who responded to these attacks were known as the Apologists. One of their main tasks was to explain why Christians could not join in the pagan cultus and especially the veneration of the emperor. This necessitated an interpretation of paganism and a statement of the proper Christian attitude toward it.

One of the most common interpretations of pagan polytheism by the Christian Apologists was that it was the work of demons. Demons were understood to be spiritual beings who were created by God but who had rebelled against him and now attempted to disrupt his creation. They were believed to cause misfortunes and diseases, and to lead men astray into immorality and idolatrous religion in which the demons themselves were the objects of worship.[13] This completely negative attitude toward paganism meant that the proper Christian approach was to destroy it or to persuade people to give it up entirely.

A somewhat more positive theory of pagan religion was that of the divine condescension and education. Here God is depicted as accommodating himself to the low religious level of the pagan world in order to lead it by stages through the religion of the Old Testament to that of Christ. Thus pagan religion and philosophy falls within God's plan of salvation, and God is presented as the patient divine teacher who leads mankind up toward the goal in Christ. "Accordingly, before the advent of the Lord, philosophy was necessary to the Greeks for righteousness. . . . For this was a schoolmaster to bring the Hellenic mind, as the law, the Hebrews, to Christ. Philosophy, therefore, was a preparation, paving the way for him who is perfected in Christ." [14]

Closely associated with this approach was the most common theory of the Apologists, which was based on the idea of the Logos. As God's agent in the creation the Logos is the pervasive divine principle of reality. Man who is created in the image of God participates in the Logos in the form of his rationality. But this participation is a matter of degree and is always in some measure distorted by sin. So all of man's cultural creations,

---

[13] See Justin Martyr, *First Apology*, 5.
[14] Clement of Alexandria, *Stromateis*, I, 5.

including religion, are understood to be informed in part by the Logos. Now the Christian gospel is that the whole Logos of God is perfectly manifest in Jesus Christ. Therefore, the more fully and faithfully a person followed the leading of the Logos in his life and thought, the more closely he approximated to the perfection of humanity in Christ. On this basis the Apologists were able to recognize in some of the greater pagans and higher aspects of pagan religion prefigurations of the Christian faith and life. "We have been taught that Christ is the first-born of God, and we have declared above that He is the Word of whom every race of men were partakers; and those who lived reasonably (according to the Logos) are Christians, even though they have been thought atheists; as, among the Greeks, Socrates and Heraclitus, and men like them." "For whatever either lawgivers or philosophers uttered well, they elaborated by finding and contemplating some part of the Word. But since they did not know the whole of the Word, which is Christ, they often contradicted themselves." [15]

We have in the Logos doctrine one typical Christian interpretation of and attitude toward other religions which we will meet again in various forms in Christian history. It is an approach which enables Christians to perceive positive elements as well as distortions in other religions, to see other religions as preparations for the Christian gospel, and to present the Christian faith as the fulfillment of other faiths.[16]

The appearance of Islam in the seventh century did not produce any new Christian attitudes or theories but rather increased the currency and extremity of the negative ones mentioned above. By the thirteenth century, however, it was possible for Thomas Aquinas to develop a more positive approach to Islam and Arabian philosophy. He states in his *Summa Contra Gentiles* that since the Muslims do not share any scripture with Christians, discussion with them must be based on natural reason alone. He argues that, apart from any revelation, man can come to know of

---

[15] Justin Martyr, *First Apology*, 46; *Second Apology*, 10.
[16] A modern example of the Logos interpretation can be found in A. C. Bouquet, *The Christian Faith and Non-Christian Religions* (New York: Harper and Brothers and Welwyn Garden City: James Nisbet & Co Ltd, 1958), Ch. VI *et passim*.

the existence and many attributes of God by the natural light of reason.[17] The implication is that any truths contained in other religions are the result of the activity of unaided human reason. But these truths of natural theology must be completed by the truths of revealed theology given in the Bible.

The spirit of the Renaissance is exemplified in the writing of Nicholas of Cusa, the fifteenth-century cardinal of the Catholic Church. In his *De Pace Fidei* he presents the idea that behind all the differences of religious practice there is one universal religion on which Jews, Christians, and Muslims can agree. It turns out, however, that this one true religion involves the doctrines of the Trinity, the Incarnation, and the Mass. But the idea of the harmony of all religions beyond the diversity of practice is a prophetic vision which we will find again in various forms, especially in theories about the "essence" of religion.

The Reformation saw the rediscovery of certain biblical themes concerning other religions, especially those of Paul. Calvin's view of other religions is very similar to Paul's approach in his letter to the Romans. God has planted in man a sense of the divine or a seed of religion, and he has also manifested himself in the glory of the creation and in the experience of man. But man in his sin does not apprehend God as he offers himself, but is led astray and constructs idols. So the seed of religion is corrupted and grows into a profusion of falsehood and superstition.[18] We will find Calvin's interpretation reflected in the selection by Emil Brunner.

Although Luther's interpretation of man's religious situation is similar to Calvin's, he lays the emphasis on a different aspect of Paul's thought, namely, his idea of justification. Luther views all religion as man's attempt to justify himself before God by his own achievement whether in moral exertion, cultic rite, or ascetic discipline. Such attempts at salvation by works he set over against the salvation by the grace of God, which is proclaimed in the Christian gospel. This did not mean, however, that Luther took no interest in other religions, for he made a special study of

---

[17] See Book I, Chs. ii, iii.
[18] See *The Institutes of the Christian Religion*, I, Chs. iii, iv.

Islam and edited a German translation of the Quran. We will find aspects of Luther's approach elaborated by Karl Barth.

The orthodox Protestant and Catholic theologians of the seventeenth century offered no new interpretations of other religions but rather tended to reproduce the ideas of early and medieval Christian thinkers. They saw man's natural rational capacity for knowledge of God as the basis of all other religions, and they asserted that these religions are fufilled and completed in the supernatural revelation in Christ. They also for the first time began to use the concept of religion to include both Christianity and other religions. These ideas became the basis of the views of other religions which were developed in the Enlightenment of the eighteenth century.

This brings us to the period covered in the selections in this volume. These selections will indicate the variety of Christian attitudes toward other religions which have appeared in the last two centuries. In order to see these views in better perspective it will be helpful to present an outline summary of the various Christian interpretations of other religions, including both those which have been surveyed above and those represented in the selections below. Critical questions will be raised about each approach.

## 6 THE VARIETY OF CHRISTIAN ATTITUDES: A SUMMARY

Needless to say, the following approaches are not absolutely distinct, and they often overlap or shade into each other. They at least represent different emphases. Moreover, probably no one attitude is represented in its purity in any one author. Each thinker usually combines two or more views in his own interpretation.

(a) *Truth–Falsehood* In its simplest form this view is that Christian faith is true and all other religions are false. We have noted the prevalence of this attitude in the Bible and the history of the Church. It was expressed sharply by Luther and is represented in one form in the selection by Karl Barth. Other religions are interpreted as simply the product of human invention, sin, attempts at self-redemption, or as the result of demonic inspiration. The resulting practical attitude toward other religions is what Hocking calls "radical displacement"; they are to be conquered and replaced by Christianity.

This view has rarely if ever been held in this simple form either in the Bible or in Christian history. The obvious difficulty here is that other religions share some beliefs with Christianity. Judaism and Islam, for example, affirm the reality of a transcendent personal creator God, so it is difficult to see how Christians can hold them to be totally false. But a valid element in this approach is that it takes the problem of truth seriously. It is sometimes asserted that all religions are equally true. But this would seem to be simply sloppy thinking, since the various religions hold views of reality which are sharply different if not contradictory. Representatives of this view sometimes go on to assert that any religion which denies that all religions are equally true is guilty of falsehood! Similar ideas will be discussed in connection with the next attitude.

(b) *Relativity*   There are several varieties of Christian attitudes toward other religions which can come under this heading. There is a cultural relativism which asserts that each religion is the appropriate expression of its own culture. Thus Christianity is the religion of Western culture and Buddhism the religion of South East Asia. There is an epistemological relativism which claims that we cannot know the absolute truth, but only the truth for us. We believe that Christianity is true for us, but we cannot go on to affirm that it is the truth for all peoples, since they must be the judges of that. Finally, there is what might be called a teleological relativism, which holds that all other religions are simply different paths to the same goal as Christianity. So which path you choose is only a matter of personal preference. The selections by Troeltsch and Toynbee represent these various types of relativism.

The attitude of cultural relativism generally assumes that religion is a by-product of culture. But we have suggested above that a more plausible view is that religion is the foundation of culture. If this is so, and if religion raises fundamental questions about the nature of reality, then cultural relativism is an avoiding of these issues. In its pure form epistemological relativism is self-stultifying. If it is asserted that we know (absolutely) that we cannot know the absolute truth, then we have a contradiction. But if this means only that it is difficult to ascertain the truth about reality, then it is simply a truism. What is really true for us must be universally true, for that is what truth means. Teleological relativism is simply not true to the facts about the other religions. Careful investigation has demonstrated that the world religions have quite different conceptions of man's fulfillment.

(c) *Essence* Many Christian thinkers have affirmed that at the heart of all religions is the same essence, one identical reality. This is the intrinsic nature which lies hidden under all the multiplicity of outward forms of religion. This essence of religion is understood in a variety of ways. It may be a matter of doctrine, morals, or experience. It is variously affirmed to be mysticism (Hocking), the feeling of absolute dependence (Schleiermacher), the numinous sense of the holy (Otto), the moral imperative (Kant), or the personal encounter with God (Farmer). Then the Christian interpretation of other religions is that they embody the essence of religion in varying degrees of imperfection and partiality, while Christian faith constitutes the purest and fullest manifestation of this essence.

Sometimes the essence is understood to have existed in its pure form at the beginning of history and then to have been progressively lost under the corrupt forms of the particular religions. Then Christianity is affirmed to be the "republication" of this essence of religion. This was the view of the Deists of the eighteenth century. Alternatively, the essence of religion is seen to be progressively manifest in more and more perfect embodiments which come to their fulfillment in Christianity (Hegel). This interpretation approaches that described in the next view.

The valid point in this aproach is that all religions must have something in common in order properly to be called religions. There must be something besides customary linguistic usage which distinguishes them from art, science, morality, and other

B

aspects of culture. The difficulty with many of the theories as to the essence of religion is that they are too abstract. The concrete religions of mankind are distorted when they are made to fit into such schemes. Also the modern study of the religions has made it extremely difficult if not impossible to demonstrate that an identical essence lies at the heart of all of them. The essence theory is found in different forms in the selections by Herbert of Cherbury, Schleiermacher, and Hocking.

(d) *Development–Fulfillment*  This approach sees the history of religion as a process of progressive development of evolution in which ever higher and purer forms emerge. Thus a scale of lower and higher forms is presented with primitive religion at the bottom, followed at the next stage by national polytheistic religions and culminating in the universal monotheistic religions of redemption. Christianity is viewed as the highest stage of development in this process or as the final or absolute form of religion. It is thus superior to all other religions as the fulfillment of all that is implicit in them. The other religions are understood to be incomplete or preliminary stages of religious development which may function as preparations for Christian faith. When the idea of fulfillment is emphasized the other religions are seen to contain elements of truth which are drawn together and completed in Christianity, or they are understood to embody aspirations and longings which are satisfied in Christian faith.

This has been a very common approach in Christian history. It is seen in Jesus' word that he came not to destroy but to fulfill the law and the prophets of the Old Testament (Matt. 5. 17), and it has been the traditional attitude of the Church toward Judaism. We have noted other forms of this view in the Logos and condescension–education theories of the Apologists and in the natural theology—revealed theology scheme of Aquinas. It received a strong impetus from the work of Hegel, who saw Christianity as the absolute religion, the culmination of a logical process of development. It is the approach found most often in the liberal Protestant theology of the nineteenth and early twentieth centuries, beginning with Schleiermacher. A book published in 1913, for example, presented Christianity as the "crown of Hinduism".

And it is obviously closely related to the next theory discussed below.

In spite of its popularity this Christian attitude toward other religions involves serious difficulties. Studies in the past century have shown that the history of religions is in no sense a story of progressive development in one direction, but rather one of change in many directions. There has been no clear line of development in the direction of higher, purer forms of religion. And of course each religion would have its own unique point of view for judging this. The so-called higher religions do not stand closer together than the earlier and lower forms, but are in fact more sharply divided from each other. Furthermore, the adherents of the other religions honestly cannot see their deepest intuitions fulfilled in Christianity. Rather the opposite is more often the case. Again, careful investigation has demonstrated that there are in fact decisive differences among the religions in regard to the nature of the divine and of human fulfillment.

(*e*) *Salvation History*   This Christian attitude toward other religions is similar to that discussed above which focusses on the idea of fulfillment, but it is set in a different framework. It is based on the Christian teaching that God is the Lord of history and that in all human history God is working out his plan of salvation for all mankind. From this point of view the other religions fall within this divine plan of salvation. They are sanctioned by God as responses to his grace, which is shown forth to all men. Their purpose in God's plan is to prepare mankind for the perfect salvation which has been accomplished in Christ. But for their individual adherents the other religions constitute real ways of salvation. Thus the Christian Church is seen as the historically visible vanguard or explicit expression of that salvation which is implicit or hidden in the other religions. The practical attitude toward other religions which results from this is that the Christian Church should not expect to triumph over the other religions and replace them. Rather the Church should enter into dialogue with the members of the other religions and testify to God's universal plan of salvation manifest in Christ.

As an explicit interpretation of other religions this approach is relatively new. But it has roots in the Bible, especially in the idea behind the covenant with Noah and in the idea of all history as comprehended in God's plan of salvation which is found in the prophets. It has come to the fore as a result of the rediscovery of the idea of the history of salvation or sacred history at the hands of the biblical scholars of this century. It is the attitude toward other religions held by a group of Roman Catholic theologians which has been associated with the progressive or liberal party at the Second Vatican Council. It is clearly represented in the selection by Hans Küng.

But as in the previous approach the main problem in this view is that it seems to overlook the radical differences between Christianity and other religions. It is difficult to see how religions with such diverse understandings of salvation as, for example, Christianity and Buddhism could both be ways to the same ultimate salvation. Furthermore, since the other religions are in fact considered to be real ways of salvation, the question is raised as to the significance of the Christian mission to the world. This becomes especially pressing when it is affirmed in this view that the only serious possibility of the loss of the ultimate fulfillment lies in the rejection of the Christian gospel. Thus it might be safer for the adherents of the other religions if the Christian message were kept a secret!

(f) *Revelation–Sin* The interpretation of other religions most widely held among contemporary Protestant theologians is based on the ideas of a general or universal divine revelation and of human sin. According to this view, God reveals himself universally in the creation and in the reason and conscience of man, but man's response to this divine self-disclosure is distorted and corrupted by his sin, which is interpreted as rebellion against God. Although man has the possibility of a faithful and obedient response to God's approach, and thus is responsible for his plight, yet in his religious response he always turns away from the true God and worships an idol, something of his own creation, whether it be a crude image or a lofty principle.

The attitude toward other religions which results from this interpretation is often called dialectical; it involves a Yes and a

No. The Christian can say Yes to other religions because he knows that they are in some way a response to the approach of the God whom he worships. But he must also say No, because he sees that they are a confused and distorted response. Thus the relation of the Christian gospel to the other religions is one of judgment and fulfillment, a judgment upon their sin and a fulfillment of their hidden origin in divine revelation. This approach, it is held, does justice to both the heights and the depths of the other religions.

Some advocates of this view hold that this dialectical relation also obtains between the Christian gospel and empirical Christianity, that Christ is the judge and fulfiller of the Christian religion as well as of other religions. This leads them to assert that Christian faith or the Christian gospel is not a religion at all and that no claims to superiority can be made on behalf of the Christian religion as such. This is an important distinction, and it underscores the common situation of Christians and the adherents of the other religions. But it is a point which is often made by interpreters of other religions as well. Furthermore, any theologian's interpretation of the Christian gospel is in fact part of the Christian religion, a sample of empirical Christianity.

This approach is most often elaborated as an interpretation of Paul's attitude as presented in the first two chapters of his letter to the Romans. It is in some ways similar to the Logos theory of the Apologists, but it was most clearly stated by Calvin. Today it is found especially among the theologians who have been influenced by Karl Barth. It finds classic expression in the selection by Emil Brunner.

One question which has to be raised about this position is, Why should God reveal himself to the adherents of the other religions sufficiently to make them guilty of idolatry but not sufficiently to save them? This interpretation often seems to have been developed from the logical implications of the doctrines of revelation and sin, and apart from direct knowledge of or contact with other religions. That is, it often tends to become an abstract theological exercise rather than a real attempt to interpret the reality of the other religions from the point of view of Christ.

(g) *New Departures*   We have looked at six main types of Christian attitudes toward other religions. It remains only to consider two further views which are comparatively new and which have not yet been formulated very clearly or completely. They can be called "Christian presence" and "Christian secularity".

The Christian-presence approach expresses a way of meeting persons of other religions, but does not specify a particular theological interpretation of other religions. It may contain an interpretation implicitly, but its intention seems to be to leave open the question of theological interpretation. This view is associated with a series of volumes on the Christian mission which is attempting to break new ground in the Christian attitude toward other religions.[19]

The basic principle of this approach is that it is the Christian's main responsibility simply to be present with the man of another faith, perceiving their common humanity with its common needs, failings, and longings. He should be a listener taking the other person and his faith as seriously as he himself hopes to be taken and attempting to see the world as he sees it. He should approach the faith of the other person with respect and reverence, for it is his response to the God who is already present with the other. Since the Christian expects to meet the presence of God in the faith and life of the other person, he should also be prepared to gain a new understanding of God. Finally, the Christian is called upon in frankness and openness to give testimony to the reality of God as he has perceived him in his own faith.

It is clear that the Christian-presence approach is an elaboration of themes which are central to Christian faith but which have too often been forgotten and betrayed in the attitude of Christians toward other religions. But it has so far avoided the difficult question of the explicit interpretation of the significance of other religions. It is represented in the selection by Warren and Taylor.

The view we have designated "Christian secularity" is derived from the thought of Karl Barth and Dietrich Bonhoeffer, especi-

---

[19] *Christian Presence Series,* ed. M. A. C. Warren (London: SCM Press Ltd, 1959 ff.).

ally from their critique of religion and the latter's call for a religionless or secular interpretation of Christian faith. Barth defines religion as unbelief, as man's attempt to order his own life and to achieve an understanding of God apart from or in opposition to the revelation of God in Christ. Bonhoeffer continues this critique and defines religion as a department of life, as an individualistic piety which turns away from the world and constructs a metaphysical framework for man's values. This is set over against the Christian gospel, which sets man in the world to serve his neighbor.

The advocates of Christian secularity see the world-wide process of secularization as the decisive fact of our time which challenges and threatens every religious world view. They also see secularization as the fruit of the Christian gospel. It is something to be welcomed, since it liberates man from all types of religious and metaphysical bondage, from the supremacy of fate, from the tyranny of cosmic powers, from the divinity of kings, and from the strictures of unquestioned ideologies. So the proper Christian attitude toward other religions is not that they should be replaced by the Christian religion. Rather Christians should help the adherents of other religions to free themselves from those aspects of their religion and culture which inhibit their freedom and responsibility, and which have caused them to accept their lot fatalistically and to turn to the eternal world for religious solace. So the function of the Christian Church in relation to the adherents of other religions is not to attempt to solve their religious problems with the Christian religion, but rather to announce to them that God has delivered them from the bondage of a sacred world view into the freedom of a secular world and that he calls them to responsibility for this world and all its human problems. Whether or not they become Christians seems to be a secondary matter in this view.[20]

This attitude toward other religions is based on those themes in the Bible which have been seen as the sources of the secularization of Western society, namely, the idea of creation which

[20] See Arend Th. van Leeuwen, *Christianity in World History* (London: Edinburgh House Press, 1964), Ch. VIII.

undercuts the sacred character of reality and the sovereignty of God which overthrows every sacred view of politics. This is also expressed in Paul's interpretation of Christ as the one who delivers man from the bondage of cosmic religious powers into freedom and responsibility for the world (see Gal. 4; Col. 2).

Christian secularity involves an almost totally negative attitude toward other religions as well as toward those aspects of Christianity which fall under its pejorative definition of religion. It is not clear whether it calls the adherents of other faiths to leave them or to try to secularize them. This view has not yet been worked out fully, but it promises to have a significant impact in the near future.

# I

# RATIONALISM
## Herbert of Cherbury

ALONGSIDE AND IN opposition to the orthodox theology of the
seventeenth century there developed a movement of thought and
belief which was known as Deism in England and as Rationalism or the Enlightenment on the Continent. "Reason" and
"nature" are the key concepts in this movement, and they are
often used interchangeably. Its dominant conviction is that
reason is the way to true knowledge in all realms, including religion. But the laws of reason are also manifest in the laws of
nature as elaborated by Newton, and the order of nature shows
forth the Author of nature, who is thus perceived by reason
either intuitively or by demonstration. Consequently, the theological views of this movement are known equally as the religion
of reason or as natural religion.

Weariness with the religious conflicts of the sixteenth and
seventeenth centuries gave impetus to this movement. The historical revelation claimed by the Christians had led not to peace
and happiness but to strife and misery. Where could man look
for an assurance in religion which would not set him against his
neighbor but rather serve as a basis for religious harmony?
The power of human reason in the new natural science had
driven the occult and the mysterious from the physical world and
laid bare the clarity and order of nature. Could not that same
power of reason purge the historical religions of superstition
and priestcraft and lay bare the pure and reasonable religion of
nature? This was the argument of the Deists and Rationalists of

the seventeenth and eighteenth centuries. Furthermore, what was taken to be evidence for the universality of this natural religion had appeared in the accounts of explorers and voyagers to non-Christian lands in distant parts of the earth.

Herbert of Cherbury (1583–1648) is generally held to be the founder of English Deism, although the movement did not come to full flower until a century later. He led a colorful life full of intrigue and escapade as a soldier, diplomat, poet, historian, and religious philosopher. He was the older brother of George Herbert, the poet. After graduation from Oxford he served as a volunteer in the Low Countries under the Prince of Orange. After some years in Italy he was appointed the English ambassador in Paris. He received the English barony of Cherbury in 1629 and was appointed to the council of war by Charles I in 1632. His later years were spent in solitary labor over his philosophical works.

The selection below is taken from his most famous work, the *De Veritate*, which was published in Paris in 1624. Descartes was impressed by it, and it anticipates some of his theories. In the face of conflicting religious doctrines, on the one hand, and the beginnings of a scientific scepticism, on the other, Herbert sought to establish a new theory of knowledge and a criterion for the determination of truth. His work is an original blending of scholastic logic and sixteenth-century Neo-Platonism, which looked upon the universe as a harmonious organism. Herbert defines truth as the conformity of a mental faculty with an object under certain conditions. The major part of his work is devoted to the analysis and classification of the faculties and their objects and of the conditions under which they come into harmonious relation.

The mental faculties fall into four classes: natural instinct, internal apprehension, external apprehension, and discursive thought or reason. The faculty of natural instinct is innate. Men are endowed with it according to the original design of nature, and thus according to God's providence. Although it is continuous with the biological instinct for self-preservation, in man it becomes a spiritual impulse for salvation. The class of truth yielded by natural instinct is called the truth of intellect, and its content is the Common Notions which are the final court of appeal for all our beliefs. These Common Notions are present in all normal healthy minds. They are, *a priori*, independent of any other principle, universal, certain, necessary for life, and apprehended immediately. They are the final criteria of truth because there is universal agreement upon them.

This is the background of the selection below on the "Common Notions Concerning Religion", which was apparently not part of the original plan of the work but was added as an afterthought. Herbert's thesis is that the five Common Notions of religion are inscribed by God in the mind of man and constitute the origin of the different religions. The religions have elaborated ceremonies, organizations, sacred books, and other institutions, but these may or may not be in accord with the Common Notions. Thus all religions are essentially the same and differ only in what has been added to their original foundation. Herbert manifests a deep concern that every man should possess the possibility of salvation, and he bases this on the universal presence of the Common Notions. Here he sides with the Arminian emphasis of his day on human freedom as against the Calvinist assertion of predestination.

Herbert's five articles of natural religion were repeated by most of the Deist authors of the later seventeenth and early eighteenth centuries. After Locke had criticized the concept of innate ideas in his *Essay Concerning Human Understanding* (1690), the Deists tended to base their idea of natural religion on what could be demonstrated by reason. The rationalist concept of the religion of nature was taken up by Voltaire in France and by Lessing in Germany and dominated the eighteenth-century view of the relations among the religions.

Herbert's theory of natural religion is one version of the "Essence" view described above, in that it sees every religion as based in varying degrees of fidelity upon the five Common Notions. The most that can be said for Christianity is that it has suffered less by way of human corruption and developed more in accord with the Common Notions than have the other religions.

Herbert attempted to justify his theory by a study of ancient religion in his work *De Religione Gentilium* (1663). But the main difficulty with his view remains that the modern study of the religions of the world has found very little to support the universality of the Common Notions. Furthermore, his static view of human nature as unaffected by history and culture is generally rejected today.

# Common Notions Concerning Religion*

BEFORE I PROCEED to discuss revelation, I think that certain assumptions which underlie our notions of revelation ought to be examined. Every religion which proclaims a revelation is not good, nor is every doctrine which is taught under its authority always essential or even valuable. Some doctrines due to revelation may be, some of them ought to be, abandoned. In this connection the teaching of Common Notions is important; indeed, without them it is impossible to establish any standard of discrimination in revelation or even in religion. Theories based upon implicit faith, though widely held not only in our own part of the world but also in the most distant regions, are here irrelevant. Instances of such beliefs are: that human reason must be discarded, to make room for Faith; that the Church, which is infallible, has the right to prescribe the method of divine worship, and in consequence must be obeyed in every detail; that no one ought to place such confidence in his private judgment as to dare to question the sacred authority of priests and preachers of God's word; that their utterances, though they may elude human grasp, contain so much truth that we should rather lay them to heart than debate them; that to God all the things of which they speak and much more are possible. Now these arguments and many other similar ones, according to differences of age and country, may be equally used to establish a false religion as to support a

* From Edward, Lord Herbert of Cherbury, *De Veritate,* trans. with introd. by Meyrick H. Carre (Bristol: J. W. Arrowsmith Ltd., 1937), pp. 289–307.

true one. Anything that springs from the productive, not to say seductive, seed of Faith will yield a plentiful crop. What pompous charlatan can fail to impress his ragged flock with such ideas? Is there any fantastic cult which may not be proclaimed under such auspices? How can any age escape deception, especially when the cunning authorities declare their inventions to be heaven-born, though in reality they habitually confuse and mix the truth with falsehood? If we do not advance toward truth upon a foundation of Common Notions, assigning every element its true value, how can we hope to reach any but futile conclusions? Indeed, however those who endeavor to base their beliefs upon the disordered and licentious codes of superstition may protest, their behavior is precisely similar to people who with the purpose of blinding the eyes of the wayfarer with least trouble to themselves offer with singular courtesy to act as guides on the journey. But the actual facts are otherwise. The supreme Judge requires every individual to render an account of his actions in the light, not of another's belief, but of his own. So we must establish the fundamental principles of religion by means of universal wisdom, so that whatever has been added to it by the genuine dictates of Faith may rest on that foundation as a roof is supported on a house. Accordingly, we ought not to accept any kind of religion lightly, without first enquiring into the sources of its prestige. And the Reader will find all these considerations depend upon Common Notions. Can anyone, I beg to ask, read the huge mass of books composed with such immense display of learning, without feeling scorn for these age-long impostures and fables, save in so far as they point the way to holiness? What man could yield unquestioning faith to a body which, disguised under the name of the Church, wastes its time over a multitude of rites, ceremonies, and vanities, which fights in so many parts of the world under different banners, if he were not led to perceive, by the aid of conscience, some marks of worship, piety, penance, reward, and punishment? Who, finally, would attend to the living voice of the preacher if he did not refer all his deeds and words to the Sovereign Deity? It would take too long to deal with every instance. It is sufficient to make

clear that we cannot establish any of them without the Common
Notions. I value these so highly that I would say that the book,
religion, and prophet which adheres most closely to them is the
best. The system of Notions, so far at least as it concerns theology,
has been clearly accepted at all times by every normal person,
and does not require any further justification. And, first of all,
the teaching of Common Notions, or true Catholic Church, which
has never erred, nor ever will err, and in which alone the glory
of Divine Universal Providence is displayed, asserts that

### There is a Supreme God

No general agreement exists concerning the Gods, but there
is universal recognition of God. Every religion in the past has
acknowledged, every religion in the future will acknowledge,
some sovereign deity among the Gods. Thus to the Romans this
supreme Power is Optimus Maximus; to the Greeks He is "'Ο ἐπὶ
πᾶσι Θεός, αὐτοφυής, παντοκράτωρ, ἀρχὴ πάντων τε τελευτὴ '";
to the Jews He is יהיה, Jehovah; to the Mohammedans, Allah;
to the Indians of the West, Pachama Viracocha, etc. The Eastern
Indians have similar names for Him. Accordingly that which is
everywhere accepted as the supreme manifestation of deity, by
whatever name it may be called, I term God. I pass on to consider His attributes, using the same method. And in the first
place I find that He is Blessed. Secondly, He is the end to which
all things move. Thirdly, He is the cause of all things, at least
in so far as they are good. From which follows, according to His
providence that, in the fourth place, He is the means by which
all things are produced; for how could we pass from the beginning
to the end but by the means provided? We need not be deterred
by the type of philosophers who have refused to grant the medium
any share of providence. Since circumstances seldom fall out in
accordance with their wishes, they make a desperate attempt to
abolish particular Providence as though the course of events
were ordained by themselves and not by the Divine will. We
must realize that writers of this kind are only wrangling about
the means by which Divine Providence acts; they are not, I
think, disputing Providence itself. Meanwhile the utmost agree-

ment exists concerning Universal Providence, or Nature. But every religion believes that the Deity can hear and answer prayers; and we are bound to assume a special Providence – to omit other sources of proof – from the universal testimony of the sense of divine assistance in times of distress. In the fifth place, He is eternal. For we are taught by a Common Notion that what is first is eternal. In the sixth place a Common Notion tells us that the Deity is good, since the cause of all good is supremely good. In the seventh place, He is just; a Common Notion, experience and history bear witness at every point that the world is ruled under His Providence with absolute justice. For as I have often observed, Common Notions, which solve the most difficult questions of philosophy and theology, teach us that all things are governed with righteousness and justice, though their causes may be hidden from us. In the eighth place, He is wise; for marks of His wisdom do not only appear in the attributes of which I have spoken but are manifest daily in His works.

In addition to these qualities there are certain attributes, such as Infinity, Omnipotence, and Liberty, concerning which I find there is much difference of opinion. But His infinity is proved by the infinity of position or space. For the supreme God penetrates all things, according to the teaching of Common Notions. His Omnipotence follows from His infinity, for it is certain that there is nothing which is beyond the power of the infinite. His omnipotence proves His liberty, since no man in his senses has ever doubted that He who can do everything is absolutely free. I think, however, that those who feel otherwise must be approached from a different angle. And here there is a Common Notion that what exists in us in a limited degree is found absolutely in God. If He is so far beyond our capacity as to be illimitable He will be infinite. If He has created all things without using any existing matter He will be omnipotent. And finally if He is the Author of our liberty He will be supremely free. The ancient Schools were wrong in holding that men were free while God was fettered to the first Sphere. The Divine Attributes prove these points as effectively when taken separately as when taken together. On the attributes and their synonyms the Schools may

usefully be consulted, and I find that in general they discuss them
very fairly. It is true that I have found that the names which they
have given these attributes are conflicting and often inappropriate. Thus the Pagans confuse the attribute of infinity with that
of unity, and invent a number of Gods. Even if you suppose
with some that under the names of Apollo, Mars, and Ceres,
various aspects of Divine Providence were recognized, you cannot deny that the fables which the ancients invented under
these names have always been thought foolish, since no one has
ever doubted (so far as I am aware) the evils of their creed. As
for the attributes which are rejected in our discussion, they are
those which make the Deity strange, physical, composite, particular, or capable of condemning men for His own pleasure. Such
a God is nothing but an idol of the imagination, and exists nowhere else. I pass now to the second Common Notion of theology.

## This Sovereign Deity Ought to be Worshipped

While there is no general agreement concerning the worship
of Gods, sacred beings, saints, and angels, yet the Common
Notion or Universal Consent tells us that adoration ought to be
reserved for the one God. Hence divine religion – and no race,
however savage, has existed without some expression of it – is
found established among all nations, not only on account of the
benefits which they received from general providence but also
in recognition of their dependence upon Grace, or particular
providence. Hence, too, men have been convinced, as I have
observed above, that they can not only supplicate that heavenly
Power but prevail upon Him, by means of the faculties implanted
in every normal man. Hence, finally, what is a more important
indication, this Power was consulted by the seers in order to
interpret the future, and they undertook no important action
without referring to it. So far the peoples were surely guided
by the teaching of Natural Instinct. The All Wise Cause of the
universe does not suffer itself to be enclosed within its own
sphere, but it bestows general Grace on all and special Grace
on those whom it has chosen. Since everyone can experience this
in himself, would it not be unjust to refuse the same power to

God? God does not suffer us to beseech Him in vain, as the universal experience of divine assistance proves, to pass over all other arguments. Although I find that the doctrine of special providence, or Grace, was only grudgingly acknowledged by the ancients, as may be gathered from their surviving works, yet since the worship of the Divine Power was recognized in every age, and carried with it this doctrine of Grace or Special Providence, I assert that this doctrine is a Common Notion. From this source spring supplications, prayers, sacrifices, acts of thanksgiving; to this end were built shrines, sanctuaries, and finally for this purpose appeared priests, prophets, seers, pontiffs, the whole order of ministers. And even if their activity has been equally evident in human affairs as in the affairs of God, since they have often been a crafty and deceitful tribe, prone to avarice, and often ineffective, this is because they have introduced much under the pretext of Religion which has no bearing upon Religion. In this way with extraordinary skill they have confused sacred matters with profane, truth with falsehood, possibility with probability, lawful worship with licentious ceremonies and senseless superstitions; with the result, I make bold to say, that they have corrupted, defiled, and prostituted the pure name of Religion. However necessary the priests were, whenever they brought contempt upon themselves, the fear of God and the respect due to sacred things diminished in proportion. Accordingly, we must give them the honor which is due to them. I obtain, then, proof of this external aspect of divine worship in any type of religion from every age, country, and race. It is therefore a Common Notion. It is no objection that temples or regions sacred to the Gods are not found among savages. For in their own fashion they consulted oracles and undertook no serious task without propitiating their Deity. I am aware that an author of reputation has said that in one remote region no religious practice can be observed. But this statement has been rejected by a later writer who pointed out that the author was ignorant of the language of that country. However, if anyone denies the assertion we must reply that the same religious faculties which anyone can experience in himself exist in every normal human being, though they appear in different forms and may be expressed without any external ceremony or ritual. And in postulating this principle I draw the conclusion that religion is the ultimate difference of man. I am not deterred by the fact that irreligious men exist, and even some who appear to be atheists. In reality they are not atheists; but because they have noticed that some people apply false and shocking attributes to God, they have preferred not to believe in God than to believe in a God of such a character. When He is endowed with true attributes, so far from not believing in Him they would pray that such a God might exist, if there were no such Being. If, however, you still maintain that irreligious persons and even atheists can be found (which I do not believe), reflect that there may be not a few madmen and fools included among those who maintain that rationality is the final difference of man. Otherwise there would hardly have been such endless disputes about Religion, nor such a multitude of martyrs; for there is no Church which does not boast of its legendary heroes, men who for the sake of religion have not only adopted lives of the utmost austerity but have endured death itself. Such conflicts would not have occurred if there had not been men so stubborn and unreasonable that they were incapable of distinguishing truth from probability, possibility, and falsity.

I pass now to aspects of worship which are universally recognized. Those which can be referred to the analogy between man and God, between man and things, and between things themselves, I include under the right conformation of the faculties. I say then that

*The connection of Virtue with Piety, defined in this work as the right conformation of the faculties, is and always has been held to be, the most important part of religious practice*

There is no general agreement concerning rites, ceremonies, traditions, whether written or unwritten, or concerning Revelation; but there is the greatest possible consensus of opinion concerning the right conformation of the faculties. The way in which this right conformation of the faculties may be established I have discussed at length above, and the Reader is invited to refer to that passage. There he will learn how Conscience guided by Common Notions produces virtue combined with piety, how from this there springs true hope, from such true hope, faith, from true faith, love, from true love, joy, and from true joy, Blessedness. Thus we now see that no faculty which leads to piety, purity of life, holiness, and virtue is not included under this heading. If I am to make some survey of these faculties, in respect of a person's years and the degree of wisdom which it has pleased God to give him, I would say that children recognize and seek God in their own way in the form of happiness, and acknowledge Him in the spontaneous gratitude which they accord their benefactors. No trait, therefore, is so excellent as gratitude, nothing so base as ingratitude. And when gratitude is expressed by more mature persons and the Common Notions gradually reveal their objects more clearly, Religion becomes enriched and appears in a greater variety of ways, though no practice emerges which is more admirable than this gratitude. With the advantage of age, piety and holiness of life take deeper roots within the conscience, and give birth to a profound love and faith in God. Very often, too, vanities and superstitions and even vices and crimes spring up and multiply together with these virtues, like tares and weeds which grow from the decaying seed of wheat. Though they blossom more slowly, they mature quickly, unless they are uprooted in good time. I assign this growth to those factors which compose the body. Accordingly, while our animal nature actually comes into being later, it reaches its completion in us before the reasoning element. This will not surprise those who notice that the animals attain their maturity in three years. Whether this fact is to be traced to their fallen state or to some other cause I will not stay to discuss. It may seem paradoxical that moral virtue which is so strict and severe is, and always has been, esteemed by men in every age and place and respected in every land, in spite of the fact that it conflicts with our physical and, I may say, agreeable feelings. But the reason for this is as follows. Since Nature unceasingly labors to deliver the soul from its physical burden, so Nature itself instils men with its secret conviction that virtue constitutes the most effective means by which our mind may be gradually separated and released from the body, and enter into its lawful realm. And though many arguments could be cited to the same purpose, I know no more convincing proof than the fact that it is only virtue that has the power to draw our soul from the delights which engulf it, and even to restore it to its native region, so that freed from the foul embrace of vice, and finally from the fear of death itself, it can apply itself to its proper function and attain inward everlasting joy.

*The minds of men have always been filled with horror for their wickedness. Their vices and crimes have been obvious to them. They must be expiated by repentance*

There is no general agreement concerning the various rites or mysteries which the priests have devised for the expiation of sin. Among the Romans, ceremonies of purification, cleansing, atonement, among the Greeks, rites of expiation and purging, and in nearly all races, sacrifices, even of human victims, a cruel and abominable device of the priests, were instituted for this purpose. Among the Egyptians and all the heathen races observances of a similar kind prevailed. I have referred to many of them in my book *On the Religion of the Gentiles* and also in my work, not yet published, *On the Causes of Errors*. Among the Mohammedans, Ramadan is held twice each year after the manner of our Forty Days. But above all other races the Eastern Indians display the most energy in exercises of this kind. At a certain sacred period of the year they gather in the forests, and taking a piece of sharp rock or stone, let forth a quantity of blood, until their spirits are on the point of leaving them, protesting at the same time that the root-causes of their sins had lain hidden in their blood and that by allowing it to gush forth they atone for their sins. But we may pass over such rites, some of which may well appear ridiculous. General agreement among religions, the nature of divine goodness, and above all conscience, tell us that our crimes may be washed away by true penitence, and that we can be restored to new union with God. For this inner witness condemns wickedness while at the same time it can wipe out the stain of it by genuine repentance, as the inner form of apprehension under proper conditions proves. I do not wish to consider here whether any other more appropriate means exists by which the divine justice may be appeased, since I have undertaken in this work only to rely on truths which are not open to dispute but are derived from the evidence of immediate perception and admitted by the whole world. This alone I assert, whatever may be said to the contrary, that unless wickedness can be abolished by penitence and faith in God, and unless the Divine goodness can satisfy the Divine justice (and no further appeal can be invoked), then there does not exist, nor ever has existed any universal source to which the wretched mass of men, crushed beneath the burden of sin, can turn to obtain grace and inward peace. If this were the case, God has created and condemned certain men; in fact, the larger part of the human race, not only without their desire, but without their knowledge. This idea is so dreadful and consorts so ill with the providence and goodness, and even the justice of God, that it is more charitable to suppose that the whole human race has always possessed in repentance the opportunity of becoming reconciled with God. And as long as men did not cut themselves off from it their damnation would not have been due to the benevolent will of God but to their own sins, nor could God have been charged with blame if they failed to find salvation. All the teaching of the greatest preachers concerning eternal salvation coincides on this issue, since every means of redress is useless except penitence and becomes, as they tell us, empty and futile. Accordingly, they hold it to be of such importance in relation to the divine goodness that they consider that when no readier way presents itself the entire secret of salvation may be revealed in this process. Some critics of Nature or Divine universal Providence object that it is not always within our power to experience remorse. I have myself pointed out that wisdom is always within our grasp. But these critics fail to notice the distinction which I have made above, between voluntary and involuntary actions, nor do they recognize that some movements cannot be prevented, and others cannot be provoked into action. Man does not remember, or keep awake, or sleep, just as he

desires. Some of these activities, like many other inner movements, admit of degrees and exceptions. But to declare that God
has cut us off from the means by which we can return to Him,
provided that we play our part to the utmost of our ability, is a
blasphemy so great that those who indulge in it seek to destroy
not merely human goodness but also the goodness of God. They
must abandon these ideas, and their ideas and utterances, at
least concerning the secret judgments of God, must be more
guarded. For they cannot deny that if not from general providence, yet from particular providence or Grace, may flow the
means by which God's favor may be won. We realize what we
owe to Grace when we reflect that by it our works are accomplished, by it they are made acceptable to God. I think that it is
chiefly by this means that God's mercy meets the demands of
His goodness. For in the mutual relationship which exists between us, when our goods are seized by plunder or theft, the
common laws of nations or universal consent requires that in
addition to repentance there should be restoration. Now, if anyone with perverted curiosity asks me why we possess the liberty
to commit sin and crime I can only answer that it is due to the
secret judgments of God. If he persists in asking what can be
known within the moderate limits of the human faculties I must
reply that man is a finite animal, and therefore cannot do anything which is absolutely good or even absolutely bad. Yet the
nature of each is modified in every action, so that the action
shares to some extent in both, though it is named according to
the element which has the larger share. Anyone who desires
further discussion on this problem may refer to what I have
said on an earlier page. I have now briefly examined the principal
Common Notions about the way of God which refer to the
journey of life. I pass on to treat of the state of the future life.
And this I shall comprise in a single proposition.

### There is Reward or Punishment after this Life

The rewards that are eternal have been variously placed in
heaven, in the stars, in the Elysian fields, or in contemplation.
Punishment has been thought to lie in metempsychosis, in hell

(which some describe as filled with fire, but the Chinese imagine pervaded with smoke), or in some infernal regions, or regions of the middle air, or in temporary or everlasting death. But all religion, law, philosophy, and, what is more, conscience teach openly or implicitly that punishment or reward awaits us after this life. Religion teaches us this explicitly when it uses the terms which I have mentioned. It teaches the same doctrine indirectly by establishing the immortality of the soul or by proving that God avenges crimes which are committed with impunity in this life. In this sense there is no nation, however barbarous, which has not and will not recognize the existence of punishments and rewards. That reward and punishment exist is, then, a Common Notion, though there is the greatest difference of opinion as to their nature, quality, extent, and mode. It is no objection that the soul perishes with the body, as some people assert. For they refer this very fact to punishment for sin, or else they mean only that part of the soul with which they have been familiar, namely, the physical senses; or finally, they must be ignored, since they talk sheer nonsense; for there is nothing in the faculties of the mind to suggest such ideas. That the soul could be immortal if God willed it is clearly a Common Notion, in that among the most distant races, seething with every type of superstition, there exists a general conviction that purity of life and courage of mind promote happiness. It is on this account that they are said to honor the bones of those who have died bravely in battle. But I do not trouble myself about such matters, since I am not concerned with superstitions and sacred rites; it is not what a large number of men assert, but what all men of normal mind believe, that I find important. Scanning the vast array of absurd fictions, I am content to discover a tiny Common Notion. And this is of the utmost importance, since when the general mass of men have rejected a whole range of beliefs which it has found valueless, it proceeds to acquire new beliefs by this method, until the point is reached where faith can be applied.

It follows from these considerations that the Dogmas which recognize a sovereign Deity enjoin us to worship Him, command

us to live a holy life, lead us to repent our sins, and warn us of
future recompense or punishment, proceed from God and are
inscribed within us in the form of Common Notions. But those
dogmas which postulate a plurality of Gods, which do not forbid
crimes and sins, which rail against penitence, and which express
doubts about the eternal state of the soul cannot be considered
either Common Notions or truths. Accordingly, every religion,
if we consider it comprehensively, is not good; nor can we admit
that salvation is open to men in every religion. For how could
anyone who believes more than is necessary, but who does less
than he ought, be saved? But I am convinced that in every
religion, and indeed in every individual conscience, either through
Grace or Nature, sufficient means are granted to men to win
God's goodwill; while all additional and peculiar features which
are found at any period must be referred to their inventors. It
is not sufficient that they should be old if they have once been
new. Ideas which are superfluous or even false may be not only
novel but ancient, and truths which are only seized by a few
cannot be essential to all. The truth which belongs to revelation
occupies a special place here; and no faith in it is in any way
disparaged by the principles which I have described. On the contrary, whatever it adds to them I hold to be valuable. The fundamental principles of Revelation itself are here established, so
that it is possible to reduce all disputes to the question, On what
faculty does the argument depend? Accordingly, so far from
these views conflicting with ordinary beliefs or depending on new
principles, I have asserted nothing but the symbol of Common
Notions and what has been universally accepted by every religion,
age, and country. I do not deny that sacred ceremonies can form
part of religion; on the contrary, I find that some ceremonies are
included in every religion and serve to embellish it; so far they
are valuable. But when they are made by the priests the essential
elements of divine worship, then religion, and we who practise
it, are the victims of imposture. Rites must be kept within bounds.
We can only accept them on the understanding that religion is
chaste and only requires such ornaments as render a matron more

venerable and respected. When she paints and dyes herself her appearance is too suggestive of the harlot.

Such, then, are the Common Notions of which the true Catholic or universal Church is built. For the church which is built of clay or stone or living rock or even of marble cannot be claimed to be the infallible Church. The true Catholic Church is not supported on the inextricable confusion of oral and written tradition to which men have given their allegiance. Still less is it that which fights beneath any one particular standard, or is comprised in one organization so as to embrace only a restricted portion of the earth, or a single period of history. The only Catholic and uniform Church is the doctrine of Common Notions which comprehends all places and all men. This Church alone reveals Divine Universal Providence, or the wisdom of Nature. This Church alone explains why God is appealed to as the common Father. And it is only through this Church that salvation is possible. The adoration which has been bestowed on every particular Church belongs to it. Every Church, as I have pointed out above, is the more exposed to error the further it is separated from it. Anyone who courts uncertain doctrines in place of the sure truths of divine providence, and forges new articles of Faith, forsakes this Church. If, however, anyone receives some truth by revelation, which I think can occur both in the waking state and in sleep, he must use it as occasion warrants, remembering that unless he is entrusted with a message of interest to all, he should reserve it to himself. For it is not likely that what is not evident to the faculties of all can have any bearing on the whole human race. I have often observed that we can take much on faith with true piety, and we need not abandon any belief as long as it does not conflict with the divine attributes. It is not the case therefore, as some critic may point out, that after examining the means by which Divine Universal Providence acts and admitting that it is universal in its operation, I then restrict it to its own kingdom. I desire that every feature which redounds to the glory of God may be added to the characteristics which have been mentioned. For my part I accept with earnest faith and gratitude all that preceding ages have uttered in praise of God's goodness and mercy. I agree with the majority of mankind that all that they tell us not merely could have come to pass but that it actually did so. But I maintain that the principles of faith are to be found in the truths of divine Universal Providence, since I cannot see that in any other way the harmony of Nature or general Providence, with Grace or particular Providence, can be preserved. This does not exclude the right of the Church to decide all matters which concern external worship, or ecclesiastical organization, or the publication for future generations of the records of earlier times, and especially those events which confirm the true attributes of God. For when these Catholic truths are received into the recesses of the soul they rest on a foundation of indubitable faith, and anything which remains can and ought to be believed with piety upon the authority of the Church; provided, that is, that all contradictions are avoided or recognized, and only those doctrines are impressed on men's minds which promote universal peace and concord, and make for purity of life. Whether these means are sufficient to prepare us for eternal salvation I leave in the hands of God. I, at least, do not seek to pry into the secret judgments of God. I am content to have shown that the human mind informed by the Common Notions has been able in every age and place to apprehend these principles. If we set aside superstitions and legends the mind takes its stand on my five articles, and upon nothing else. To deny this would be to allow less sense to men than to sheep; for they at least when they are let into the pastures avoid those herbs which are harmful and only eat those which are good for them. Whether indeed human wisdom has undertaken this examination in any age or place, or whether, even if it has done so, all who have rejected the inferior and trifling portions of religion, or possibly have accepted a mystical interpretation of them on the authority of their priests, equally enjoy the supreme happiness, I have not attempted to discuss. I firmly maintain, however, that it is, and always has been, possible for all men to reach the truths I have described. But whether they have been manifest, or whether, even when they are manifest, they are immediately accepted, I am so far from wishing to discuss that all matters of this nature which depend upon the secret counsels of God, I leave to be inferred from the Divine wisdom and goodness. But if anyone calls them in dispute I am prepared stoutly to defend them. For by no other method could the existence of Divine Universal Providence, the highest attribute of God, be proved by the principles of common reason. If we abandon these principles – and as I have often pointed out Nature or the Common Providence of the world does not operate beyond the means at its disposal – and if we give way to wicked blasphemies, terrible crimes, and finally to impenitence, to which we are sacramentally bound; if we defile the purity of Religion with foolish superstitions and degrading legends; it would be wholly unjust to blame the Supreme Goodness for our sins. It would be like accusing a host who provides a feast set out with a splendid profusion of dishes, of encouraging drunkenness, gluttony, and license. For what is sufficient is due to God, excess is due to us. Why, then, as I have said elsewhere, following the law of common reason, can we not apply the same rule to the perfect sphere of the religion of God that we apply to any circle? If anything is added to it or taken from it its shape is destroyed, and its perfection ruined. I do not, however, wish to decide too hastily on this question. I would, indeed, firmly maintain that it is impossible to remove any feature from religion. But whether anything can suitably be added to the orb of religion, as is possible with a circle, I am not so certain; though the shape of a visible circle is continuous so that no part of it is hidden. The fair form of Divine Universal Providence ought to stand forth in all its beauty and not lurk behind a mask. Whatever feature is added to this circular shape should fitly and exactly correspond in a form which is harmonious and congruent both with its centre and its circumference. The chief reason for this is that no other genuine and Almighty God can be accepted but He who directs universal providence to those ends which essentially concern the salvation of the soul. But since no other clear pattern of that Providence can be found than that which lies open to the whole human race in these Articles, and in these alone, we ought to consider whether it is possible to conceive of any stricter or purer religion, or of any means by which it is possible for a man to become more virtuous or more just, than is contained in these Catholic Articles. Accordingly, if the priests have agreed to emphasize for the sake of Universal Peace not merely these principles (since Dogmas are permissible in matters of faith) but have further resolved to add those parts of beliefs in historical events which display great mercy toward the human race, a procedure with which I am in full accord, yet they should not suffer elements to be introduced which disparage the work of Universal Providence or confine it within strict or narrow limits. But neither must they allow features to be introduced which, through too hasty a desire for forgiveness, soften or destroy the austere outline of religion; otherwise men may relapse more quickly and with less foresight into sin. I humbly recommend these considerations to the judgment of the priests, with the hope that they may abandon their mysteries, and direct themselves to accomplishing their function toward God and His interests in accordance with the most sacred maxims given us to that end, and so exert themselves on behalf of the people. Anyone may add for himself, their substance, quality, quantity, mode, etc., to these articles. I shall now discuss what may be derived from Revelation.

# 2

# ROMANTICISM
## Friedrich Schleiermacher

THE ROMANTIC MOVEMENT of the late eighteenth and early nineteenth centuries in Germany arose in reaction to the rationalism of the Enlightenment. The Romanticists were concerned to recover the elements of intuition, imagination, and feeling in human life and culture which had been subordinated to the activity of pure reason. They stressed the significance of the concrete, organic, historical individual as against what they believed to be the abstractions of Rationalism. At the center of attention was man's passionate mystical relation to the natural universe understood as an eternally active whole. In theology the Romantic spirit was mediated by Friedrich Schleiermacher (1768–1834).

Schleiermacher brought to Romanticism the deep influence of his early education at the hands of the Moravians. This background in German pietism led to his study for ordination. In 1796 he was appointed chaplain at a hospital in Berlin and was introduced to the circle of the Romanticists in which the spirit of Goethe was dominant. This group included Novalis and Schlegel, and it was with the latter in mind that Schleiermacher published his *Speeches on Religion to its Cultured Despisers* in 1799 at the age of thirty-one. As a professor at the University of Halle and later at the new University of Berlin, he lectured on philosophy and theology while continuing as a preacher. During these years he published works on ethics, logic, and hermeneutics, and in 1821 appeared his famous systematic theology, *The Christian Faith*.

There is little doubt that Schleiermacher was the most influential Protestant theologian of the nineteenth century. He was attacked by the rationalist theologians of the Enlightenment and by the orthodox, but he opened a new era in Protestant thought and is rightly known as the father of modern liberal theology. Although he has passed out of favor because of the severe criticism by the neo-orthodox theologians of the second quarter of this century, this criticism itself has kept him close to the center of theological attention.

In the *Speeches on Religion* Schleiermacher is concerned to correct the current understanding of religion as a set of rational and moral doctrines about God, human freedom, and immortality, i.e. the "natural religion" of the Enlightenment. What has been forgotten is the longing of the human heart for communion with the universe and the Infinite or God. Religion cannot be reduced to metaphysics, morals, or science; it is essentially a matter of man's sense of the Infinite in all his experience. The seat of religion is not in reason, conscience, or will, but in feeling, in immediate self-consciousness. This has often been understood to mean that religion is essentially emotion or a psychological state, and Schleiermacher has been criticized as a psychological subjectivist. But this is a misinterpretation, since by "feeling" Schleiermacher probably meant an awareness or immediate apprehension of that which is beyond the self.

On the basis of this definition of religion Schleiermacher asserts that real religion is found only in the positive or historical religions of mankind. Furthermore, the very nature of religion as an awareness of the Infinite in the finite requires that religion can be completely manifest only in a multiplicity of religions. In each positive religion one particular relation of mankind to the Infinite is selected and placed at the center. In Christianity this relation is the universal resistance of the finite to the Infinite and the overcoming of this resistance in God's redemption. Because this relation is the most fundamental, Christianity is the highest form of religion, "the religion of religions". Yet Christianity does not seek to be the sole religion, but willingly sees other forms of religion produced outside itself.

In *The Christian Faith* Schleiermacher carries these lines of thought somewhat further. Religion is defined as the "feeling of absolute dependence" which is a consciousness of being in relation to God. The various religions are arranged on a scale of development moving from idol-worship up through polytheism to monotheism. Of the three examples of monotheism Islam represents the aesthetic type, while Judaism and Christianity represent the teleological or ethical type. But since Judaism is a less perfect form, retains elements of idol-worship, and is in the process of extinction, Christianity remains "the most perfect of the most highly developed forms of religion". Yet other religions are not simply false, since all religions contain some relation to truth and an obscure awareness of God (see Section 7–9).

Schleiermacher's interpetation of and attitude toward other religions combines elements of the approaches described above under the headings "Essence" and "Development–Fulfillment". He defines an essence of religion which is found at the heart of all religions, and he places all religions on a scale of development from lower to higher or more perfect forms. Thus his view is open to the difficulties which have been raised about these approaches.

# Religion and the Religions*

IN ORDER TO make quite clear to you what is the original and characteristic possession of religion, it resigns, at once, all claims on anything that belongs either to science or morality. Whether it has been borrowed or bestowed it is now returned. What, then, does your science of being, your natural science, all your theoretical philosophy, in so far as it has to do with the actual world, have for its aim? To know things, I suppose, as they really are; to show the peculiar relations by which each is what it is; to deter-

* From Friedrich Schleiermacher, *On Religion: Speeches to Its Cultured Despisers*, trans. by J. Oman, introd. by R. Otto (New York: Harper Torchbooks, 1958), pp. 35–39, 45–46, 211–218, 222–224, 237–238, 241–243, 250–252. Reprinted with the permission of Harper & Row, Publishers, Inc.

mine for each its place in the Whole, and to distinguish it rightly from all else; to present the whole real world in its mutually conditioned necessity; and to exhibit the oneness of all phenomena with their eternal laws. This is truly beautiful and excellent, and I am not disposed to depreciate it. Rather, if this description of mine, so slightly sketched, does not suffice, I will grant the highest and most exhaustive you are able to give.

And yet, however high you go; though you pass from the laws to the Universal Lawgiver, in whom is the unity of all things; though you allege that nature cannot be comprehended without God, I would still maintain that religion has nothing to do with this knowledge, and that, quite apart from it, its nature can be known. Quantity of knowledge is not quantity of piety. Piety can gloriously display itself, both with originality and individuality, in those to whom this kind of knowledge is not original. They may only know it as everybody does, as isolated results known in connection with other things. The pious man must, in a sense, be a wise man, but he will readily admit, even though you somewhat proudly look down upon him, that, in so far as he is pious, he does not hold his knowledge in the same way as you.

Let me interpret in clear words what most pious persons only guess at and never know how to express. Were you to set God as the apex of your science, as the foundation of all knowing as well as of all knowledge, they would accord praise and honour, but it would not be their way of having and knowing God. From their way, as they would readily grant, and as is easy enough to see, knowledge and science do not proceed.

It is true that religion is essentially contemplative. You would never call anyone pious who went about in impervious stupidity, whose sense is not open for the life of the world. But this contemplation is not returned, as your knowledge of nature is, to the existence of a finite thing, combined with and opposed to another finite thing. It has not even, like your knowledge of God – if for once I might use an old expression – to do with the nature of the first cause, in itself and in its relation to every other cause and operation. The contemplation of the pious is the immediate consciousness of the universal existence of all finite things, in and through the Infinite, and of all temporal things in and through the Eternal. Religion is to seek this and find it in all that lives and moves, in all growth and change, in all doing and suffering. It is to have life and to know life in immediate feeling, only as such an existence in the Infinite and Eternal. Where this is found religion is satisfied, where it hides itself there is for her unrest and anguish, extremity and death. Wherefore it is a life in the infinite nature of the whole, in the One and in the All, in God, having and possessing all things in God, and God in all. Yet religion is not knowledge and science, either of the world or of God. Without being knowledge, it recognizes knowledge and science. In itself it is an affection, a revelation of the Infinite in the finite, God being seen in it and it in God.

Similarly, what is the object of your ethics, of your science of action? Does it not seek to distinguish precisely each part of human doing and producing, and at the same time to combine them into a whole, according to actual relations? But the pious man confesses that, as pious, he knows nothing about it. He does, indeed, contemplate human action, but it is not the kind of contemplation from which an ethical system takes its rise. Only one thing he seeks out and detects, action from God, God's activity among men. If your ethics are right, and his piety as well, he will not, it is true, acknowledge any action as excellent which is not embraced in your system. But to know and to construct this system is your business, ye learned, not his. If you will not believe, regard the case of women. You ascribe to them religion, not only as an adornment, but you demand of them the finest feeling for distinguishing the things that excel: do you equally expect them to know your ethics as a science?

It is the same, let me say at once, with action itself. The artist fashions what is given him to fashion, by virtue of his special talent. These talents are so different that the one he possesses another lacks; unless someone, against heaven's will, would possess all. But when anyone is praised to you as pious, you are not accustomed to ask which of these gifts dwell in him by virtue of his piety. The citizen – taking the word in the sense of the ancients, not in its present meagre significance – regulates, leads,

c

and influences in virtue of his morality. But this is something different from piety. Piety has also a passive side. While morality always shows itself as manipulating, as self-controlling, piety appears as a surrender, a submission to be moved by the Whole that stands over against man. Morality depends, therefore, entirely on the consciousness of freedom, within the sphere of which all that it produces falls. Piety, on the contrary, is not all bound to this side of life. In the opposite sphere of necessity, where there is no properly individual action, it is quite as active. Wherefore the two are different. Piety does, indeed, linger with satisfaction on every action that is from God, and every activity that reveals the Infinite in the finite, and yet it is not itself this activity. Only by keeping quite outside the range both of science and of practice can it maintain its proper sphere and character. Only when piety takes its place alongside of science and practice, as a necessary, an indispensable third, as their natural counterpart, not less in worth and splendor than either, will the common field be altogether occupied and human nature on this side complete.

But pray understand me fairly. I do not mean that one could exist without the other, that, for example, a man might have religion and be pious, and at the same time be immoral. That is impossible. But, in my opinion, it is just as impossible to be moral or scientific without being religious. But have I not said that religion can be had without science? Wherefore, I have myself begun the separation. But remember, I only said piety is not the measure of science. Just as one cannot be truly scientific without being pious, the pious man may not know at all, but he cannot know falsely. His proper nature is not of that subordinate kind, which, according to the old adage that like is only known to like, knows nothing except semblance of reality.

His nature is reality which knows reality, and where it encounters nothing it does not suppose it sees something. And what a precious jewel of science, in my view, is ignorance for those who are captive to semblance. If you have not learned it from my Speeches or discovered it for yourselves, go and learn it from your Socrates. Grant me consistency at least. With ignorance your knowledge will ever be mixed, but the true and proper opposite of knowledge is presumption of knowledge. By piety this presumption is most certainly removed, for with it piety cannot exist.

Such a separation of knowledge and piety, and of action and piety, do not accuse me of making. You are only ascribing to me, without my deserving it, your own view and the very confusion, as common as it is unavoidable, which it has been my chief endeavor to show you in the mirror of my Speech. Just because you do not acknowledge religion as the third, knowledge and action are so much apart that you can discover no unity, but believe that right knowing can be had without right acting, and *vice versa*. I hold that it is only in contemplation that there is division. There, where it is necessary, you despise it, and instead transfer it to life, as if in life itself objects could be found independent one of the other. Consequently, you have no living insight into any of these activities. Each is for you a part, a fragment. Because you do not deal with life in a living way, your conception bears the stamp of perishableness, and is altogether meagre. True science is complete vision; true practice is culture and art self-produced; true religion is sense and taste for the Infinite. To wish to have true science or true practice without religion, or to imagine it is possessed, is obstinate, arrogant delusion, and culpable error. It issues from the unholy sense that would rather have a show of possession by cowardly purloining than have secure possession by demanding and waiting. What can man accomplish that is worth speaking of, either in life or in art, that does not arise in his own self from the influence of this sense for the Infinite? Without it, how can anyone wish to comprehend the world scientifically, or if, in some distinct talent, the knowledge is thrust upon him, how should he wish to exercise it? What is all science, if not the existence of things in you, in your reason? What is all art and culture if not your existence in the things to which you give measure, form, and order? And how can both come to life in you except in so far as there lives immediately in you the eternal unity of Reason and Nature, the universal existence of all finite things in the Infinite? ...

There then you have the three things about which my Speech

has so far turned – perception, feeling, and activity, and you now understand what I mean when I say they are not identical and yet are inseparable. Take what belongs to each class and consider it by itself. You will find that those moments in which you exercise power over things and impress yourselves upon them form what you call your practical, or, in the narrower sense, your moral life; again the contemplative moments, be they few or many, in which things produce themselves in you as intuition, you will doubtless call your scientific life. Now can either series alone form a human life? Would it not be death? If each activity were not stimulated and renewed by the other, would it not be self-consumed? Yet they are not identical. If you would understand your life and speak comprehensibly of it, they must be distinguished. As it stands with these two in respect of one another, it must stand with the third in respect of both. How, then, are you to name this third, which is the series of feeling? What life will it form? The religious as I think, and as you will not be able to deny, when you have considered it more closely.

The chief point in my Speech is now uttered. This is the peculiar sphere which I would assign to religion – the whole of it, and nothing more. Unless you grant it, you must either prefer the old confusion to clear analysis or produce something else, I know not what, new and quite wonderful. Your feeling is piety, in so far as it expresses, in the manner described, the being and life common to you and to the All. Your feeling is piety in so far as it is the result of the operation of God in you by means of the operation of the world upon you. This series is not made up either of perceptions or of objects of perception, either of works or operations or of different spheres of operation, but purely of sensations and the influence of all that lives and moves around, which accompanies them and conditions them. These feelings are exclusively the elements of religion, and none are excluded. There is no sensation that is not pious, except it indicate some diseased and impaired state of the life, the influence of which will not be confined to religion. Wherefore, it follows that ideas and principles are all foreign to religion. This truth we here come upon for the second time. If ideas and principles are to be anything they must belong to knowledge, which is a different department of life from religion. . . .

At present I have something else to deal with, a new opposition to vanquish. I would, as it were, conduct you to the God that has become flesh; I would show you religion when it has resigned its infinity and appeared, often in sorry form, among men; I would have you discover religion in the religions. Though they are always earthly and impure, the same form of heavenly beauty that I have tried to depict is to be sought in them.

The divisions of the Church and the difference of religion are almost always found together. The connection seems inseparable. There are as many creeds and confessions as churches and religious communions. Glancing at this state of things, you might easily believe that my judgment on the plurality of the Church must also be my judgment on the plurality of religion. You would, however, entirely mistake my opinion. I condemned the plurality of the Church, but my argument presupposed the plurality of religion. I showed from the nature of the case that in the Church all rigid outline should be lost, that all distinct partition should disappear. Not only did I hold that all should be one indivisible whole in spirit and sympathy but that the actual connection should have larger development and ever approach the highest, the universal unity. Now if there is not everywhere plurality of religion, if the most marked difference is not necessary and unavoidable, why should the true Church need to be one? Is it not that everyone in the religion of others may see and share what he cannot find in his own? And why should the visible Church be only one, if it is not that everyone may seek in it religion in the form best fitted to awake the germ that lies asleep in him? And if this germ can only be fertilized and made to grow by one definite kind of influence it must itself be of a definite kind.

Nor can these different manifestations of religion be mere component parts, differing only in number and size, and forming, when combined, a uniform whole. In that case everyone would by natural progress come to be like his neighbor. Such religion as he acquired would change into his own, and become identical with it. The Church, this fellowship with all believers which I consider indispensable for every religious man, would be merely provisional. The more successful its work, the quicker would it end – a view of the institution I have never contemplated. I therefore find that multiplicity of the religions is based in the nature of religion.

That no man can perfectly possess all religion is easy to see. Men are determined in one special way, religion is endlessly determinable. But it must be equally evident that religion is not dismembered and scattered in parts by random among men, but that it must organize itself in manifestations of varying degrees of resemblance. Recall the several stages of religion to which I drew your attention. I said that the religion of a person, to whom the world reveals itself as a living whole, is not a mere continuation of the view of the person who only sees the world in its apparently hostile elements. By no amount of regarding the Universe as chaotic and discrete can the higher view be attained. These differences you may call kinds or degrees of religion, but in either case you will have to admit that, as in every similar case, the forms in which an infinite force divides itself are usually characteristic and different.

Wherefore, plurality of religions is another thing than plurality of the Church. The essence of the Church is fellowship. Its limit, therefore, cannot be the uniformity of religious persons. It is just difference that should be brought into fellowship. You are manifestly right when you believe that the Church can never in actuality be completely and uniformly one. The only reason, however, is that every society existing in space and time is thereby limited and losing in depth what it gains in breadth, falls to pieces. But religion, exactly by its multiplicity, assumes the utmost unity of the Church. This multiplicity is necessary for the complete manifestation of religion. It must seek for a definite character, not only in the individual but also in the society. Did the society not contain a principle to individualize itself, it could have no existence. Hence we must assume and we must search for an endless mass of distinct forms. Each separate religion claims to be such a distinct form revealing religion, and we must see whether it is agreeable to this principle. We must make clear to ourselves wherein it is peculiar. Though the difference be hidden under strange disguises, though it be distorted not only by the unavoidable influence of the transitory to which the enduring has condescended but also by the unholy hand of sacrilegious men, we must find it.

To be satisfied with a mere general idea of religion would not be worthy of you. Would you then understand it as it really exists and displays itself, would you comprehend it as an endlessly progressive work of the Spirit that reveals Himself in all human history, you must abandon the vain and foolish wish that there should only be one religion; you must lay aside all repugnance to its multiplicity; as candidly as possible you must approach everything that has ever, in the changing shapes of humanity, been developed in its advancing career, from the ever fruitful bosom of the spiritual life.

The different existing manifestations of religion you call positive religions. Under this name they have long been the object of a quite pre-eminent hate. Despite your repugnance to religion generally, you have always borne more easily with what for distinction is called natural religion. You have almost spoken of it with esteem.

I do not hesitate to say at once that from the heart I entirely deny this superiority. For all who have religion at all and profess to love it, it would be the vilest inconsequence to admit it. They would thereby fall into the openest self-contradiction. For my own part, if I only succeeded in recommending to you this natural religion I would consider that I had lost my pains.

For you, indeed, to whom religion generally is offensive, I have always considered this preference natural. The so-called natural religion is usually so much refined away, and has such metaphysical and moral graces, that little of the peculiar character of religion appears. It understands so well to live in reserve, to restrain, and to accommodate itself that it can be put up with anywhere. Every positive religion, on the contrary, has certain strong traits and a very marked physiognomy, so that its every movement, even to the careless glance, proclaims what it really is.

If this is the true ground of your dislike you must now rid yourself of it. If you have now, as I hope, a better estimate of religion it should be no longer necessary for me to contend against it. If you see that a peculiar and noble capacity of man underlies religion, a capacity which, of course, must be educated, it cannot be offensive to you to regard it in the most definite forms in which it has yet appeared. Rather you must the more willingly grant a form your attention the more there is developed in it the characteristic and distinctive elements of religion.

But you may not admit this argument. You may transfer all the reproaches you have formerly been accustomed to bestow on religion in general to the single religions. You may maintain that there are always, just in this element that you call positive, the occasion and the justification of those reproaches, and that in consequence the positive religions cannot be as I have sought to represent, the natural manifestations of the true religion. You would show me how, without exception, they are full of what, according to my own statement, is not religion. Consequently, must not a principle of corruption lie deep in their constitution? You will remind me that each one proclaims that it alone is true, and that what is peculiar to it is absolutely the highest. Are they not distinguished from one another by elements they should as much as possible eliminate? In disproving and contending, be it with art and understanding or with weapons stranger and more unworthy, do they not show themselves quite contrary to the nature of true religion? You would add that, exactly in proportion as you esteem religion and acknowledge its importance, you must take a lively interest in seeing that it everywhere enjoys the greatest freedom to cultivate itself on all sides. You must, therefore, hate keenly those definite religious forms that hold all their adherents to the same type and the same word, withdraw the freedom to follow their own nature and compress them in unnatural limits. In contrast, you would praise mightily the superiority in all these points of the natural to the positive religions.

Once more I say, I do not deny that misunderstandings and perversions exist in all religions, and I raise no objections to the dislike with which they inspire you. Nay, I acknowledge there is in them all this much bewailed degeneration, this divergence into alien territory. The diviner religion itself is, the less would I embellish its corruptions, or admiringly cherish its excrescences. But forget for once this one-sided view and follow me to another. Consider how much of this corruption is due to those who have dragged forth religion from the depths of the heart into the civil world. Acknowledge that much of it is unavoidable as soon as the Infinite, by descending into the sphere of time and submitting to the general influence of finite things, takes to itself a narrow shell. And however deep-rooted this corruption may be, and however much the religions may have suffered thereby, consider this also: if the proper religious view of all things is to seek even in things apparently common and base every trace of the divine, the true and the eternal, and to reverence even the faintest, you cannot omit what has the justest claims to be judged religiously.

And you would find more than remote traces of the Deity. I invite you to study every faith professed by man, every religion that has a name and a character. Though it may long ago have degenerated into a long series of empty customs, into a system of abstract ideas and theories, will you not, when you examine the original elements at the source, find that this dead dross was once the molten outpourings of the inner fire? Is there not in all religions more or less of the true nature of religion, as I have presented it to you? Must not, therefore, each religion be one of the special forms which mankind, in some region of the earth and at some stage of development, has to accept?

I must take care not to attempt anything systematic or complete, for that would be the study of a life, and not the business of a discourse. Yet you must not be allowed to wander at hazard in this endless chaos. That you may not be misled by the false ideas that prevail; that you may estimate by a right standard the true content and essence of any religion; that you may have some definite and sure procedure for separating the inner from the outer, the native from the borrowed and extraneous, and the sacred from the profane, forget the characteristic attributes of single religions and seek, from the centre outwards, a general

view of how the essence of a positive religion is to be comprehended and determined.

You will then find that the positive religions are just the
definite forms in which religion must exhibit itself – a thing to
which your so-called natural religions have no claim. They are
only a vague, sorry, poor thought that corresponds to no reality,
and you will find that in the positive religions alone a true
individual cultivation of the religious capacity is possible. Nor
do they, by their nature, injure the freedom of their adherents.

Why have I assumed that religion can only be given fully in
a great multitude of forms of the utmost definiteness? Only on
grounds that naturally follow from what has been said of the
nature of religion. The whole of religion is nothing but the sum
of all relations of man to God, apprehended in all the possible
ways in which any man can be immediately conscious in his life.
In this sense there is but one religion, for it would be but a
poverty-stricken and halting life if all these relations did not exist
wherever religion ought to be. Yet all men will not by any means
apprehend them in the same way, but quite differently. Now this
difference alone is felt and alone can be exhibited while the
reduction of all differences is only thought.

You are wrong, therefore, with your universal religion that is
natural to all, for no one will have his own true and right religion,
if it is the same for all. As long as we occupy a place, there must
be in these relations of man to the whole a nearer and a farther,
which will necessarily determine each feeling differently in each
life. Again, as long as we are individuals, every man has greater
receptiveness for some religious experiences and feelings than for
others. In this way everything is different. Manifestly then, no
single relation can accord to every feeling its due. It requires the
sum of them. Hence, the whole of religion can be present only
when all those different views of every relation are actually
given. This is not possible, except in an endless number of
different forms. They must be determined adequately by a
different principle of reference to the others, and in each the same
religious element must be characteristically modified. In short,
they must be true individuals....

Let me say then at once that the only remaining way for a truly individual religion to arise is to select some one of the great relations of mankind in the world to the Highest Being, and, in a definite way, make it the center and refer to it all the others. In respect of the idea of religion, this may appear a merely arbitrary proceeding, but, in respect of the peculiarity of the adherents, being the natural expression of their character, it is the purest necessity. Hereby a distinctive spirit and a common character enter the whole at the same time, and the ambiguous and vague reach firm ground. By every formation of this kind one of the endless number of different views and different arrangements of the single elements, which are all possible and all require to be exhibited, is fully realized. Single elements are all seen on the one side that is turned toward this central point, which makes all the feelings have a common tone and a livelier closer interaction.

The whole of religion can only be actually given in the sum of all the forms possible in this sense. It can therefore be exhibited only in an endless series of shapes that are gradually developed in different points of time and space, and nothing adds to its complete manifestation that is not found in one of those forms. Where religion is so moulded that everything is seen and felt in connection with one relation to the Deity that mediates it or embraces it, it matters not in what place or in what man it is formed or what relation is selected, it is a strictly positive religion. In respect of the sum of the religious elements – to use a word that should again be brought to honor – it is a heresy, for from many equals one is chosen to be head of the rest. In respect, however, of the fellowship of all participants and their relation to the founder of their religion who first raised this central point to clear consciousness, it is a school and a discipleship.

But if, as is to be hoped, we are agreed that religion can only be exhibited in and by such definite forms, only those who with their own religion pitch their camp in some such positive form, have any fixed abode, and, if I might so say, any well-earned right of citizenship in the religious world. They alone can boast of contributing to the existence and the progress of the whole, and they alone are in the full sense religious persons, on one side belonging by community of type to a kindred, on the other being distinguished by persistent and definite traits from everyone else....

Never forget that the fundamental intuition of a religion must be some intuition of the Infinite in the finite, some one universal religious relation, found in every other religion that would be complete, but in this one only place in the center.

I beg you also not to regard everything found in the heroes of religion or in the sacred sources as religion. Do not seek in everything the decisive spirit of that religion. Nor do I exclude trifles merely, or things that on any estimate are foreign to religion, but things often mistaken for it. Recollect how undesignedly those sources were prepared, so that it was impossible to provide for the exclusion of everything not religion. And recall how the authors lived in all sorts of circumstances in the world, and could not say at every word they wrote, this does not belong to the faith. When they speak worldly wisdom and morality, or metaphysics and poetry, therefore, do not at once conclude that it must be forced into religion, or that in it the character of religion is to be sought. Morality, at least, should be everywhere only one, and religion which should not be anywhere one cannot be distinguished by the differences of morality, which are always something to be got rid of.

Above all, I beg you not to be misled by the two hostile principles that everywhere, and almost from the earliest times, have sought to distort and obscure the spirit of religion. Some would circumscribe it to a single dogma, and exclude everything not fashioned in agreement with it; others, from hatred of polemics, or to make religion more agreeable to the irreligious, or from misunderstanding and ignorance of the matter, or from lack of religious sense, decry everything characteristic as dead letter. Guard yourselves from both. With rigid systematizers or shallow indifferentists you will not find the spirit of a religion. It is found only among those who live in it as their element, and ever advance in it without cherishing the folly that they embrace it all.

Whether with these precautions you will succeed in discovering the spirit of the religions I do not know. I fear religion is only comprehensible through itself, and that its special architecture and characteristic difference will not become clear till you yourself belong to some one religion.

How you may succeed in deciphering the rude and undeveloped religions of remote peoples, or in unravelling the manifold, varied religious phenomena lying wrapped up in the beautiful mythologies of Greece and Rome, I care very little. May your gods guide you! But when you approach the holiest in which the Universe in its highest unity and comprehensiveness is to be perceived, when you would contemplate the different forms of the highest stage of religion which is not foreign or strange, but more or less existent among ourselves, I cannot be indifferent as to whether or not you find the right point of view....

The original intuition of Christianity is more glorious, more sublime, more worthy of adult humanity, penetrates deeper into the spirit of systematic religion and extends itself further over the whole Universe. It is just the intuition of the Universal resistance of finite things to the unity of the Whole, and of the way the Deity treats this resistance. Christianity sees how He reconciles the hostility to Himself, and sets bounds to the ever-increasing alienation by scattering points here and there over the whole that are at once finite and infinite, human and divine. Corruption and redemption, hostility and mediation, are the two indivisibly united, fundamental elements of this type of feeling, and by them the whole form of Christianity and the cast of all the religious matter contained in it are determined. With ever-increasing speed the spiritual world has departed from its perfection and imperishable beauty. All evil, even this that the finite must decay before it has completed the circuit of its existence, is a consequence of the will, of the self-seeking endeavor of the isolated nature that, everywhere rending itself from its connection with the Whole, seeks to be something by itself. Death itself has come on account of sin. The spiritual world, going from bad to worse, is incapable of any production in which the Divine Spirit actually lives. The understanding being darkened has swerved from the truth; the heart is corrupt and has no praise before God; the image of the Infinite in every part of finite nature has gone extinct.

In accordance with this state of the spiritual world, all dealings of Divine Providence are calculated. They are never directed to the immediate results for feeling; they do not consider the happiness or suffering which they produce; they are not even for hindering or forwarding certain actions. They are simply calculated to check corruption in the great masses, to destroy, without mercy, what can no more be restored, and with new powers to give birth to new creations. Wherefore He does signs and wonders that interrupt and shake the course of things, and sends ambassadors, with more or less of divine spirit indwelling, to pour out divine powers upon men.

And when man does seek through self-consciousness to enter into fellowship with the unity of the Whole, the finite resists him, and he seeks and does not find and loses what he has found. He is defective, variable, and attached to details and non-essentials. He wills rather than gives heed, and his aim vanishes from his eyes. In vain is every revelation. Everything is swallowed up by the earthly sense, everything is swept away by the innate irreligious principle. The Deity finds ever new devices. By His power alone, ever more glorious revelations issue from the bosom of the old. He sets up ever more exalted mediators between Himself and men. In every later ambassador the Deity unites with humanity ever more closely, that men may learn to know the Eternal Being. Yet the ancient complaint that man cannot comprehend what is from the Spirit of God is never taken away.

This is how Christianity most and best is conscious of God, and of the divine order in religion and history. It manipulates religion itself as matter for religion. It is thus a higher power of religion, and this most distinguishes its character and determines its whole form. Because it presupposes a widely extended godlessness, it is through and through polemical. It is polemical in its outward communication, for, to make its deepest nature evident, every corruption must be laid bare, be it in morals or in thinking. Above all, it must expose the hostility to the consciousness of the Highest Being, which is the irreligious principle itself. Relentlessly it unmasks every false morality, every bad religion, every unhappy union of both for mutual covering of nakedness. Into the inmost secrets of the corrupt heart it presses and illumines, with the sacred torch of personal experience, every evil that creeps in darkness. Almost its first work on appearing was to destroy the last expectation of its pious contemporaries, saying it was irreligious and godless to expect any other restoration than restoration to purer faith, to the higher view of things, and to eternal life in God. Boldly it led the heathen beyond the separation they had made between the world of the gods and the world of men. Not to live and move and have the being in God is to be entirely ignorant of Him. If this natural feeling, this inner consciousness is lost amid a mass of sense impressions and desires no religion has yet entered the narrow sense. Everywhere, then, its heralds tore open the whited sepulchres and brought the dead bones to light. Had these first heroes of Christianity been philosophers, they would have spoken as strongly against the corruption of philosophy. They never failed to recognize the outlines of the divine image. Behind all distortions and degradations they saw hidden the heavenly germ of religion. But as Christians they were chiefly concerned with the individual who was far from God and needed a mediator....

The fundamental idea of every positive religion, being a component part of the infinite Whole in which all things must be eternal, is in itself eternal and universal, but its whole development, its temporal existence, may not, in the same sense, be either universal or eternal. For to put the centre of religion just in that idea, it requires not only a certain mental attitude but a certain state of mankind. In this state, in the free play of the universal life, gone, never to return, that relation which, by its worth, made all others dependent on it can no longer maintain itself in the feeling, and this type of religion can no more endure. This is the case with all childlike religions, as soon as men lose the consciousness of their essential power. They should be collected as monuments of the past and deposited in the magazine of history, for their life is gone, never to return. Christianity, exalted above them all, more historical and more humble in its glory, has expressly acknowledged this transitoriness of its temporal existence. A time will come, it says, when there shall no more be any mediator, but the Father shall be all in all. But when shall this time come? I, at least, can only believe that it lies beyond all time.

One half of the original intuition of Christianity is the corruptibleness of all that is great and divine in human things. If a time should come when this – I will not say can no more be discovered, but no more obtrudes, when humanity advances so uniformly and peacefully that only the navigator who calculates its course by the stars knows when it is somewhat driven back on the great ocean it traverses by a passing contrary wind, and the unarmed eye, looking only at what is taking place, can no more directly observe the retrogression of human affairs, I would gladly stand on the ruins of the religion I honour.

The other half of the original Christian faith is that certain brilliant and divine points are the source of every improvement in this corruption and of every new and closer union of the finite with the Deity. Should a time ever come when the power that draws us to the Highest was so equally distributed among the great body of mankind that persons more strongly moved should cease to mediate for others, I would fain see it, I would willingly help to level all that exalteth itself. But this equality of all equalities is least possible. Times of corruption await all human things, even though of divine origin. New ambassadors from God will be required with exalted power to draw the recreant to itself and purify the corrupt with heavenly fire, and every such epoch of humanity is a palingenesis of Christianity, and awakes its spirit in a new and more beautiful form.

And if there are always to be Christians, is Christianity, therefore, to be universal and, as the sole type of religion, to rule alone in humanity? It scorns this autocracy. Every one of its elements it honors enough to be willing to see it the centre of a whole of its own. Not only would it produce in itself variety to infinity but would willingly see even outside all that it cannot produce from itself. Never forgetting that it has the best proof of its immortality in its own corruptibleness, in its own often sad history, and ever expecting a redemption from the imperfection that now oppresses it, it willingly sees other and younger, and, if possible, stronger and more beautiful types of religion arise outside of this corruption. It could see them arise close beside it, and issue from all points, even from such as appear to it the utmost and most doubtful limits of religion. The religion of religions cannot collect material enough for its pure interest in all things human. As nothing is more irreligious than to demand general uniformity in mankind, so nothing is more unchristian than to seek uniformity in religion.

In all ways the Deity is to be contemplated and worshipped. Varied types of religion are possible, both in proximity and in combination, and if it is necessary that every type be actualized at one time or another it is to be desired that, at all times, there should be a dim sense of many religions. The great moments must be few in which all things agree to ensure to one among them a wide-extended and enduring life, in which the same view is developed unanimously and irresistibly in a great body, and many persons are deeply affected by the same impression of the divine....

# 3

# RELATIVISM
## Ernst Troeltsch

IF SCHLEIERMACHER STANDS at the beginning of the liberal Protestant theology of the last century, then Ernst Troeltsch (1865–1923) stands at its end, or at least at the end of its dominance. Troeltsch is known primarily for his massive two-volume study, *The Social Teaching of the Christian Church* (1912), but his interests and researches covered a wide field, including the philosophy of religion, theology, history, and especially the problem of historical method and its impact upon Christianity. In his theological studies Troeltsch was most deeply influenced by Albrecht Ritschl, the main figure in German Protestant theology in the latter part of the nineteenth century. After a Lutheran pastorate in Munich, Troeltsch taught philosophy and theology at the universities of Heidelberg and Berlin.

The two fundamental and closely related problems which engaged Troeltsch's concern in most of his work were the significance of the modern historical consciousness for interpreting Christianity and western culture and the problem of relating the Christian tradition to the modern cultural situation. The rise of historical consciousness and of the new discipline of scientific historical research in the latter half of the nineteenth century placed all theological and philosophical problems in a new light. All cultural phenomena were now seen as elements in a continuous development with deep roots in the past and the possibility of endless growth in the future. The historian perceived the transitoriness and relativity of all things. The canons of historical research forbade the interpretation of any event or person as of absolutely unique significance. This attitude came to be called "historicism" or "historical relativism", and Troeltsch was its main representative in the theological field.

Troeltsch interpreted the nature of religion in the tradition of Schleiermacher and German idealism. He affirmed a "religious *a priori*", an autonomous or self-sufficient element in the experience of man which cannot be reduced to moral, or social, or biological factors. Religion is a participation in the presence of the Divine, a communion of the human spirit with the absolute Spirit which discloses itself in the history of human culture. But the history of religion does not indicate a single uniform development in the direction of a perfect manifestation, but rather a diversity of concrete individual forms which are ever-changing. Christianity is simply one of these forms.

Over against this relativity of religious forms Troeltsch also perceived the demand of the religious consciousness for certainty, the practical need for assurance and peace. It was this conflict between religious conviction and radical historical criticism which lay behind his later writings mentioned in the essay below. This essay was written for presentation at Oxford University in 1923. In the first part Troeltsch traces his struggles with this problem during the last twenty years of his life. At first he based the superiority of Christianity upon the uniqueness of its claim to absolute validity, namely, the revelation of God in the lives of men. But he became gradually more aware of the sharpness of the conflict between the radical individuality and relativity of the great religions and any kind of claim for supreme validity.

His conclusions on the relations of Christianity and other religions constitute a combination of the types of relativism described in the Introduction. Our conviction about the truth of Christianity is based upon "the evidence of a profound inner experience". This has final and unconditional validity, but only for us. Other civilized peoples with other high religions are in exactly the same situation. Thus the proper attitude among the religions cannot be one of seeking conversion, but rather one of mutual understanding and helpfulness.

Yet Troeltsch can also assert that all the higher religions are tending in the same direction toward a common goal. How is this "teleological relativism" to be reconciled with his concept of the radical individuality of the religions? Furthermore, how can something be "very Truth" for us and not for all mankind? Are human beings fundamentally different in the various cultures? Since there is no objective way of settling the question of validity, is the only alternative a "leap of faith"? It is to Troeltsch's great credit that in his complete honesty he was willing to face any and all difficulties in his own positions, although he was perhaps not aware of them all.

# The Place of Christianity Among the World Religions*

IT HAS LONG been my great desire to visit the famous University of Oxford, which shines across to us in my country with the splendor of its medieval days, and is most closely associated for us with the problem of the development of Nominalism and Empiricism out of the Scholastic philosophy. But that it would be my privilege to survey it from the height of an Oxford lecture-platform was a thing which exceeded my boldest aspirations. I am indebted for this high honor to Professor Clement C. J. Webb, and to the kind interest which you have shown in my literary work. I am deeply conscious how great an honor it is, and I should like to offer you and Mr Webb my very sincere thanks. I can only hope that you will not miss today the wisdom and learning of your ordinary teacher.

In view of these unusual circumstances, I could not select any other subject than the one which contains the center and starting-point of my academic work. This central theme is most clearly,

---

* From Ernst Troeltsch, *Christian Thought: Its History and Application* (New York: Meridian Books and London: University of London Press, Ltd, 1957), pp. 35–63.

I think, set forth in my little book on *The Absolute Validity of Christianity*, which forms the conclusion of a series of earlier studies and the beginning of new investigations of a more comprehensive kind in the philosophy of history. Moreover, this subject is for me the point at which my own original interests and the problems presented by the modern religious situation have met together. It was recognized as such by a countryman of your own, Mr A. C. Bouquet, in his book *Is Christianity the Final Religion?* and I am indebted to him for a very able statement and criticism of the position. I should like, therefore, to occupy this hour in explaining the position I adopted in my little book, and in elucidating the further development of my thought by means of this small work.

To put it briefly, the central meaning of this book consists in a deep and vivid realization of the clash between historical reflection and the determination of standards of truth and value. The problem thus arising presented itself to me at a very early age. I had had a predominantly humanistic and historical education, from which I had been led to extend my studies and interests over a wide field of historical investigation, using the terms "history" and "humanity" in the sense we in Germany have been wont to attribute to them in our best periods – namely, in the objective sense of a contemplation of objects which covers as far as possible the whole extent of human existence, and which finds its delight in all the abundant diversity and ceaseless movement characteristic of human existence, and this without seeking any precise practical ends. It seems to us that it is the wealth of moral life and development that manifests itself in this endlessly diversified world of history, and imparts some of its own loftiness and solemnity to the soul of the observer.

I was, however, inspired by smaller interest, which was quite as strong and quite as much a part of my natural endowment as the first, I mean the interest in reaching a vital and effective religious position, which could alone furnish my life with a center of reference for all practical questions, and could alone give meaning and purpose to reflection upon the things of this world. This need of mine led me to theology and philosophy, which I devoured with an equally passionate interest. I soon discovered, however, that the historical studies which had so largely formed me, and the theology and philosophy in which I was now immersed, stood in sharp opposition, indeed even in conflict, with one another. I was confronted, upon the one hand, with the perpetual flux of the historian's data and the distrustful attitude of the historical critic toward conventional traditions, the real events of the past being, in his view, discoverable only as a reward of ceaseless toil, and then only with approximate accuracy. And, upon the other hand, I perceived the impulse in men toward a definite practical standpoint – the eagerness of the trusting soul to receive the divine revelation and to obey the divine commands. It was largely out of this conflict, which was no hypothetical one, but a fact of my own practical experience, that my entire theoretical standpoint took its rise.

Though this conflict was a personal one, however, it was no mere accident of my personal experience. It was rather the personal form in which a vital problem characteristic of the present stage of human development presented itself to me. I am, of course, aware that the sting of this problem is not equally felt in all parts of the civilized world of Europe and America. As Bouquet has explained in the work I have already mentioned, we must not apply without reservation to England, still less to America with its very undeveloped historical sense, what is true, in this respect, of other countries.

Nevertheless, there exists at bottom, everywhere, an impression that historical criticism and the breadth of historical interest are fraught with danger to the recognition of simple standards of value, be they of rational or traditional origin. In the Anglo-Saxon countries it is especially ethnography and the comparative study of religion, together with careful philosophical criticism, that produce this attitude. In my own country it is primarily an examination of European civilization itself that has impressed us with the relativity and transitoriness of all things, even of the loftiest values of civilization. The effect, however, is very similar in the two cases. Whether we approach it from the standpoint of Herbert Spencer and the theory of evolution, or from that of Hegel and Ranke and German romanticism, history presents a spectacle of bewildering diversity, and of historical institutions as all in a perpetual state of movement from within.

Indeed, the comparative study of religion, which gives an additional impulse to the tendency to relativity produced by historical reflection, has been pre-eminently the work of the great colonizing nations, especially of the English and the Dutch. And the criticism of the Bible and of dogma is not without representatives in England; and thus a growing feeling of uncertainty has been created here in this department also. The difference between this English line of reflection and the historical thought of Germany really consists simply in the fact that the latter is less wont to consider the practical needs and interests of society, while in theory it is determined more by the concept of individuality than by sociological or evolutionary principles which tend to regard all processes as leading to a single goal presented by nature.

Important as these differences are, however, they are all but different aspects of the one fundamental conflict between the spirit of critical scepticism generated by the ceaseless flux and manifold contradictions within the sphere of history and the demand of the religious consciousness for certainty, for unity, and for peace. Whether this conflict becomes more apparent in the critical analysis of details or in the challenging of fundamental principles, the cause and the general effect remain very much the same.

In my book on *The Absolute Validity of Christianity* I examined the means whereby theology is able to defend itself against these difficulties. This, of course, involved an examination of the fundamental concepts of theology as such. I believed that I could here determine two such concepts, both of which claimed to establish the ultimate validity of the Christian revelation in opposition to the relativities revealed by the study of history.

The first of these concepts was the theory that the truth of Christianity is guaranteed by miracles. In our times we are no longer primarily concerned here with miracles in the external

world, i.e. with the so-called "nature-miracles", involving an in-
fringement of natural law, but with the miracles of interior conversion and the attainment of a higher quality of life through
communion with Jesus and His community. In this connection, it
is claimed, an entirely different type of causation comes into
operation from that which is operative anywhere else in the
world. The Christian life may indeed be compared to an island
in the midst of the stream of history, exposed to all the storms of
secular life, and lured by all its wiles, yet constituting, in reality,
a stronghold of experience of quite another order. The absolute
validity of Christianity rests upon the absoluteness of God Himself, who is made manifest here directly in miracles but who
manifested Himself beyond this island only as a *causa remota* –
as the ground of the interconnection of all relative things. In this
way both a natural and a supernatural theology are possible,
the latter resting upon the new birth and experience of the inner
man, while natural theology is based upon the facts and forces of
the external world. This theory is simply a restatement of the old
miracle apologetic in the more intimate and spiritual form which
is acquired under the influence of Methodism and Pietism.

The second fundamental concept of theology, which I have
called the concept of evolution, presents a considerable contrast to
the first. Its most important exponent is Hegel. According to this
view, Christianity is simply the perfected expression of religion as
such. In the universal process of the unfolding of Spirit, the
fundamental impulse toward salvation and communion with
God overcomes all the limitations of sense experience, of the
natural order, of mythological form, until it attains perfect expression in Christianity, and enters into combination with the
loftiest and most spiritual of all philosophies, namely, that of
Platonism. Christianity, it is maintained, is not *a particular* religion, it is *religion*. It is no isolated manifestation of Spirit, but
the flower of spiritual life itself. All religion implies salvation
and rebirth, but outside Christianity these are subject to the limitations of physical nature and are baulked by human selfishness.
In the prophets and in Christ the Divine Life breaks through
these limits and flows unrestrained into the thirsty world, which

finds therein the solution of all its conflicts and the goal of all its striving. The whole history of religion and its obvious trend are thus a completely adequate proof of Christianity. The historical process does not stand in opposition to it. When regarded as a whole, and as one process, it rather affords a demonstration of its supreme greatness and all-embracing power. The miracles which attend its development are partly explicable, as in other religions, as mythical elements, accumulated during the growth of tradition, but they are partly effects of the shock produced by the spiritual revolution traceable here. They are thus not so much its credentials as its attendant phenomena, and as such they may be left without anxiety in the hands of the historical critic.

I found myself obliged to dismiss both these views as untenable. The former I rejected on the ground that an inward miracle, though it is indeed a powerful psychical upheaval, is not a miracle in the strict sense of the term. Are we justified in tracing the Platonic *Eros* to a natural cause, while we attribute a supernatural origin to the Christian *Agape*? And how can we prove such origin, even if we care to assume it? This would only be possible by having recourse once more to the visible signs which accompany these inward miracles, which would be again to treat the accompaniment as if it were itself the melody. Moreover, we should then be faced with the competition furnished by similar miracles in non-Christian religions, not to mention the negative results of historical criticism and the trouble attendant upon every theory of miracles.

If, however, we turn for this reason to the second view we find the difficulties to be different, indeed, but no less formidable. The actual history of religion knows nothing of the common character of all religions, or of their natural upward trend toward Christianity. It perceives a sharp distinction between the great world-religions and the national religions of heathen tribes, and further discovers certain irresolvable contradictions between these world-religions themselves which render their ultimate fusion and reconciliation in Christianity highly improbable, either in theory or in practice. Moreover, Christianty is itself a theoretical abstraction. It presents no historical uniformity, but displays a different character in every age, and is, besides, split up into many different denominations, hence it can in no wise be represented as the finally attained unity and explanation of all that has gone before, such as religious speculation seeks. It is rather a particular, independent, historical principle, containing, similarly to the other principles, very diverse possibilities and tendencies.

This leads us finally to a conception which has, I think, obtained less recognition in other countries than in Germany – I mean the conception which dominates the whole sphere of history, viz. Individuality. History cannot be regarded as a process in which a universal and everywhere similar principle is confined and obscured. Nor is it a continual mixing and remixing of elemental psychical powers, which indicate a general trend of things toward a rational end or goal of evolution. It is rather an immeasurable, incomparable profusion of always-new, unique, and hence individual tendencies, welling up from undiscovered depths, and coming to light in each case in unsuspected places and under different circumstances. Each process works itself out in its own way, bringing ever-new series of unique transformations in its train, until its powers are exhausted, or until it enters as component material into some new combination. Thus the universal law of history consists precisely in this, that the Divine Reason, or the Divine Life, within history, constantly manifests itself in always-new and always-peculiar individualizations – and hence that its tendency is not toward unity or universality at all, but rather toward the fulfillment of the highest potentialities of each separate department of life. It is this law which, beyond all else, makes it quite impossible to characterize Christianity as the reconciliation and goal of all the forces of history, or indeed to regard it as anything else than a historical individuality.

These are the historical ideas which have been handed down to us from German Romanticism, the great opposition movement to Rationalism and to all the clumsy miracle apologetic. They illustrate the special character and significance of German Romanticism, considered as a part of the great Romantic Movement of

Europe. They form the starting-point of all the German history and most of the German theology of the nineteenth century. They present our problem in its most crucial form, and explain why it became a more burning problem in Germany than elsewhere, except where it was envisaged in the same way, either as a result of independent reflection or under German influence.

What, then, is the solution? This is the question which I attempted to answer in my book. I first endeavored to show that it was in any case impossible to return to the old miracle apologetic. This has been rendered untenable, not by theories but by documents, by discoveries, by the results of exploration. The force of such evidence cannot be resisted by anyone whose sense of truth has been educated by philology, or even by anyone possessing an average amount of ordinary "common sense". I then submitted that the mere fact of the universality of Christianity – of its presence in all the other religions – would, even if true – be irrelevant. The point at issue was not whether Christianity was as a matter of fact universal or at least implicit in all religion, but whether it possessed ultimate truth, a truth which might easily depend upon a single instance of itself.

This formed a position for further reflection. It is quite possible, I maintained, that there is an element of truth in every religion, but that this is combined with innumerable transitory, individual features. This element of truth can only be disentangled through strife and disruption, and it should be our constant endeavor to assist in this process of disentanglement. The recognition of this truth is, however, an intuition which is born of deep personal experience and a pure conscientiousness. No strict proof of it is possible, for to demonstrate the actual presence of this truth in all the other cases would not be to establish its validity, even if this demonstration were easier than it is. Such an intuition can only be confirmed retrospectively and indirectly by its practical fruits, and by the light that it sheds upon all the problems of life. Thus in relation to Christianity such an intuition can only arise from immediate impression and personal conviction. Its claim to universal validity can only be felt and believed, in the first instance, and must be confirmed retrospectively through its genuine ability to furnish a solution of the various problems of life.

Now, validity of this kind seems always to rest upon the fine point of personal conviction. We still require a broader foundation upon actual, objective facts. I believed that I had discovered such a foundation for Christianity in the terms in which its claim to ultimate validity finds instinctive and immediate expression; in other words, in its faith in revelation and in the kind of claim it makes to truth. I thought it necessary to compare it from this point of view with other religions, whose belief in revelation and claim to validity were in every case of quite a different kind. If we examine any of the great world-religions we shall find that all of them, Judaism, Islam, Zoroastrianism, Buddhism, Christianity, even Confucianism, indeed claim absolute validity, but quite naïvely, and that in a very different manner in each case, the differences being illustrative of differences in their inner structure. These claims are always naïve – simple and direct. They are not the outcome of an apologetic reasoning, and the differences they exhibit in their naïve claims to absolute validity indicate the varying degree of such absolute validity as they really mean and intend within their own minds. This seemed to me to be nearly the most important point in every comparison between the religions, and the one which furnished the most searching test of the character of the dogmatic contents to be compared – contents which, in themselves, reveal so little as to the manner of their foundation in immediate religious experience.

A similar line of thought is to be found in the excellent book on *National and Universal Religions*, by the Dutch writer, Abraham Kuenen. If we make his distinction the basis of our investigation and comparison we at once perceive that Judaism and Zoroastrianism were explicitly national religions, associated with a particular country and concerned with tasks presented by a particular type of civilization – in the case of the Jews primarily with questions of national loyalty and national aspiration. Islam, too, is at bottom the national religion of the Arab peoples, compelling by the sword recognition of the prophetic claims of

Mohammed in all the countries to which the Arab races have penetrated. Where, on the other hand, it has spread beyond the boundaries of Arabian territory, it has not as a rule attempted to convert unbelievers, but has simply maintained them as a source of revenue. And where Islam has developed great missionary activity, as, for example, in Africa and in the islands of the Malay Archipelago, it shows itself to be bound to certain conditions of civilization which render it more readily acceptable to primitive races than Christianity, but which prove it, at the same time, to be indissolubly connected with a particular type of civilization. Finally, where it has adopted Persian or Indian mysticism, or Greek or modern philosophy, it loses its essential character, and becomes no more than a sign and a proof of national autonomy. Confucianism and Buddhism again are rather philosophies than religions, and owe their claim to absolute validity more to the common character of thought than to belief in a specific religious revelation, while Confucianism is essentially a national movement and Buddhism is, as a matter of fact, bound to the conditions of life in tropical countries.

Now, the naïve claim to absolute validity made by Christianity is of quite a different kind. All limitation to a particular race or nation is excluded on principle, and this exclusion illustrates the purely human character of its religious ideal, which appeals only to the simplest, the most general, the most personal and spiritual needs of mankind. Moreover, it does not depend in any way upon human reflection or a laborious process of reasoning, but upon an overwhelming manifestation of God in the persons and lives of the great prophets. Thus it was not a theory but a life – not a social order but a power. It owes its claim to universal validity not to the correctness of its reasoning nor to the conclusiveness of its proofs, but to God's revelation of Himself in human hearts and lives. Thus the naïve claim to absolute validity of Christianity is as unique as its conception of God. It is indeed a corollary of its belief in a revelation within the depths of the soul, awakening men to a new and higher quality of life, breaking down the barriers which the sense of guilt would otherwise set up, and making a final breach with the egoism obstinately centered

in the individual self. It is from this point of view that its claim
to absolute validity, following as it does from the content of its
religious ideal, appears to be vindicated. It possesses the highest
claim to universality of all the religions, for this its claim is
based upon the deepest foundations, the nature of God and of
man.

Hence we may simply leave aside the question of the measure
of validity possessed by the other religions. Nor need we trouble
ourselves with the question of the possible further development of
religion itself. It suffices that Christianity is itself a developing
religion, constantly striving toward a fresh and fuller expression.
We may content ourselves with acknowledging that it possesses the
highest degree of validity attained among all the historical religions which we are able to examine. We shall not wish to become
Jews, nor Zoroastrians, nor Mohammedans, nor again Confucian-
ists, nor Buddhists. We shall rather strive continually to bring
our Christianity into harmony with the changing conditions of
life, and to bring its human and divine potentialities to the fullest
possible fruition. It is the loftiest and most spiritual revelation we
know at all. It has the highest validity. Let that suffice.

Such was the conclusion I reached in the book which I wrote
some twenty years ago, and, from the practical standpoint at least,
it contains nothing that I wish to withdraw. From the point of
view of theory, on the other hand, there are a number of points
which I should wish to modify today, and these modifications
are, of course, not without some practical effects.

My scruples arise from the fact that, while the significance for
history of the concept of Individuality impresses me more forcibly
every day, I no longer believe this to be so easily reconcilable
with that of supreme validity. The further investigations, especially into the history of Christianity, of which I have given the
results in my *Social Teachings (Die Soziallehren der christlichen
Kirchen und Gruppen,* 1912), have shown me how thoroughly
individual is historical Christianity after all, and how invariably
its various phases and denominations have been due to varying
circumstances and conditions of life. Whether you regard it as a

whole or in its several forms, it is a purely historical, individual, relative phenomenon, which could, as we actually find it, only have arisen in the territory of the classical culture, and among the Latin and Germanic races. The Christianity of the Oriental peoples – the Jacobites, Nestorians, Armenians, Abyssinians – is of quite a different type, indeed even that of the Russians is a world of its own. The inference from all that is, however, that a religion, in the several forms assumed by it, always depends upon the intellectual, social, and national conditions among which it exists. On the other hand, a study of the non-Christian religions convinced me more and more that their naïve claims to absolute validity are also genuinely such. I found Buddhism and Brahminism especially to be really humane and spiritual religions, capable of appealing in precisely the same way to the inner certitude and devotion of their followers as Christianity, though the particular character of each has been determined by the historical, geographical, and social conditions of the countries in which it has taken shape.

The subject to which I devoted most attention, however, was that of the relation of individual historical facts to standards of value within the entire domain of history in connection with the development of political, social, ethical, aesthetic, and scientific ideas. I have only lately published the results of these investigations in my new book on *The Historical Standpoint and its Problems* (*Der Historismus und seine Probleme*, 1922). I encountered the same difficulties in each of these provinces – they were not confined to religion. Indeed, even the validity of science and logic seemed to exhibit, under different skies and upon different soil, strong individual differences present even in their deepest and innermost rudiments. What was really common to mankind, and universally valid for it, seemed, in spite of a general kinship and capacity for mutual understanding, to be at bottom exceedingly little, and to belong more to the province of material goods than to the ideal values of civilization.

The effect of these discoveries upon the conclusions reached in my earlier book was as follows:

The individual character of European civilization, and of the

Christian religion which is intimately connected with it, receives now much greater emphasis, while the somewhat rationalistic concept of validity, and specifically of *supreme validity*, falls considerably into the background. It is impossible to deny facts or to resist the decrees of fate. And it is historical facts that have welded Christianity into the closest connection with the civilizations of Greece, Rome, and Northern Europe. All our thoughts and feelings are impregnated with Christian motives and Christian presuppositions; and, conversely, our whole Christianity is indissolubly bound up with elements of the ancient and modern civilizations of Europe. From being a Jewish sect Christianity has become the religion of all Europe. It stands or falls with European civilization; while, on its own part, it has entirely lost its Oriental character and has become hellenized and westernized. Our European conceptions of personality and its eternal, divine right, and of progress toward a kingdom of the spirit and of God, our enormous capacity for expansion and for the interconnection of spiritual and temporal, our whole social order, our science, our art – all these rest, whether we know it or not, whether we like it or not, upon the basis of this deorientalized Christianity.

Its primary claim to validity is thus the fact that only through it have we become what we are, and that only in it can we preserve the religious forces that we need. Apart from it we lapse either into a self-destructive titanic attitude, or into effeminate trifling, or into crude brutality. And at the same time our life is a consistent compromise, as little unsatisfactory as we can manage, between its lofty spirituality and our practical everyday needs – a compromise that has to be renewed at every fresh ascent and every bend in the road. This tension is characteristic of our form of human life and rouses us to many a heroic endeavour, though it may also lead us into the most terrible mendacity and crime. Thus we are, and thus we shall remain, as long as we survive. We cannot live without a religion, yet the only religion that we can endure is Christianity, for Christianity has grown up with us and has become a part of our very being.

Now, obviously we cannot remain in these matters at the level of brute fact. Christianity could not be the religion of such a

D

highly developed racial group if it did not possess a mighty spiritual power and truth; in short, if it were not, in some degree, a manifestation of the Divine Life itself. The evidence we have for this remains essentially the same, whatever may be our theory concerning absolute validity – it is the evidence of a profound inner experience. This experience is undoubtedly the criterion of its validity, but, be it noted, only of its validity *for us*. It is God's countenance as revealed to us; it is the way in which, being what we are, we receive, and react to, the revelation of God. It is binding upon us, and it brings us deliverance. It is final and unconditional for us, because we have nothing else, and because in what we have we can recognize the accents of the divine voice.

But this does not preclude the possibility that other racial groups, living under entirely different cultural conditions, may experience their contact with the Divine Life in quite a different way, and may themselves also possess a religion which has grown up with them, and from which they cannot sever themselves so long as they remain what they are. And they may quite sincerely regard this as absolutely valid for them, and give expression to this absolute validity according to the demands of their own religious feeling. We shall, of course, assume something of this kind only among nations which have reached a relatively high stage of civilization, and whose whole mental life has been intimately connected with their religion through a long period of discipline. We shall not assume it among the less developed races, where many religious cults are followed side by side, nor in the simple animism of heathen tribes, which is so monotonous in spite of its many variations. These territories are gradually conquered by the great world religions which possess a real sense of their own absolute validity. But among the great spiritual religions themselves the fundamental spiritual positions which destiny has assigned to them persist in their distinctness. If we wish to determine their relative value it is not the religions alone that we must compare but always only the civilizations of which the religion in each case constitutes a part incapable of severance from the rest. But who will presume to make a really final pronouncement here? Only God Himself, who has determined these differences, can do that. The various racial groups can only seek to purify and enrich their experience, each within its own province and according to its own standards, and to win the weaker and less-developed races for their own faith, always remembering that the religion thus adopted by another people will individualize itself anew.

The practical bearing of this new manner of thinking differs but little from that of my earlier view, or indeed from that of any theology which seeks to retain the essential basis of Christianity, and intends merely to substantiate and to interpret it. Its detailed application, however, brings to light one or two important consequences.

In the first place, it has a considerable influence upon the question of foreign missions. Missionary enterprise has always been in part simply a concomitant of the political, military, and commercial expansion of a state or nation, but in part also an outcome of the religious enthusiast's zeal for conversion. The former aspect is exceedingly important as a factor in human history, but is irrelevant in the present connection. The latter aspect, on the other hand, is intimately connected with the claim to absolute validity. But here we have to maintain, in accordance with all our conclusions hitherto, that directly religious missionary enterprise must stand in quite a different relation to the great philosophical world religions from that in which it stands to the crude heathenism of smaller tribes. There can be always only a spiritual wrestling of missionary Christianity with the other world religions, possibly a certain contact with them. The heathen races, on the other hand, are being morally and spiritually disintegrated by the contact with European civilization; hence they demand a substitute from the higher religion and culture. We have a missionary duty toward these races, and our enterprise is likely to meet with success among them, although Christianity, be it remembered, is by no means the only religion which is taking part in this missionary campaign. Islam and Buddhism are also missionary religions. But in relation to the great world religions we

need to recognize that they are expressions of the religious consciousness corresponding to certain definite types of culture, and
that it is their duty to increase in depth and purity by means of
their own interior impulses, a task in which the contact with
Christianity may prove helpful, to them as to us, in such processes of development from within. The great religions might
indeed be described as crystallizations of the thought of great
races, as these races are themselves crystallizations of the various
biological and anthropological forms. There can be no conversion
or transformation of one into the other, but only a measure of
agreement and of mutual understanding.

The second practical consequence of my new trend of thought
concerns the inner development of Christianity itself. If my theory
is correct this development is closely related to the whole spiritual and cultural development of European civilization. True, the
religious consciousness, whose object is God and eternal peace,
is less exposed to restlessness and change than are the purely temporal constituents of the movement; hence it has become insti-
tutionalized in the various large denominations which, because
of these internal reasons, constitute the most conservative element
in the life of Europe. Nevertheless, Christianity is drawn into the
stream of spiritual development even within the Churches, and
still more outside and beyond them, in the free speculation of
literature and philosophy. Moreover, it contains, like all the world
religions, and perhaps more than any other world religion, an
impulse and the power to a continual self-purification and self-
deepening, for it has been assigned to that Spirit which shall lead
men into all truth, and which seeks its fulfillment in the coming
Kingdom of God; and again, because it has been bound up from
the first with all the intellectual forces of Hellenism.

Under these circumstances the course of its development is
unpredictable, for it is capable of assuming always new individualizations. A new era in the world's history is beginning
for it at this moment. It has to ally itself anew to a new conception of nature, a new social order, and a profound interior transformation of the spiritual outlook, and has to bring to the suffering world a new peace and a new brotherhood. How this can be

accomplished it is not for me to say here; indeed, the answer is as yet very far from clear. All that is certain is that Christianity is at a critical moment of its further development, and that very bold and far-reaching changes are necessary, transcending anything that has yet been achieved by any denomination. I have, in this respect, become more and more radical and super-denominational while, at the same time, I have come more and more to regard the specific kernel of religion as a unique and independent source of life and power.

Can we, then, discover no common goal of religion, nothing at all that is absolute, in the objective sense of constituting a common standard for mankind? Instinctive conviction makes us reluctant to admit such a sceptical conclusion, and it will especially be combated on the ground of the reality of the subjective validities which we have discovered. These are not simply illusions or the products of human vanity. They are the products of the impulse toward absolute objective truth, and take effect in the practical sphere under constant critical self-purification and effort at self-improvement. I have already drawn attention to this fact in my earlier work. I only wish to emphasize now more strongly than I did then that this synthesis cannot as yet be already attained in any one of the historical religions, but that they all are tending in the same direction, and that all seem impelled by an inner force to strive upward toward some unknown final height, where alone the ultimate unity and the final objective validity can lie. And, as all religion has thus a common goal in the Unknown, the Future, perchance in the Beyond, so, too, it has a common ground in the Divine Spirit ever pressing the finite mind onward toward further light and fuller consciousness, a Spirit Which indwells the finite spirit, and Whose ultimate union with it is the purpose of the whole many-sided process.

Between these two poles, however – the divine Source and the divine Goal – lie all the individual differentiations of race and civilization, and, with them also, the individual differences of the great, comprehensive religions. There may be mutual understanding between them if they are willing to renounce those sorry things, self-will and the spirit of violent domination. If each strives to fulfil its own highest potentialities, and allows itself to be influenced therein by the similar striving of the rest, they may approach and find contact with each other. Some striking examples of such contact are recorded in Canon Streeter's *The Sadhu*, and in a book called *On the Verge of the Primitive Forest*, by the Alsatian physician and writer on the philosophy of religion, Albert Schweitzer. But, so far as human eye can penetrate into the future, it would seem probable that the great revelations to the various civilizations will remain distinct, in spite of a little shifting of their several territories at the fringes, and that the question of their several relative values will never be capable of objective determination, since every proof thereof will presuppose the special characteristics of the civilization in which it arises. The conception of personality itself is, for instance, different in the east and in the west, hence arguments starting from it will lead to different conclusions in the two cases. Yet there is no other concept which could furnish a basis for argument concerning practical values and truths save this concept of personality, which is always itself already one of the fundamental positions of the several religions, and is determined by them according to these respective general attitudes of theirs.

This is what I wish to say in modification of my former theories. I hope you feel that I am not speaking in any spirit of scepticism or uncertainty. A truth which, in the first instance, is *a truth for us* does not cease, because of this, to be very Truth and Life. What we learn daily through our love for our fellow-men, viz. that they are independent beings with standards of their own, we ought also to be able to learn through our love for mankind as a whole – that here too there exist autonomous civilizations with standards of their own. This does not exclude rivalry, but it must be a rivalry for the attainment of interior purity and clearness of vision. If each racial group strives to develop its own highest potentialities we may hope to come nearer to one another. This applies to the great world religions, but it also applies to the various religious denominations, and to individuals in their intercourse with one another. In our earthly experience the Divine Life is not One, but Many. But to apprehend the One in the Many constitutes the special character of love.

# 4

# EXCLUSIVISM
## Karl Barth

IF TROELTSCH'S RELATIVISM signifies the end of the dominance of the liberal Protestant theology on the Continent, then a major cause of this end can be found in the work of Karl Barth (1886–   ). Since Barth's career helps to illuminate the theological change occasioned by his thought, some account must be taken of it. A Swiss by birth, Barth received most of his theological education at the universities of Berlin and Marburg at the hands of the leading liberal theologians of the day, Adolf von Harnack and Wilhelm Herrmann, both disciples of Ritschl. But after a few years as a pastor in a small Swiss village he began to discover that his liberal theology was inadequate to interpret the crises of industrialization and World War I. This led him to renewed study of the Bible, not as an object of historical research but as the living word of God which is to be attested in preaching.

The result of this study and the influence of Dostoevsky and Kierkegaard was the publication in 1918 of Barth's commentary on Paul's letter to the Romans, which has been described as the greatest prophetic theological work of this century. It signified the beginning of a new departure in Protestant theology which has been called neo-orthodoxy or dialectical theology. Barth's prophetic themes were the transcendence and sovereignty of God, the sin and misery of man apart from God, and the salvation of man through Christ by grace alone. His thought thus signalled an intensive and extensive attack on the fundamental ideas of the liberal theology initiated by Schleiermacher. His writings led to teaching posts at the universities of Göttingen, Münster, and Bonn. Because of his attacks on the Nazi régime in the early thirties, he was dismissed from his professorship at Bonn and moved to the University of Basel from which he retired in 1961. The main fruit of his theological labor has taken the form of his twelve-volume *Church Dogmatics*, which has now run to over seventy-five hundred pages and is less than four-fifths complete, although he has ceased work on it. Barth is also the author of *Anselm: Fides quaerens intellectum* (1931), *The Knowledge of God and the Service of God* (1938), *Dogmatics in Outline* (1947), *Protestant Thought from Rousseau to Ritschl* (1947), and *Evangelical Theology* (1963), as well as several volumes of essays and sermons.

The work of Barth and his colleagues has produced a major revolution in Protestant theology in this century. Although the influence of his own thought has waned considerably since mid-century, the succeeding movements of theology have developed as positive or negative reactions to Barth. In particular, many of the so-called "new theologians" started off as followers of Barth. And their patron saint Dietrich Bonhoeffer stated that Barth's greatest service was the beginning of the criticism of religion in the selection reproduced below.

This selection is taken from the second volume of Barth's *Church Dogmatics*, which was published in 1938. It is a part of the two-volume introduction entitled "The Doctrine of the Word of God", in which part he is treating the revelation of God under the concept of the gift of the Holy Spirit. The first part of this section (which is not included) is entitled "The Problem of Religion in Theology". Here Barth presents a radical criticism of the way in which the liberal theology has placed the concept of religion at the center of theology. He begins by affirming that the revelation of God in Christ is an event in human experience, and thus in the realm of religion, which can be investigated historically and psychologically. Therefore, the Christian religion is not unique or unparalleled, but in fact only a particular instance of the universal reality called religion. Men have always been aware of a power beyond them, and have responded in the various forms of the religious life. The elements and problems in all religions are the same as those in Christianity.

But this fact has caused the Protestant theology of the last two centuries, including Schleiermacher and Troeltsch, to fall into the temptation of considering man's religion as the norm or principle by which we are to interpret the revelation of God. Thus liberal theology attempted to understand revelation in the light of religion, rather than vice versa. This, asserts Barth, is heresy and unbelief. This is not said, however, from the point of view of conservatism or fear of free scientific investigation, but exactly for the sake of free theological investigation. Barth sees the necessity and importance of a scientific investigation of religion, but he states that this must in no way be confused with theology. The correct order in theology is to interpret man's religion in the light of God's revelation in Christ, which he now sets out to do.

Barth's thesis in the rest of this section is that religion, including Christianity, is unbelief, the manifestation of man's rebellion against God, and that Christianity can be called the true religion only because of the miracle of grace whereby the sinner is justified by God. The selection below includes only about one-sixth of the original, which contains many extended excursuses on the Bible and the history of religion and of Christian theology. The section also includes an analysis of mysticism and atheism which claim to be radical criticisms of religion but are really dependent upon it.

Barth's view of the relation of Christianity to other religions is one form of the "Truth–Falsehood" approach described above and has many antecedents in the Bible and Christian history, especially in Luther. It has been rejected out of hand by many as pure perversity or as a dialectical sleight-of-hand. Other critics have pointed out that Barth's view in this section is not consistent with what he says in other places. Here he has nothing good to say about religion at all. "It is never the truth. It is a complete fiction, which has not only little but no relation to God." Yet it is implied in this section and stated more explicitly in other parts of the *Church Dogmatics* that religion does in fact have something to do with God, that it is man's distorted and perverted response to God's approach. Barth has also been taken to task for his strained interpretation of key biblical passages, such as the first chapter of Romans. Finally, Barth's interpretation of religion smacks more of the abstract assertion of a theological axiom than of the sensitive analysis of the complex reality of man's religion.

# The Revelation of God as the Abolition of Religion*

THE REVELATION OF God in the outpouring of the Holy Spirit is the judging but also reconciling presence of God in the world of human religion, that is, in the realm of man's attempts to justify and to sanctify himself before a capricious and arbitrary picture of God. The Church is the locus of true religion, so far as through grace it lives by grace....

## 2. RELIGION AS UNBELIEF

A theological evaluation of religion and religions must be characterized primarily by the great cautiousness and charity of its assessment and judgments. It will observe and understand and take man in all seriousness as the subject of religion. But it will not be man apart from God, in a human *per se*. It will be man for whom (whether he knows it or not) Jesus Christ was born, died, and rose again. It will be man who (whether he has already heard it or not) is intended in the Word of God. It will be man who (whether he is aware of it or not) has in Christ his Lord. It will always understand religion as a vital utterance and activity of this man. It will not ascribe to this life-utterance and activity of his a unique "nature", the so-called "nature of religion", which

* From Karl Barth, *Church Dogmatics*, ed. by G. W. Bromiley and T. F. Torrance (Edinburgh: T. & T. Clark, 1956), Vol. I, Part 2, pp. 280, 297–303, 307–310, 325–328, 332–333, 337–338, 353–354.

it can then use as a gauge to weigh and balance one human thing against another, distinguishing the "higher" religion from the "lower", the "living" from the "decomposed", the "ponderable" from the "imponderable". It will not omit to do this from carelessness or indifference toward the manifoldness with which we have to do in this human sphere, nor because a prior definition of the "nature" of the phenomena in this sphere is either impossible or in itself irrelevant, but because what we have to know of the nature of religion from the standpoint of God's revelation does not allow us to make any but the most incidental use of an immanent definition of the nature of religion. It is not, then, that this "revealed" nature of religion is not fitted in either form or content to differentiate between the good and the bad, the true and the false in the religious world. Revelation singles out the Church as the *locus* of true religion. But this does not mean that the Christian religion as such is the fulfilled nature of human religion. It does not mean that the Christian religion is the true religion, fundamentally superior to all other religions. We can never stress too much the connection between the truth of the Christian religion and the grace of revelation. We have to give particular emphasis to the fact that through grace the Church lives by grace, and to that extent it is the *locus* of true religion. And if this is so, the Church will boast of its "nature", i.e. the perfection in which it fulfils the "nature" of religion, as it can attribute that nature to other religions. We cannot differentiate and separate the Church from other religions on the basis of a general concept of the nature of religion. . . .

A truly theological treatment of religion and religions, as it is demanded and possible in the Church as the *locus* of the Christian religion, will need to be distinguished from all other forms of treatment by the exercise of a very marked tolerance toward its object. Now this tolerance must not be confused with the moderation of those who actually have their own religion or religiosity, and are secretly zealous for it, but who can exercise self-control, because they have told themselves or have been told that theirs is not the only faith, that fanaticism is a bad thing, that love must always have the first and the last word. It must not be confused with the clever aloofness of the rationalistic Know-All – the typical Hegelian belongs to the same category – who thinks that he can deal comfortably and in the end successfully with all religions in the light of a concept of a perfect religion which is gradually evolving in history. But it also must not be confused with the relativism and impartiality of an historical scepticism, which does not ask about truth and untruth in the field of religious phenomena, because it thinks that truth can be known only in the form of its own doubt about all truth. That the so-called "tolerance" of this kind is unattainable is revealed by the fact that the object, religion and religions, and therefore man, are not taken seriously, but are at bottom patronized. Tolerance in the sense of moderation, or superior knowledge, or scepticism is actually the worst form of intolerance. But the religion and religions must be treated with a tolerance which is informed by the forbearance of Christ, which derives therefore from the knowledge that by grace God has reconciled to Himself godless man and his religion. It will see man carried, like an obstinate child in the arms of its mother, by what God has determined and done for his salvation in spite of his own opposition. In detail, it will neither praise nor reproach him. It will understand his situation – understand it even in the dark and terrifying perplexity of it – not because it can see any meaning in the situation as such, but because it acquires a meaning from outside, from Jesus Christ. But confronted by this object it will not display the weak or superior or weary smile of a quite inappropriate indulgence. It will see that man is caught in a way of acting that cannot be recognized as right and holy, unless it is first and at the same time recognized as thoroughly wrong and unholy. Self-evidently, this kind of tolerance, and therefore a theological consideration of religion, is possible only for those who are ready to abase themselves and their religion together with man, with every individual man, knowing that they first, and their religion, have need of tolerance, a strong forbearing tolerance.

We begin by stating that religion is unbelief. It is a concern, indeed, we must say that it is the one great concern, of godless man. . . .

In the light of what we have already said, this proposition is not in any sense a negative value-judgment. It is not a judgment of religious science or philosophy based upon some prior negative judgment concerned with the nature of religion. It does not affect only other men with their religion. Above all, it affects ourselves also as adherents of the Christian religion. It formulates the judgment of divine revelation upon all religion. It can be explained and expounded, but it cannot be derived from any higher principle than revelation, nor can it be proved by any phenomenology or history of religion. Since it aims only to repeat the judgment of God, it does not involve any human renunciation of human values, any contesting of the true and the good and the beautiful which a closer inspection will reveal in almost all religions, and which we naturally expect to find in abundant measure in our own religion, if we hold to it with any conviction. What happens is simply that man is taken by God and judged and condemned by God. That means, of course, that we are struck to the very roots, to the heart. Our whole existence is called in question. But where that is the case there can be no place for sad and pitiful laments at the non-recognition of relative human greatness. . . .

To realize that religion is really unbelief, we have to consider it from the standpoint of the revelation attested in Holy Scripture. There are two elements in that revelation which make it unmistakably clear.

1. Revelation is God's self-offering and self-manifestation. Revelation encounters man on the presupposition and in confirmation of the fact that man's attempts to know God from his own standpoint are wholly and entirely futile; not because of any necessity in principle, but because of a practical necessity of fact. In revelation God tells man that He is God, and that as such He is his Lord. In telling him this, revelation tells him something utterly new, something which apart from revelation he does not know and cannot tell either himself or others. It is true that he could do this, for revelation simply states the truth. If it is true that God is God and that as such He is the Lord of man, then it is also true that man is so placed toward Him, that he could

know Him. But this is the very truth which is not available to man, before it is told him in revelation. If he really can know God this capacity rests upon the fact that he really does know Him, because God has offered and manifested Himself to him. The capacity, then, does not rest upon the fact, which is true enough, that man could know him. Between "he could" and "he can" there lies the absolute decisive "he cannot", which can be removed and turned into its opposite only by revelation. The truth that God is God and our Lord, and the further truth that we could know Him as God and Lord, can only come to us through the truth itself. This "coming to us" of the truth is revelation. It does not reach us in a neutral condition, but in an action which stands to it, as the coming of truth, in a very definite, indeed a determinate relationship. That is to say, it reaches us as religious men; i.e. it reaches us in the attempt to know God from our standpoint. It does not reach us, therefore, in the activity which corresponds to it. The activity which corresponds to revelation would have to be faith; the recognition of the self-offering and self-manifestation of God. We need to see that in view of God all our activity is in vain even in the best life; i.e. that of ourselves we are not in a position to apprehend the truth, to let God be God and our Lord. We need to renounce all attempts even to try to apprehend this truth. We need to be ready and resolved simply to let the truth be told us, and therefore to be apprehended by it. But that is the very thing for which we are not resolved and ready. The man to whom the truth has really come will concede that he was not at all ready and resolved to let it speak to him. The genuine believer will not say that he came to faith from faith, but – from unbelief, even though the attitude and activity with which he met revelation, and still meets it, is religion. For in faith, man's religion as such is shown by revelation to be resistance to it. From the standpoint of revelation religion is clearly seen to be a human attempt to anticipate what God in His revelation wills to do and does do. It is the attempted replacement of the divine work by a human manufacture. The divine reality offered and manifested to us in revelation is replaced by a concept of God arbitrarily and wilfully evolved by man. . . .

"Arbitrarily and wilfully" means here by his own means, by his own human insight and constructiveness and energy. Many different images of God can be formed once we have engaged in this undertaking, but their significance is always the same....

The image of God is always that reality of perception or thought in which man assumes and asserts something unique and ultimate and decisive either beyond or within his own existence, by which he believes himself to be posited or at least determined and conditioned. From the standpoint of revelation, man's religion is simply an assumption and assertion of this kind, and as such it is an activity which contradicts revelation – contradicts it, because it is only through truth that truth can come to man. If a man tries to grasp at truth of himself he tries to grasp at it *a priori*. But in that case he does not do what he has to do when the truth comes to him. He does not believe. If he did, he would listen; but in religion he talks. If he did, he would accept a gift; but in religion he takes something for himself. If he did, he would let God Himself intercede for God: but in religion he ventures to grasp at God. Because it is a grasping, religion is the contradiction of revelation, the concentrated expression of human unbelief, i.e. an attitude and activity which is directly opposed to faith. It is a feeble but defiant, an arrogant but hopeless, attempt to create something which man could do, but now cannot do, or can do only because and if God Himself creates it for him: the knowledge of the truth, the knowledge of God. We cannot therefore interpret the attempt as a harmonious co-operating of man with the revelation of God, as though religion were a kind of outstretched hand which is filled by God in His revelation. Again, we cannot say of the evident religious capacity of man that it is, so to speak, the general form of human knowledge, which acquires its true and proper content in the shape of revelation. On the contrary, we have here an exclusive contradiction. In religion man bolts and bars himself against revelation by providing a substitute, by taking away in advance the very thing which has to be given by God....

He has, of course, the power to do this. But what he achieves and acquires in virtue of this power is never the knowledge of

God as Lord and God. It is never the truth. It is a complete fiction, which has not only little but no relation to God. It is an anti-God who has first to be known as such and discarded when the truth comes to him. But it can be known as such, as a fiction, only as the truth does come to him. . . .

Revelation does not link up with a human religion which is already present and practised. It contradicts it, just as religion previously contradicted revelation. It displaces it, just as religion previously displaced revelation; just as faith cannot link up with a mistaken faith, but must contradict and displace it as unbelief, as an act of contradiction. . . .

2. As the self-offering and self-manifestation of God, revelation is the act by which in grace He reconciles man to Himself by grace. As a radical teaching about God, it is also the radical assistance of God which comes to us as those who are unrighteous and unholy, and as such damned and lost. In this respect, too, the affirmation which revelation makes and presupposes of man is that he is unable to help himself either in whole or even in part. But again, he ought not to have been so helpless. It is not inherent in the nature and concept of man that he should be unrighteous and unholy and therefore damned and lost. He was created to be the image of God, i.e. to obedience toward God and not to sin, to salvation and not to destruction. But he is not summoned to this as to a state in which he might still somehow find himself, but as one in which he no longer finds himself, from which he has fallen by his own fault. But this, too, is a truth which he cannot maintain: it is not present to him unless it comes to him in revelation, i.e. in Jesus Christ, to be declared to him in a new way – the oldest truth of all in a way which is quite new. He cannot in any sense declare to himself that he is righteous and holy, and therefore saved, for in his own mouth as his own judgment of himself it would be a lie. It is truth as the revealed knowledge of God. It is truth in Jesus Christ. Jesus Christ does not fill out and improve all the different attempts of man to think of God and to represent Him according to his own standard. But as the self-offering and self-manifestation of God He replaces and completely outbids those attempts, put-

ting them in the shadows to which they belong. Similarly, in so far as God reconciles the world to Himself in Him, He replaces all the different attempts of man to reconcile God to the world, all our human efforts at justification and sanctification, at conversion and salvation. The revelation of God in Jesus Christ maintains that our justification and sanctification, our conversion and salvation, have been brought about and achieved once and for all in Jesus Christ. And our faith in Jesus Christ consists in our recognizing and admitting and affirming and accepting the fact that everything has actually been done for us once and for all in Jesus Christ. He is the assistance that comes to us. He alone is the Word of God that is spoken to us. There is an exchange of status between Him and us: His righteousness and holiness are ours, our sin is His; He is lost for us, and we for His sake are saved. By this exchange (καταλλαγή, 2 Cor. 5. 19) revelation stands or falls. It would not be the active, redemptive self-offering and self-manifestation of God, if it were not centrally and decisively the *satisfactio* and *intercessio Jesu Christi.*

And now we can see a second way in which revelation contradicts religion, and conversely religion necessarily opposes revelation. For what is the purpose of the universal attempt of religions to anticipate God, to foist a human product into the place of His Word, to make our own images of the One who is known only where He gives Himself to be known, images which are first spiritual, and then religious, and then actually visible? What does the religious man want when he thinks and believes and maintains that there is a unique and ultimate and decisive being, that there is a divine being (θεῖον), a godhead, that there are gods and a single supreme God, and when he thinks that he himself is posited, determined, conditioned, and overruled by this being? Is the postulate of God or gods, and the need to objectify the Ultimate spiritually or physically, conditioned by man's experience of the actual superiority and lordship of certain natural and supernatural, historical and eternal necessities, potencies, and ordinances? Is this experience (or the postulate and need which correspond to it) followed by the feeling of man's impotence and failure in face of this higher world, by the urge to put himself on peaceful and friendly terms with it, to interest it on his behalf, to assure himself of its support, or, better still, to enable himself to exercise an influence on it, to participate in its power and dignity and to co-operate in its work? Does man's attempt to justify and sanctify himself follow the attempt to think of God and represent Him? Or is the relationship the direct opposite? Is the primary thing man's obscure urge to justify and sanctify himself, i.e. to confirm and strengthen himself in the awareness and exercise of his skill and strength to master life, to come to terms with the world, to make the world serviceable to him? Is religion with its dogmatics and worship and precepts the most primitive, or better perhaps, the most intimate and intensive part of the technique, by which we try to come to terms with life? Is it that the experience of that higher world, or the need to objectify it in the thought of God and the representation of God, must be regarded only as an exponent of this attempt, that is, as the ideal construction inevitable within the framework of this technique? Are the gods only reflected images and guarantees of the needs and capacities of man, who in reality is lonely and driven back upon himself and his own willing and ordering and creating? Are sacrifice and prayer and asceticism and morality more basic than God and the gods? Who is to say? In face of the two possibilities we are in a circle which we can consider from any point of view with exactly the same result. What is certain is that in respect of the practical content of religion it is still a matter of an attitude and activity which does not correspond to God's revelation, but contradicts it. At this point, too, weakness and defiance, helplessness and arrogance, folly and imagination are so close to one another that we can scarcely distinguish the one from the other. Where we want what is wanted in religion, i.e. justification and sanctification as our own work, we do not find ourselves – and it does not matter whether the thought and representation of God has a primary or only a secondary importance – on the direct way to God, who can then bring us to our goal at some higher stage on the way. On the contrary, we lock the door against God, we alienate ourselves from Him, we come into direct opposition to Him. God in His revelation will not allow man to try to come to terms with life, to justify and sanctify himself. God in His revelation, God in Jesus Christ, is the One who takes on Himself the sin of the world, who wills that all our care should be cast upon Him, because He careth for us....

It is the characteristically pious element in the pious effort to reconcile Him to us which must be an abomination to God, whether idolatry is regarded as its presupposition or its result, or perhaps as both. Not by any continuing along this way, but only by radically breaking away from it, can we come, not to our own goal but to God's goal, which is the direct opposite of our goal....

### 3. TRUE RELIGION

The preceding expositions have established the fact that we can speak of "true" religion only in the sense in which we speak of a "justified sinner".

Religion is never true in itself and as such. The revelation of God denies that any religion is true, i.e. that it is in truth the knowledge and worship of God and the reconciliation of man with God. For as the self-offering and self-manifestation of God, as the work of peace which God Himself has concluded between Himself and man, revelation is the truth beside which there is no other truth, over against which there is only lying and wrong. If by the concept of a "true religion" we mean truth which belongs to religion in itself and as such, it is just as unattainable as a "good man", if by goodness we mean something which man can achieve on his own initiative. No religion is true. It can only become true, i.e. according to that which it purports to be and for which it is upheld. And it can become true only in the way in which man is justified, from without; i.e. not of its own nature and being but only in virtue of a reckoning and adopting and separating which are foreign to its own nature and being, which are quite inconceivable from its own standpoint, which come to it quite apart from any qualifications or merits. Like justified man, true religion is a creature of grace. But grace is the revelation of God.

No religion can stand before it as true religion. No man is righteous in its presence. It subjects us all to the judgment of death. But it can also call dead men to life and sinners to repentance. And similarly in the wider sphere where it shows all religion to be false, it can also create true religion. The abolishing of religion by revelation need not mean only its negation: the judgment that religion is unbelief. Religion can just as well be exalted in revelation, even though the judgment still stands. It can be upheld by it and concealed in it. It can be justified by it, and – we must at once add – sanctified. Revelation can adopt religion and mark it off as true religion. And it not only can. How do we come to assert that it can, if it has not already done so? There is a true religion: just as there are justified sinners. If we abide strictly by that analogy – and we are dealing not merely with an analogy, but in a comprehensive sense with the thing itself – we need have no hesitation in saying that the Christian religion is the true religion.

In our discussion of "religion as unbelief" we did not consider the distinction between Christian and non-Christian religion. Our intention was that whatever we said about the other religions affected the Christian similarly. In the framework of that discussion we could not speak in any special way about Christianity. We could not give it any special or assured place in face of that judgment. Therefore the discussion cannot be understood as a preliminary polemic against the non-Christian religions, with a view to the ultimate assertion that the Christian religion is the true religion. If this were the case our task now would be to prove that, as distinct from the non-Christian religions, the Christian is not guilty of idolatry and self-righteousness, that it is not therefore unbelief but faith, and therefore true religion; or, which comes to the same thing, that it is no religion at all, but as against all religions, including their mystical and atheistical self-criticism, it is in itself the true and holy and as such the unspotted and incontestable form of fellowship between God and man. To enter on this path would be to deny the very thing we have to affirm. If the statement is to have any content we can dare to state that the Christian religion is the true one only as we listen to the divine revelation. But a statement which we dare to make as we listen to the divine revelation can only be a statement of faith. And a statement of faith is necessarily a statement which is thought and expressed in faith and from faith, i.e. in recognition and respect of what we are told by revelation. Its explicit and implicit content is unreservedly conditioned by what we are told. But that is certainly not the case if we try to reach the statement that the Christian religion is the true religion by a road which begins by leaving behind the judgment of revelation, that religion is unbelief, as a matter which does not apply to us Christians but only to others, the non-Christians, thus enabling us to separate and differentiate ourselves from them with the help of this judgment. On the contrary, it is our business as Christians to apply this judgment first and most acutely to ourselves: and to others, the non-Christians, only in so far as we recognize ourselves in them, i.e. only as we see in them the truth of this judgment of revelation which concerns us, in the solidarity, therefore, in which, anticipating them in both repentance and hope, we accept this judgment to participate in the promise of revelation. At the end of the road we have to tread there is, of course, the promise to those who accept God's judgment, who let themselves be led beyond their unbelief. There is faith in this promise, and, in this faith, the presence and reality of the grace of God, which, of course, differentiates our religion, the Christian, from all others as the true religion. This exalted goal cannot be reached except by this humble road. And it would not be a truly humble road if we tried to tread it except in the consciousness that any "attaining" here can consist only in the utterly humble and thankful adoption of something which we would not attain if it were not already attained in God's revelation before we set out on the road.

We must insist, therefore, that at the beginning of a knowledge of truth of the Christian religion there stands the recognition that this religion, too, stands under the judgment that religion is unbelief, and that it is not acquitted by any inward worthiness, but only by the grace of God, proclaimed and effectual in His revelation. But concretely this judgment affects the whole practice of

our faith: our Christian conceptions of God and the things of
God, our Christian theology, our Christian worship, our forms
of Christian fellowship and order, our Christian morals, poetry,
and art, our attempts to give individual and social form to the
Christian life, our Christian strategy and tactics in the interest
of our Christian cause, in short our Christianity, to the extent
that it is *our* Christianity, the human work which we undertake
and adjust to all kinds of near and remote aims and which as
such is seen to be on the same level as the human work in other
religions. This judgment means that all this Christianity of ours,
and all the details of it, are not as such what they ought to be
and pretend to be, a work of faith, and therefore of obedience to
the divine revelation. What we have here is in its own way – a
different way from that of other religions, but no less seriously
– unbelief, i.e. opposition to the divine revelation, and therefore
active idolatry and self-righteousness. It is the same helplessness
and arbitrariness. It is the same self-exaltation of man which
means his most profound abasement. But this time it is in place
of and in opposition to the self-manifestation and self-offering of
God, the reconciliation which God Himself has accomplished, it
is in disregard of the divine consolations and admonitions that
great and small Babylonian towers are erected, which cannot as
such be pleasing to God, since they are definitely not set up to
His glory. . . .

We are here concerned with an order which can be forgotten
or infringed only to the detriment of a real knowledge of the truth
of the Christian religion. Again, to ascribe the demonstrative
power for this truth to the religious self-consciousness as such
is to the dishonoring of God and the eternal destruction of souls.
Even outwardly, in its debate with non-Christian religions, the
Church can never do more harm than when it thinks that it must
abandon the apostolic injunction, that grace is sufficient for us.
The place to which we prefer to look is only mist, and the reed
upon which we have to lean will slip through our fingers. By
trying to resist and conquer other religions, we put ourselves on
the same level. They, too, appeal to this or that immanent truth
in them. They, too, can triumph in the power of the religious

self-consciousness, and sometimes they have been astonishingly successful over wide areas. Christianity can take part in this fight. There is no doubt that it does not lack the necessary equipment, and can give a good account of itself alongside the other religions. But do not forget that if it does this it has renounced its birthright. It has renounced the unique power which it has as the religion of revelation. This power dwells only in weakness. And it does not really operate, nor does the power with which Christianity hopes to work, the power of religious self-consciousness which is the gift of grace in the midst of weakness, unless Christianity has first humbled instead of exalting itself. By its neglect of this order, Christianity has created great difficulties for itself in its debate with other religions....

We must not allow ourselves to be confused by the fact that a history of Christianity can be written only as a story of the distress which it makes for itself. It is a story which lies completely behind the story of that which took place between Yahweh and His people, between Jesus and His apostles. It is a story whose source and meaning and goal, the fact that the Christian is strong only in his weakness, that he is really satisfied by grace, can in the strict sense nowhere be perceived directly. Not even in the history of the Reformation! What can be perceived in history is the attempt which the Christian makes, in continually changing forms, to consider and vindicate his religion as a work which is in itself upright and holy. But he continually feels himself thwarted and hampered and restrained by Holy Scripture, which does not allow this, which even seems to want to criticize this Christian religion of his. He obviously cannot shut out the recollection that it is in respect of this very work of his religion that he cannot dispense with the grace of God and therefore stands under the judgment of God. At this point we are particularly reminded of the history of the Reformation. But in the very light of that history we see that the recollection has always been there, even in the pre- and post-Reformation periods. Yet the history of Christianity as a whole reveals a tendency which is quite contrary to this recollection. It would be arbitrary not to recognize this, and to claim that the history of Christianity, as

distinct from that of other religions, is the story of that part of
humanity, which, as distinct from others, has existed only as
the part which of grace lives by grace. In the strict sense there
is no evidence of this throughout the whole range of Christianity.
What is evident is in the first instance a part of humanity which
no less contradicts the grace and revelation of God because it
claims them as its own peculiar and most sacred treasures, and
its religion is to that extent a religion of revelation. Contradiction
is contradiction. That it exists at this point, in respect of the
religion of revelation, can be denied even less than at other points.
Elsewhere we might claim in extenuation that it simply exists
in fact, but not in direct contrast with revelation. But in the
history of Christianity, just because it is the religion of revelation,
the sin is, as it were, committed with a high hand. Yes, sin! For
contradiction against grace is unbelief, and unbelief is sin, indeed
it is *the* sin. It is therefore a fact that we can speak of the truth
of the Christian religion only within the doctrine of the *iustificatio
impii*. The statement that even Christianity is unbelief gives rise
to a whole mass of naïve and rationalizing contradiction. Church
history itself is a history of this contradiction. But it is this very
fact which best shows us how true and right the statement is. We
can as little avoid the contradiction as jump over our own
shadow.

We cannot expect that at a fourth or fifth or sixth stage the
history of Christianity will be anything but a history of the
distress which Christianity creates for itself. May it not lack in
future reformation, i.e. expressions of warning and promise deriv-
ing from Holy Scripture! But before the end of all things we
cannot expect that the Christian will not always show himself an
enemy of grace, in spite of all intervening restraints.

Notwithstanding the contradiction and therefore our own existence, we can and must perceive that for our part we and our
contradiction against grace stand under the even more powerful
contradiction of grace itself. We can and must – in faith. To
believe means, in the knowledge of our own sin to rely upon
the righteousness of God which makes an infinite satisfaction
for our sin. Concretely, it means, in the knowledge of our own

contradiction against grace to cleave to the grace of God which infinitely contradicts this contradiction. In this knowledge of grace, in the knowledge that it is the justification of the ungodly, that it is grace for the enemies of grace, the Christian faith attains to its knowledge of the truth of the Christian religion. There can be no more question of any immanent rightness or holiness of this particular religion as the ground and content of the truth of it than there can be of any other religion claiming to be the true religion in virtue of its inherent advantages. The Christian cannot avoid abandoning any such claim. He cannot avoid confessing that he is a sinner even in his best actions as a Christian. And that is not, of course, the ground, but the symptom of the truth of the Christian religion. The abandoning and confessing means that the Christian Church is the place where, confronted with the revelation and grace of God, by grace men live by grace. . . .

There is, of course, one fact which powerfully and decisively confirms the assertion, depriving it of its arbitrary character and giving to it a necessity which is absolute. But to discern this fact, our first task – and again and again we shall have to return to this "first" – must be to ignore the whole realm of "facts" which we and other human observers as such can discern and assess. For the fact about which we are speaking stands in the same relationship to this realm as does the sun to the earth. That the sun lights up this part of the earth and not that means for the earth no less than this, that day rules in the one part and night in the other. Yet the earth is the same in both places. In neither place is there anything in the earth itself to dispose it for the day. Apart from the sun, it would everywhere be enwrapped in eternal night. The fact that it is partly in the day does not derive in any sense from the nature of the particular part as such. Now it is in exactly the same way that the light of the righteousness and judgment of God falls upon the world of man's religion, upon one part of that world, upon the Christian religion, so that that religion is not in the night but in the day, it is not perverted but straight, it is not false religion but true. Taken by itself, it is still human religion and therefore unbelief, like all other religions. Neither in the root nor in the crown of this particular tree, neither at the source nor at the outflow of this particular stream, neither on the surface nor in the depth of this particular part of humanity can we point to anything that makes it suitable for the day of divine righteousness and judgment. If the Christian religion is the right and true religion the reason for it does not reside in facts which might point to itself or its own adherents, but in the fact which as the righteousness and the judgment of God confronts it as it does all other religions, characterizing and differentiating it and not one of the others as the right and true religion. ...

# 5

# DIALECTIC
## Emil Brunner

THE NAME MOST closely associated with that of Barth in the
leadership of the dialectical theology is that of his fellow countryman Emil Brunner (1889–1966). Although he was over-shadowed
by Barth, it was in fact Brunner who published the first extensive
treatments of the doctrines of salvation, ethics, and man from
the point of view of the dialectical theology [*The Mediator* (1927),
*The Divine Imperative* (1932), *Man in Revolt* (1937)]. He was
also the first of this school to complete a *Dogmatics* (1946–60).
Brunner remains perhaps the most representative figure in the
theological revival of the twenties and thirties, standing between
Barth on the right and Bultmann and Tillich on the left.

Brunner was deeply involved in the religious socialist movement from his student days at the Universities of Zürich and
Berlin, and he continued this political and cultural interest
throughout his career. Like Barth he began as a pastor in a
small Swiss village, but he was soon called to the University
of Zürich where he was professor of theology from 1924 to 1955
and Rector of the University from 1942 to 1944. He travelled
widely, taught in England and the United States, and worked in
many phases of the ecumenical movement. He ended his teaching career at the International Christian University in Japan.
Beside those mentioned above, his most important books include
*Philosophy of Religion* (1927), *The Divine-Human Encounter*
(1938), *Justice and the Social Order* (1943), and *Christianity and
Civilization*, 2 vols. (1947–48).

Although he worked with Barth during the twenties on the journal *Zwischen den Zeiten*, the house organ of the dialectical theology, issues soon arose between them which culminated in a sharp exchange in 1934 published under the title *Natural Theology* and comprising an essay by Brunner entitled "Nature and Grace" and a response from Barth entitled "No! An Angry Answer to Emil Brunner". The points at issue here are basic to the Christian attitude toward other religions, namely, whether there is a revelation outside the Bible, whether man can come to know God apart from the biblical revelation, and whether therefore there is a point of contact in man for God's revelation in Christ. Brunner argued affirmatively on the basis of Bible and tradition, and Barth rejected all his arguments. Thus in these two documents we can see the fundamental divergence between Barth's negative attitude toward other religions and Brunner's dialectical attitude.

In 1941 Brunner published his most thorough treatment of this subject under the title *Revelation and Reason*. The first half of the book is devoted to an analysis of the idea of revelation in which he affirms a general revelation of God to all men through the creation. The second half is concerned with the relation of the Christian revelation to the functions of reason in science, philosophy, and other aspects of culture. Three chapters are devoted to the interpretation of religion. The first is entitled "The World Religions and Their Claim to Revelation". Here Brunner asserts that whereas primitive, polytheistic, and mystical religions make no claim to a revelation of universal validity, three world religions do make this claim. Of these Zoroastrianism and Islam really reduce to a rationalistic moralistic theism with no mystery of redemption. Judaism either awaits the Messiah, and thus does not claim a final revelation, or else it too reduces to the same type of theism. Brunner concludes that the claim of a universally valid revelation is in fact quite rare and that it appears in its fullness only in Christian faith.

In the second chapter, entitled "Revelation and the Naturalistic Theory of Religion", Brunner investigates the psychological interpretation of religion by Freud, the sociological interpretations of Feuerbach and Durkheim, and the transcendental or idealistic interpretations of Kant, Hegel, Schleiermacher, and Otto. Brunner concludes that while these theories point to real elements in the religions, they distort them, and in any case cannot make sense of Christian faith. He discusses these theories further in the third chapter, which is the selection below. Here his thesis is that the religions are the product of the original divine revelation in the creation and of human sin.

It is important to note that Brunner's view of the other religions is practically identical to that of Hendrik Kraemer, whose writings have had a world-wide impact on the discussion of this question. His first book, *The Christian Message in a Non-Christian World* (1938), was written for the meeting that year of the International Missionary Council in Madras, India. It was largely directed against a study of American missions in Asia entitled *Rethinking Missions* (1932), edited by W. E. Hocking, and it was the first major challenge to the attitude toward other religions reflected in that volume which represented the prevailing liberal theology.

Brunner's interpretation of other religions is a clear example of the view which has been discussed above under the heading "Revelation–Sin".

# Revelation and Religion*

THE CHRISTIAN FAITH, faith in the God revealed by Jesus Christ, is not *"one"* of the religions of the world". A religious and geographical survey of the world would, of course, include "Christianity" under the general concept of religion. It is impossible for a non-Christian to take that which distinguishes the Christian faith from "the other religions" so seriously that on that account

* From Emil Brunner, *Revelation and Reason: The Christian Doctrine of Faith and Knowledge,* trans. O. Wyon (Philadelphia: The Westminster Press, 1946 and London: SCM Press Ltd, 1947), pp. 258–273. Copyright 1946 by W. L. Jenkins. Used by permission.

he would give up his general concept of "religion". But the Christian faith itself cannot recognize this general conception, without losing its own identity. It cannot admit that its faith is one species of the genus "religion", or if it does so, only in the sense in which it regards itself as the true religion in contrast to the other false religions.[1] To the outsider this looks like narrow-minded or fanatical intolerance; actually, it is a necessary expression of sober truth. The Christian faith alone lives by the Word of God, by the revelation in which God imparts Himself. We have already shown how erroneous is the idea that these "other religions" make the same claim to revelation. This can be proved to be incorrect; not one of them dares to assert, "The Word became flesh, and we beheld His glory, the glory of the only begotten Son of the Father, full of grace and truth." Therefore, because the Christian faith stands on this foundation, it is something wholly different from "the other religions".

But this judgment becomes complete only when we go a step farther, and from the standpoint of faith state clearly what the "other religions" are, and what the phenomenon "religion" really means. Thus in the following pages we shall contrast the naturalistic explanations of religion which we were discussing in the last chapter with the Christian understanding of the "other religions".

1. This contrast is not merely an antithesis. The naturalistic, psychological explanation of religion has its own right to exist. A whole mass of religious facts can, in actual fact, be explained as due to fear, desire, the longing for happiness, the "myth-forming imagination", and to projections of the unconscious. Indeed, we are particularly grateful for the illuminating light which modern psychoanalysis has thrown upon certain religious phenomena. The sociological explanation of religion has also produced an impressive amount of material in support of its argument, which, for anyone who has even a slight knowledge

---

[1] This is the Reformation idea of religion. Thus Zwingli entitles his main work *De vera religione;* thus Luther speaks of the Christian faith as the *vera et unica religio* (*W.A.*, 25, 287); this is the meaning of Calvin in his *Institutio Christianae religionis.*

of the subject, possesses convincing power. The fact that religion is influenced by social conditions, which, on their part, are due to various accidents of geography, climate, race, or history, cannot be contested. Further, we must note that in making this admission we do not think that the psychological or the sociological explanations need be confined only to the non-Christian religions but that even in the history of Christianity there is a mass of phenomena which may, and should, be explained in the same way.

In spite of this, however, it is wrong to conclude that this admission means that the phenomenon of religion as a whole, or some particular religious system, has now been completely explained. On the contrary, in all religious phenomena one constant factor is involved which cannot be included in any naturalistic explanation. In *all* forms of religion, in addition to fear there is reverence; as well as the human desire for happiness, there is also a real longing for divine perfection; in addition to social usefulness there is also a genuine striving after communion with the deity, and a genuine submission to a higher, holy command; and behind all the rank fantasy growths of affective thought there is an element which cannot be derived from fantasy at all: the knowledge of something which is unconditioned, ultimate, normative, supramundane, supratemporal.

Behind the bare formula, "The wish is simply made into a god", there lies the problem, How can we in any way "make" anything "into a god"? Animals also have wishes, but they have no gods. To "make a god" something is required which is not self-evident.[2] To do this we need more than the mere power of abstraction, more than the capacity to enlarge sense images, to intensify dimensions into the infinite by means of fantasy. A wish that has been made into a god is a problem that far surpasses all the psychology of Hume, Feuerbach, or Freud, because something lies behind it which transcends psychology: an awareness of an Absolute, of a Holy, of something which is more than the world, more than human. This is the point at which the transcen-

---

[2] Luther, *Nisi enim divinitatis notitiam habuissent, non potuissent eam tribuere idolis nec nomen Dei usurpare* (*W.A.*, 14, 588).

E

dental explanation of religion comes into its own.

Whether in the form in which it has been expressed by Kant, Hegel, Schleiermacher, Fries, or Otto, it always emphasizes the same point, namely, that religion is as much part of the essential, spiritual nature of man as logic, ethics, or art.[3] This is stated, it is true, not merely as a fact of anthropology (as in Feuerbach's view), as something which man cannot ignore, but it is related to all that is valid, true, normative, and absolutely essential.

2. It will not do to regard Feuerbach, from the Christian angle, as the necessary final point of the transcendental philosophy.[4] There is truth in the theory of Transcendentalism, as a whole, as well as in its theory of religion in particular, namely, to put it quite simply, the truth which lies in the distinction between what is psychologically real and what is spiritually valid. Hence the transcendental interpretation of the theory of religion also contains an important element of truth, namely, that in religion the Unconditioned, the Valid, the Eternal, the Absolute – that which lies at the bottom of everything spiritual as spiritual – pierces directly into human consciousness. This will be denied only by one who fails to understand it. Therefore, to a great extent, Kant is right: in all religion there is something of the "conception of the moral as a divine command"; Hegel is right: in the religious element there is something of a "relation of the spirit to the absolute Spirit", just as Schleiermacher's doctrine of "the feeling of absolute dependence" emphasizes an important aspect of religion. Who can seriously deny that Otto's interpretation of religion as the experience of the Numinous does emphasize an important element in all religion, and that in point of fact, as

[3] Hence Schlatter, *Das christliche Dogma*, pp. 25 ff., rightly speaks of the "impossibility of avoiding the consciousness of God", and in so doing is simply following Reformation doctrine: "That within the human spirit there is a *sensus divinatis*, a feeling for the Divine, and, moreover, through natural instinct, stands beyond question" (*Institutes*, I, 3, i). See also Kähler, *Die Wissenschaft der chr. Lehre*, p. 113. The naturalistic explanation of religion can evade this difficulty only by its (philosophically impossible) derivation of all that is "ideal" from sense data, that is, through a defective theory of knowledge.

[4] Karl Barth in his essay on "Feuerbach" in *Zwischen den Zeiten*, 1927, pp. 11–33.

Otto says, profound reverence, the trembling awe produced by the Numinous, is a feeling that cannot be derived from any natural experience. In religion man is feeling after that which is above him, and yet, so long as he is a human being, makes itself known to him as near him and in him. The transcendental theory of religion brings out the fact which the Christian faith, even if in a different sense, likewise acknowledges: that human existence always, and necessarily, consists in a relation with God.

But the theory of transcendental philosophy is too abstract and rational to do justice to real religion. For in real religion – and here I refer to the content of all non-Christian religions – man always has to do with powers which meet him in an irrational way outside himself. The immanental religious interpretation of the transcendental philosophy can find no real explanation of this aspect of religion – for the sense of revelation, for the powerful character of the gods. Quite improperly, it rationalizes and depersonalizes religion. For the fact that in these religions man is dealing with a "god" or with "gods" and not with "the Divine", that these deities intervene in human life, and make themselves known, and are discovered, not merely on a basis of reflection but on the basis of inner or outer reality, philosophy has no other explanation than this: that this happens to be the primitive way of thinking, a product of the myth-forming imagination. It is at this point that the Christian explanation of religion[5] begins.

3. The Christian interpretation is the most complex of all. It

[5] Unfortunately no one has yet worked out a complete Christian doctrine of the non-Christian religions, based on the concrete material provided by these religions, and their religious testimony, which is conceived and carried out from the standpoint of the Biblical faith. Most people who deal with the problem of religion in general are either quite remote from the Christian faith or they hold a rather relative point of view of Christianity. The others, who really know what the Christian faith is, in contrast to all other forms of religion, do not see the problem, and content themselves with making some quite general statements. The nearest to that which is assumed here is Kähler, *op. cit.*, pp. 109–177; von Oettingen, *Lutherische Dogmatik*, I, pp. 158–228, and, especially instructive, even although with a Hegelian streak of evolutionistic optimism, Dorner, *Christl. Glaubenslehre*, I, pp. 672–696. Apart from Dorner, however, they remain in the sphere of abstractions.

includes the naturalistic, psychological theory, the sociological theory, and that of transcendental philosophy, but it also brings with it a new element, by means of which the other elements of explanation are in part transformed, and in part differently integrated. This new element is a twofold thesis: the religions, the religious life of the natural man, are the product of the original divine revelation and of human sin. Apart from real revelation, the phenomenon of religion cannot be understood. Even the most primitive polytheistic or prepolytheistic idolatrous religion is unintelligible without the presupposition of the universal revelation of God which has been given to all men through the Creation. Therefore the Apostle, when he explains the nature of the pagan religion, speaks, first of all, of this universal self-manifestation of God to all men without exception through the works of creation and through the writing of the law upon their hearts. Likewise he admits that the Athenians "ignorantly worship" "an unknown God", and that this is possible because they were created in order that they should seek after the Lord, and because, as he says in another passage, "He has not left Himself without a witness among them." [6] The Holy Scriptures teach us to understand all pagan religion from the standpoint of the revelation through the Creation.

The original revelation[7] is not a historical entity. Like the creation, it is the presupposition of every individual and collective existence. Men know something of God – γνόντες τόν Θεόν – because "God has revealed it unto them". This revelation is

[6] Acts 14. 17; 17. 27.

[7] For the whole of Christian theology the doctrine of the original revelation, which forms part of the Biblical history (Gen., chs. 1 ff.) is taken for granted. Luther, for instance, in his exposition of Gen., ch. 2, expounds in detail the religion which was possible and real upon the basis of this original revelation. Now, it is very remarkable that a school of theology which lays so much store by the Bible and the Reformers should skate so lightly over the question of this original revelation. Sin no more destroys the "primitive state" and the original revelation than it makes man no longer a creature created by God. It is obvious that our changed view of history must involve a reformulation of the doctrine of the primitive state, and also of the original revelation; but to ignore it altogether can lead only to the greatest confusion. Cf. *Der Mensch im Widerspruch*, pp. 101 ff. [English trans., *Man in Revolt*, by O. Wyon. Tr.]

not something that took place long, long ago, and has now been relegated to the far-distant past, but, as Paul says, it is a present reality – even when men turn its truth into illusion. Behind all religion, therefore, there lies, on the side of God, truth, communication, the testimony of the Creator-God to himself.[8] The heathen, says Calvin, are never wholly left without any knowledge of God, "since God reveals Himself to them – admittedly only in a dim and veiled manner – or at least He has given them a little taste of His truth. ..." "Even at the time when He confined the grace of His covenant to Israel, still He did not withhold the knowledge of Himself so completely from the heathen that not a little spark of it reached them."[9] Luther says, "For God has implanted such light and intelligence in human nature, that it may give a token, and moreover a picture of His divine Governance, that He is the sole Lord and Creator of all creatures."[10]

"We must either deny heathenism the right to bear the name of religion at all or we must admit that in it we see God's acts, and His revelation, even though this is said in a broad sense."[11] There are phenomena in the religions of non-Christian peoples which "we must refer back to stirrings of the divine Spirit in their hearts."[12] The most important of these "effects" of the original revelation is the sense of God, in general. Men have always had a certain knowledge (*notitia*) of God, and this knowledge of God "will not allow itself to be stifled. There may indeed have been people like the Epicureans, Pliny, and the like, who deny it with their mouth ... but this does not help them; their conscience tells them otherwise" (Luther).[13] Calvin teaches that this sense of God is so deeply interwoven with the nature of man that "the

[8] Kähler and other modern theologians who take their stand on the Bible have replaced the concept of the original revelation by that of the "religious disposition". But this does not solve the problem; it only pushes it farther back, and diverts it into a subjective and anthropological direction. The question should be put like this: What are the influences coming from outside of man which urge him to the formation of religious ideas and of religious phenomena? Kähler, for instance, recognizes this question (*op. cit.*, pp. 117, 185), but he does not answer it in a satisfactory manner.

[9] Calvin, 49, 208.    [10] Luther, *E.A.*, 9, 4.    [11] Dorner, *op. cit.*, p. 679.
[12] *Ibid.*, p. 677.    [13] Luther, *W.A.*, 19, 206.

knowledge (*notitia*) of God and of ourself is connected by a mutual bond"[14] Hence the transcendental theory of religion is both right and wrong: right, in so far as it sees the sense of God as an integral element in the nature of man; and wrong, in so far as the original revelation is different from anything that man can come to know by his own efforts. For the Biblical Christian doctrine of the original revelation is only one half of the truth; the other half is the doctrine of original sin.

This first, positive, point having been made, we must make the second, negative, point equally clear: "Religion" is the product of man's sinful blindness. In the same passage, and indeed in the same sentence, in which Paul speaks of the original revelation, he also speaks of the original sin of all men: "Because that, knowing God, they glorified Him not as God ... but became vain in their reasonings ... and changed the glory of the incorruptible God for the likeness of an image of corruptible man, and of birds, and four-footed beasts, and creeping things."[15] The God of the "other religions" is always an idol. The religious forms of the imagination always follow the law of secularization, either in the form of making finite – idolatry in the ordinary, polytheistic sense – or in the form of depersonalization, in which the idea of God is dissolved into an abstraction. The paradoxical truth of the Living God – that He is absolute Person – is torn asunder into non-paradoxical parts. Religions of one kind "personalize" God, and make Him finite, in the form of myths; the other kind dissolves Him into abstract speculation. The reason for this transformation of the divine revelation into human illusion, however, is not an undeveloped consciousness, a condition of childish immaturity, but it is due to the fact that "they glorified Him not as God, neither gave Him thanks". If the secularization, the blending of God with nature and man, is the first phenomenon, then the *cor incurvatum in se*, egocentricity, or anthropocentrism, or eudaemonism, that is, the failure to give glory to God, or self-seeking, is the deepest motive of all the "other religions", and indeed of man as a whole. The original sin of man breaks out first of all, and mainly, in his religion: the essence of original

[14] Calvin, *Institutes*, I, i, 3.    [15] Rom. 1. 21 ff.

sin is man's apostasy and his inveterate tendency to be absorbed in himself. Neither this original revelation nor original sin can be placed within the historical category. This fact of original sin is always at work beneath the surface of human life; it is the fundamental principle within human history as a whole, and within the life of each individual.

All empirical religion, to use mathematical terms, is the "product" of these two factors" [16] combined with others, which through this are brought into play. These two original elements, however, are so closely interwoven that in our efforts to explain we cannot always distinguish the one from the other. For this very reason the Naturalistic and the Idealistic theories of religion are equally right and equally wrong: the Naturalistic theory, which sees religion only from "below", and the Idealistic theory, which sees it only from "above". Naturalism does not know how very much "from below" the all-too-human element in religion is – it only knows the concept of nature, but not that of sin, which here receives a new name, the daemonic. And Idealism does not know how very much "from above" the divine element is, for indeed it does not know the concept of creation, but only of immanence; hence in unconscious arrogance it makes a divine gift into an attribute of human nature.

Only from the standpoint of the Word of God can we understand the phenomenon of human religion, with all that it contains of wonderful and terrible, sublime and gruesome elements. From that standpoint alone can we do justice to its impressive, as well as to its repellent, elements, to those which are divinely true and to those which are demoniacally false. In all religion there is a recollection of the divine truth which has been lost; in all there is a longing after the divine Light and the divine Love; but in all religion also there yawns an abyss of daemonic distortion of

---

[16] The Reformation doctrine of the "other religions" consists essentially in this dual thesis. When one element in this dialectic is removed, then there arises a perversion of this doctrine – either in a Naturalistic or in an Idealistic sense. Hence what we need is a Christian "philosophy of mythology", like that of Schelling, from which indeed we can learn a great deal, but which breaks down at the decisive point, the understanding of sin.

the truth, and of man's effort to escape from God. In all religion,[17] even in the most primitive form of idolatry, there is something of reverence and gratitude toward a Power on which man knows himself to be dependent, which is different from his dependence on natural facts; but in all religion too, even in the "higher religions", this reverence is mingled with fear of the absolutely Terrible, which only leads to a slavish submission to overwhelming Power, while gratitude is mingled with a selfish longing for happiness, for which the Deity is "used".

All religion is aware of God, that is, of something that is neither the world nor man – or it would not be religion; but it is always at the same time a blend of God and the world, or of God and the self. Thus it is the deification of the world, or the deification of the self, and often both at once. The equally false separation between God and the world in Deism is no longer religion, but a rationalistic negation of religion, which leads directly to agnosticism or to atheism; yet even self-deification, as in original Buddhism, leading to the "negative mysticism" of nirvana, becomes "religious atheism". Strict monotheism alone makes a distinction between the creatures and God, without separating the two in a Deistic manner; but a monotheism of this kind flourishes only on the soil of Biblical revelation. All "approximations" to it are colored by the tendency to blur the distinction. This destruction of the idea of God is closely related to the destruction of the direction of the will: all non-Biblical religion is essentially eudaemonistic and anthropocentric in tendency, if not actually self-centered. Even in his worship of God man seeks himself, his own salvation; even in his surrender to the Deity he wants to find his own security. All these elements are contained in the brief Pauline formula, and in so doing the nature of religion is adequately characterized. But his final judgment is: illusion, unreality. The distinctive mark of non-Biblical religion is its lack of realism. Man cannot, dare not, see himself as he is; therefore

[17] On the following cf. especially Kraemer, *The Christian Message in a Non-Christian World*, a work which combines in a unique way erudition and an independent view of the religions with solid Reformation and Biblical theology.

he cannot and will not see God as He is. The moment that the sinner sees himself as a sinner his sin falls away from him; but he cannot do this of himself: he can do this only when God reveals him to himself, and reveals Himself in such a way that the sinner dares to open himself to the truth. This is the secret of *that* truth of revelation which is also called the forgiveness of sins. "Therefore the true and only religion, the only true divine worship, is to believe in the free forgiveness of our sins, without works, out of pure grace alone. ... To trust in this God, who is gracious to us out of pure love and who does us good 'for nothing', that is the true religion and the true righteousness" (Luther).[18] All human religion, because, and in so far as, it does not know this God, is *falsa religio*; it means leaving God out of account. We will now proceed to deal with this question in more detail.

4. The first fact that we have to consider is the universal extent of religion, on the one hand, and the possibility and reality of irreligion and atheism, on the other hand. All attempts to find a people without a religion have proved unsuccessful. Discoveries made during the excavation of ancient sites give clear evidence of the existence of religious views and customs.[19] Among the peoples of the ancient world in particular, and among primitive peoples, religion is taken for granted; indeed, it naturally takes a prominent place in their individual and social life. The same is true of the individual human being of the present day. The consciousness of something sacred, the sense of reverence, and the idea of God are never wholly absent from any human being. It is true that education and tradition play a great part in all this, but tradition itself cannot be ultimately derived from tradition, and education cannot create anything; it can only develop what was already there in germ.

But whereas among the primitive peoples of antiquity, and almost down to modern times, irreligion was an exception, an anomaly within the society which took religion for granted as part of its life, the course of modern development reveals more and more the phenomenon of mass atheism and collective irreli-

---

[18] Luther, *W.A.*, 25, 287.
[19] Cf. P. Wilhelm Schmidt, *Der Ursprung der Gottesidee*.

gion. This fact is a great embarrassment[20] for the Idealistic theory of religion, while from the standpoint of the Christian faith this possibility was always, from the outset, taken into account. It is true that atheism or irreligion does not extend, even in a society bereft of religion, to the loss of the idea of God, or to complete callousness toward the idea of the Holy,[21] but on occasions it does come very near to this extreme.

At the same time the following facts should be borne in mind. First, atheism is often more truly "religious" than the religiosity it attacks.[22] Those who know religion only in its worst and most distorted forms, as hypocrisy or as a cover for the "all-too-human" element, cannot express their consciousness of the Holy in any other form save that of protest. Atheistic objectors, accusers of the divine Governance of the world, are as a rule not "godless" at all; very often the bitter invectives which they hurl at what they call the "injustice" of "heaven" actually contain a passionate love of justice. In the name of the divine justice they protest against the world's injustice, which, however, they identify with their own idea of God. Similarly, the godlessness of the modern labor movement, which found such a terrible expression in the Bolshevist Revolution, can be understood only when we realize its passionate hatred of a bourgeois society which justifies its unjust and inhuman enjoyment of privilege by religious theories, and defends its privileges by means of ecclesiastical politics. Finally, we must say that it is precisely the consciously "godless" man who always lives on the idea of God, in the very fact of his negation. The most difficult thing to explain is not this aggressive atheism but complete religious indifference.

[20] Since for Idealism and for every kind of transcendental philosophical view of religion the sense of God and religion are identical, and thus both necessarily belong to the nature of man, the fact of godlessness has to be reinterpreted in the sense of being merely a feebly developed religious sense. Godlessness differs from religion only in quantity and in a dynamic understanding of it. It is then a result of defective intellectual development; actually it appears oftener among highly educated people than among the less educated.

[21] See above what Luther says (p. 121) about the Epicureans.

[22] We can see this root of atheism very plainly, especially in classical philosophy, but it is also visible in Nietzsche and Marx.

But when we start from the Christian conception of sin, then godlessness of all kinds – both the polemically aggressive kind (the passionate hatred of God and of religion) and complete religious indifference – lies, from the outset, within the realm of possibility. "The mind of the flesh is enmity against God."[23] The sinful man, in spite of the fact that God makes Himself known to him in the Creation and in conscience, can not only flee from Him, but he can do the opposite and intensify his striving for independence to the point of denying God. The titanic revolt against the very existence of God is *one* form of sin; another form is the effort to escape from God, which extends to complete forgetfulness of Him.[24] The sinful human being is able to turn his back upon God, and to immerse himself so completely in the affairs of this life that in the end he forgets God entirely. Spiritual sterility, indeed, may reach such a pitch that human beings may no longer have any interest in anything beyond the immediate and purely natural fulfillment of human needs; this loss of interest produces a state of almost total insensibility to the claims of any higher sphere.

Above all, we must not overlook the fact that the religious consciousness may clothe itself in apparently purely secular forms. When God is got rid of, something else has to take His place – blood and soil, state and nation, eros, art, science, technics, sport.[25] The religious element is always present where people become fanatical, where absolute values are concerned, even though the things themselves may be small and insignificant enough. People who have got rid of God are usually their own god, and all the passion which should serve the glory of God is devoted to the interests of the self. A parallel phenomenon, which has been brought to light by the discoveries of modern psychoanalysis, is this: the religious element which has been repressed asserts its presence all the more strongly in the unconscious. It comes out in dreams, in neuroses, in depravity, in criminal

[23] Rom. 8. 7.
[24] Cf. the degrees of unspirituality in Kierkegaard, *Sickness Unto Death.*
[25] See Luther's *Larger Catechism* on the First Commandment.

tendencies, and in illness of all kinds.[26] Unfortunately the pscho-
logy and phenomenology of the repression of the religious instinct
has not yet been written; it would be an amazing science, which
would throw a great deal of light upon perplexing phenomena
in human life.

Man may indeed try to escape from God, but God never lets
him go completely. Man may be godless – that is indeed the
proper *telos* of sin – but he cannot prevent himself making an
idol to take the place of God. "The heart of man must have
a god, that is, something in which he puts his confidence, something which is a comfort to him. . . . Now he must have either the
true God or a false god" (Luther). The story of modern humanity
is full of temples erected to substitute deities. Theophil Spoerri has
shown this very plainly in his book *Götter des Abendlandes*
(*Gods of the West*). It is still probably true that, as Luther says,
"man must always have either a god or an idol".[27]

5. The dialectical Christian conception of religion makes it
clear that all religious forms of life, whether primitive or highly
cultivated, ancient or modern, individual or collective, ideas or
actions, reveal a dichotomy.[28] Polytheism divides the nature of
the one God into two groups of gods, good and evil, loving and
cruel. The more personal the conception of the gods, the more
impotent do they become, the more are they dominated by an
impersonal destiny of fate; the more intellectual the religion,
the more abstract and impersonal it becomes; it then develops
into a rational "religion without revelation", either in the form of
speculative mysticism or of religious moralism. The more the
moral element predominates, the weaker does the religious ele-

[26] See the very interesting detailed example of a neurosis with an
unconscious religious basis in Jung's *Psychology and Religion.*

[27] ["*Gott oder Abgott.*" Tr.]

[28] In recent days attempts have been made also from the theological side
to construct a typology of religions (cf. Søderblom, *Natürliche Theologie
und Religionsgeschichte*). Since, however, they usually start from the
axiom that "religion, in spite of the differences and contrasts, forms a
connected whole . . . to which also Christianity must be reckoned" (Søderblom, p. 77), behind these attempts almost without exception there is a
more or less Idealistic concept of religion, which does not allow the
Christian truth of the nature of the religions to appear.

ment become, and the converse is also true. Primitive religion still contains all these elements, undifferentiated, but here too the connection of the religious element with the instinctive and the chaotic irrational elements reaches its zenith. The history of religion cannot show any religious system that is fully spiritual and yet contains within itself both personal and revealed elements; nor can it point to an ethical movement that does not drift away from true religion, nor does it know a religious life that becomes more human as it becomes more religious, a religion in which the truly divine and the truly human are combined, and indeed are one. This oneness can be found only in that which is more than religion, in the divine revelation in Jesus Christ.

6. Jesus Christ is both the Fulfillment of all religion and the Judgment on all religion. As the Fulfiller, He is the Truth which these religions seek in vain. There is no phenomenon in the history of religion that does not point toward Him: the bloody sacrifice of expiation, the sacred meal, the ecstatic element, the seeking of the Holy Spirit, the magical element, the indication of the *dynamis* of God in the reality of His revelation, prayer, the divine Father, and the divine Judge. All this the world of religions knows in a fragmentary and distorted form, as almost unrecognizable "relics" of an "original" revelation. From the standpoint of Jesus Christ, the non-Christian religions seem like stammering words from some half-forgotten saying. None of them is without a breath of the Holy, and yet none of them is the Holy. None is without its impressive truth, and yet none of them is the Truth; for their Truth is Jesus Christ.

But the atheistic protest against religion is also fulfilled in Jesus Christ. All religion creates a gulf between the sacred and the secular; it is religion in contrast to the secular. In Jesus this contrast is explicitly denied; nothing is secular, all is sacred, for all belongs to God. Jesus rejects holy seasons, holy persons, holy places, specially holy acts, and indeed, too, the holy gods; for what the religions know as "gods" are not truly holy, not truly divine. In Jesus the protest of the atheist has as much right as religion.

For Jesus Christ is not only the Fulfillment; He is also the

Judgment on all religion. Viewed in His light, all religious systems appear untrue, unbelieving, and indeed godless. In sacrifice man seeks to placate God; in prayer he seeks to make use of Him; the very fact of the multiplicity of the gods is an insult to the idea of God; their supposed sacredness is mixed with that which is cruel and horrible, their kindness with moral laxity and favoritism. Their supramundane nature is too earthly, too human, too close to nature. And the higher religions – what is mysticism other than the self-deification of man? What is religious moralism other than the self-confidence of man who believes he can redeem himself? The higher the intellectual development of a religion, the more intense is its opposition to the truth revealed in Christ. The Jews, not the pagans; the high priests and the scribes, not the pagan representative of the emperor, willed the crucifixion of Jesus. There is only one religion that rivals Judaism in its hatred of Christ, and that is Islam.

None of the religions knows the self-communication of the holy and merciful God. Hence in the last resort they are all religions of self-redemption. There is, it is true, the "grace" religion of India, with its gentle practice of bhakti, of the love of God, and its doctrine that the divine grace is not appropriated by man, but that it appropriates him, as a mother cat picks up and carries off her kitten in her mouth, in contrast to the mother monkey to whom the baby clings by his own efforts.[29] But the "grace" which is here meant is not the forgiveness of sin; thus it is not the grace of the holy God, in whose presence sin is guilt and who takes guilt seriously. It is not the grace that comes to us in the self-acting intervention of God in the history of mankind, but a grace that is discovered upon a mystical "way" of meditative recollection by man. Nor is this "grace" communion with God, and through Him with all creatures, but it is union with God, and forgetfulness of all that is creaturely, which is a mere illusion.

In the history of religion, in Eastern Buddhism there is the doctrine of grace of the Amita Buddha. But this Amita Buddha,

[29] Cf. Otto, *Die Gnadenreligion Indiens und das Christentum*, and Konow in Chantepie's *Lehrbuch*, II, p. 159.

to call on whom brings salvation, is not the Creator, the Lord of heaven and earth, not the Holy God, who will not allow Himself to be mocked; and this salvation is not the vision of God face to face, not the fulfillment of the creaturely in fellowship with the divine Person, but nirvana, dissolution into nothingness. The Eastern religions of grace come no less under the judgment of Christ than the two Semitic monotheistic religions which lay so much stress on the will, and on righteousness through "works." [30]

The only power that in principle unconditionally excludes self-redemption is the message of the mediation of Jesus Christ, who has given Himself for us, and who gives to those who believe in Him eternal life. Here is the "religion" in which the truly divine is at the same time the truly human; the Absolute at the same time personal; the religious at the same time the ordinary-human; the historical revelation which is at the same time the original revelation; the "religion" in which alone there is shown to us the glory and the love of God, His power, and the responsibility of man, the mercy which gives all, and the holiness which demands all.

But this revelation ought not to be called "religion", nor should faith in it bear this name. For in Jesus Christ "the Christian religion" is judged as much as the other religions. This precisely is the center of the "doctrine of justification", of the *sola gratia* and *sola fide*: that even the Christian and religious man is not "justified" by his piety, that even his piety needs the forgiving grace of Christ. Indeed, the touchstone of true faith is the fact that the Christian thus believes beyond his own faith, that he is aware of his own sinfulness, even though he is Christian and genuinely "devout". "True religion" can therefore consist only in the fact that our trust is not in "religion" at all but wholly and solely in that divine mercy which meets us in God's revelation, and that all our rightful practices of piety are shot through and through with

[30] Luther included all non-Christocentric religion under the one heading, "righteousness of works, self-redemption". In so far as even the "religions of grace" are ultimately based upon a eudaemonistic striving and therefore are anthropocentric and not theocentric in tendency, he is right; but this difference should be borne in mind. Cf. Vossberg, *Luthers Kritik aller Religion.*

this conviction. It lies in the nature of sin that it even captures the highest in man. It is possible for man to understand the Christian faith in such a way that in it he seeks himself instead of God; that he seeks to assert himself and to "realize" himself, instead of seeking the glory of God. The history of Christianity, of the "Christian religion", is only too full of proofs of this statement. Only when we accept this judgment on our Christianity, and in spite of this are in good heart, do we show that we have understood what is true and what is false in religion. The judgment cannot be other than this: "I am the Truth" – and He is also "the Way and the Life".

# 6

## RECONCEPTION
## William Ernest Hocking

IN SPITE OF the widespread influence of the theological movement inspired by the dialectical theology of Barth and Brunner various patterns of liberal theology persisted among theologians and philosophers of religion, especially in America. Outstanding among these, particularly for his interest in attitudes toward other religions, is the American philosopher, William Ernest Hocking (1873–1966). Hocking grew up in the Middle West in a family of strong Methodist piety. An early interest in William James led him to study at Harvard, where he came under the influence of the idealist philosopher Josiah Royce. A year's study in Germany brought him into contact with the phenomenology of Edmund Husserl. Upon completion of his graduate study at Harvard, Hocking taught comparative religion at Andover Theological Seminary and philosophy at the University of California and at Yale. After service in World War I he returned to Harvard as professor of philosophy until his retirement in 1943.

Hocking is the author of more than twenty books on philosophy, psychology, political science, law, education, and religion. In 1912 he published his most famous work, *The Meaning of God in Human Experience*, which is an interpretation of religion from the point of view of a philosophy of personal idealism. In 1930 he confronted the problem of the relations among the world religions as the chairman of a commission of laymen whose task was to study the foreign mission work of six Protestant denominations in Asia. He edited the commission's report, which was published in 1932 under the title *Rethinking Missions*, and wrote its introductory section on general principles. Here we find the themes which are elaborated more fully in his later works. The religions of the world should see each other no longer as antagonists but as partners in the struggle against the growing secular spirit. This is possible because all the religions contain a common core of religious truth which is "the inalienable religious intuition of the human soul". Thus the relation among the religious should be one of mutual help in the search for the completest religious truth.

The selection below is taken from Hocking's Hibbert Lectures delivered in 1936 at Oxford and Cambridge and published in 1940 under the title *Living Religions and a World Faith*. The first chapter is devoted to an investigation of the nature of religion, its universality and particularity, its communal and individual character. Here religion is defined as "a passion for righteousness, and for the spread of righteousness, conceived as a cosmic demand". A second chapter treats the characteristics of oriental religions. Today the emergence of a world culture through the means of a world science and a world commerce raises the question of the possibility of a world faith. In the third chapter Hocking discusses three possible ways to a world faith: the way of radical displacement, the way of synthesis, and the way of reconception.

Radical displacement, which Hocking associates with Barth and Kraemer, is the traditional approach of Christian missions. It requires a complete break with the old allegiances. Hocking rejects it on the basis of its results, its pedagogy, its psychology, and its presupposition of a special revelation of the only way of salvation. The way of synthesis is the adoption of what one finds to be true in other religions. Although he is much more in sympathy with this way, Hocking believes that even if it can avoid the danger of a romantic syncretism, this way is inadequate, since it cannot solve the basic issues between the religions. It is in fact a preliminary stage of the way of reconception.

Reconception is the deepening of one's understanding of the essence of his own religion in the light of the valid insights of other religions. It is the true way to a world faith, since the essence of all religions is the same. A final chapter assesses the present and future prospects of the way of reconception and the place of Christianity in this way. Hocking holds that in its ideal character Christianity is the "anticipation of the essence of all religion, and so contains potentially all that any religion has". Our actual or empirical Christianity, however, falls far short of this, and Hocking offers suggestions as to the values in other religions which Christianity lacks.

Twenty years later Hocking returned to these questions in a volume entitled *The Coming World Civilization* (1956). While continuing to reject relativism and indifferentism in the relations between the religions and to stress the importance of the historic identity of the religions, he foresees a growing convergence among the great faiths of the world. The basis of this is that at the heart of the world religions lies a mysticism which is essentially identical. Thus "the several universal religions are already fused together, so to speak, at the top". The difficulties in the "Essence" view of the relations among the religions have been discussed in the Introduction.

# The Way of Reconception*

IN THE NATURAL order of experience, broadening is preliminary to deepening.

The first business of childhood is the accumulation of riches – wide collection of facts, names, ideas, with no particular concern for their order or their nature. The stage of insight which we call "understanding" follows slowly; the ambition to master things by penetrating their "nature" arrives with maturity.

The religious experience of the race follows a similar pattern. The many gods of the early world belong to the stage of accumu-

* From William Ernest Hocking, *Living Religions and a World Faith* (New York: The Macmillan Co., 1940), pp. 190–208. Used by permission of the estate of William Ernest Hocking.

lation: they are records of the wide variety of primitive religious experience, care-free in respect to order, careful only for the faithful preservation of every inkling of the divine. They are preparations for that stage of "understanding" which discerns that the many gods are one. This rhythm of broadening and deepening recurs. In the later world, when the several great systems of faith are brought, as now, into intimate contact, there is a new era of broadening, in which each religion extends its base to comprise what it finds valid in other strands of tradition. But this also must serve as preliminary to that deepening which is a search for better grasp of its own essence.

For broadening necessarily stimulates the deepening process. One's conceptions have been inadequate; they have not anticipated these new vistas and motives: we require to understand our own religion better – we must *reconceive it* – then we shall see how the new perspectives belong quite naturally to what has always been present in its nature, unnoticed or unappreciated by us.

We are at the dawn of this new stage of deepening. In the contemporary epoch, in which the position and meaning of religion are in constant question, inclusiveness in the content of faith becomes a secondary aim. All the sails of the mind have for some time been set for exploration and acquisition; there are really few who need any longer to be admonished not to reject what is good in what to them is foreign. The great effort now required is the effort to discern the substance of the matter underlying all this profusion of religious expression, to apprehend the generating principle of religious life and of each particular form of it.

The word "essence" refers to this generating principle, the single germ from which the many expressions are derived and can therefore be understood. As every living thing has its germ-cell-group,[1] so has every project, undertaking, institution, histori-

---

[1] The organic analogy is fairly precise, even to its tantalizing ambiguities. We cannot understand the oak from the acorn without also understanding the acorn from the oak; growth is no mere unpacking of a magic parcel in which every subsequent development is precontained, it is the appropriation of novelty and adventure, it is also creation; the germ is but the

cal movement its essence. This essence can easily be ungrasped or
misunderstood; and if a leader or statesman misapprehends the
essence of his business, fails to know what can be thrown over-
board in storm, and what must on no account be surrendered,
he heads for disaster. To know the essence of a religion is peculiarly difficult (as the succession of early church councils may
witness). It is always a matter of degree and an unfinished enterprise, so that we must now and again return to it. In proportion
as we grasp it, we can distinguish what is indispensable from
what is relatively accidental and variable. To possess the essence
would be to have sureness, and therefore freedom and courage,
in recognizing truth wherever there is truth, as well as in rejecting
encumbrances, retained antiquities, excess, pretence, accretion. It
would be to give to our impulsive sympathy the discriminating
power of unerring instinct.

How is the essence to be found? Not by comparison, nor by
analysis – though these help: it is found by what the logician
calls "induction", namely a *perception of the reason* why a given
group of facts or experiences do belong together. For this perception (which is often the work of genius) no rules can be given;
it comes as a discovery, an illumination. "Induction" is but a
word which covers the uncommandable insight; induction is the
discovery of essence.

But the broadening of the base of experience aids in discerning
the essence. For it is just these anticipatory warmings of the mind
toward what is felt to be kindred in other faiths which begin to
release us from bondage to the accidental in our own.

One day I was visiting, with a companion of unimpeachable ortho-
doxy, the temple of the Sleeping Buddha near Colombo. A woman
was praying, not at the immense recumbent image of the Buddha, but
at a small standing image at its feet. We questioned the attendant
priest. "Do you not pray to the Buddha?" "No; the Buddha has

opportunity upon which time gathers its undreamed-of spoils; hence all
this reading backward into the germ of what has developed is subject
to illusion. Nevertheless, there is a germ, which is the core of identity;
and we *keep learning about it* from the very novelties which it has made
possible.

entered Nirvana; he is no longer concerned with the affairs on this earth." "To whom do you pray?" "To the Bodhisattvas. This standing image represents a Bodhisattva. He is now in the Universe, and will some day come to the earth to renew the knowledge of the truth, which men are always forgetting." "Does that coming of the Bodhisattva mean anything to you?" asked my companion. "O yes. When he comes, there will be an end of war and hatred; there will be a time of peace and kindness. I hope for his coming. I long for his coming!" There was fervour in the answer. To my surprise, my orthodox companion said, "I join in your hope!" He had swiftly accepted, across wide differences of concepts and imagery, an identity of meaning: to this extent he was coming upon the essence of a symbol common to the two faiths.

The intimations of Synthesis are the natural preparation for Reconception. And the deepenings of Reconception render Synthesis less a separate process than a spontaneous movement of life.

The relation between the three methods may be clarified by a figure – the diagram being, as Whitehead says, the modern form of the Platonic myth!

The way of Reconception has its own dangers. It may be supposed that the essence is sufficient. In that case the search for essence might be a reduction of religion to bare bones, and a discarding of everything but the centre. If the essence seems to present itself as a small group of general principles, the particular aspects of religion are especially likely to be taken as extraneous, and one reverts to religion-in-general.

This is an obvious misuse of the method. To find the life which runs to the various members is not to cancel the members. To find the law which describes the growth of a tree is not to cancel the tree. To discover the premiss from which conclusions follow is not to escape the conclusions; on the contrary, it is to keep those conclusions, to possess them more perfectly. To perceive in any measure the essence of a religion is to be more rather than less alive to all of its functions, and to all its implications.

With this warning, the way of Reconception is peculiarly fitted to meet the groping of an age which, with a certain prevalent dullness, doubts whether it can have any religion at all; and supposing that it can set up its own conditions for accepting religion, requires it not alone to be useful and intelligible, but above all to be brief! It is not in a position to perform an Induction, but it calls for Reduction, and inclines to assume that the two are one.

Such demands, no doubt, like the philistine's demands on art, lack the modesty which would be appropriate to dullness; they

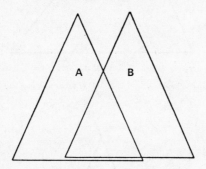

Two religions, A and B, are represented as being partly coincident or overlapping in their present teaching and character. The subsequent diagrams will represent the three ways to a world faith which we have now discussed, as practised by A — religion B being assumed for simplicity's sake to remain passive.

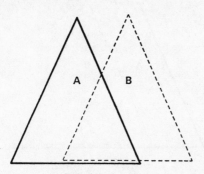

1. Radical Displacement

A hardens its own outline, excluding all of B except what is now included in A

forget that the only God whom man can use is a God who makes demands on *him*. Nevertheless, the human demand also has its place in God's world; and the very dullness of the cry for Reduction may act as a guide in the search for essence. What the

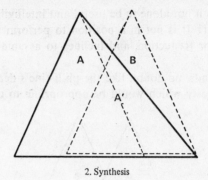

2. Synthesis

A reaches over to include what it finds valid in B, but with some distortion in its own shape.

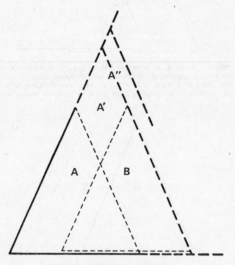

3. Inclusion by Reconception

The apex of the cone A, its conceived essence, moves upward, until without distortion the cone A includes what is valid of B, and indefinitely more, as self-understanding deepens.

demand rightly calls for is what this search may supply – not an impoverishment of religion, but a recovery of proportion and vitality.

The search for essence is progressive. It comes to no final

stopping place; for every Reconception, there is conceivably a better one still to be had.[2] It is the natural process of religious growth, because it is growth *within sameness*; each new discernment of the "essence" is but a better sense of what has all along been seen and taught; it is a new grasp of the eternal identity of the faith.

It thus escapes the fallacy of that Modernism which insisted on the relativity of all stages of religious teaching, and failed to see that religion in its nature must unite men with the everlasting and changeless.[3] The change is in our apprehension; we can hardly pretend that this our finite apprehension needs no improvement! [4] All our judgments of the essence of Christianity contain an element of certainty, and also of uncertainty – an ingredient of hypothesis. On account of this factor of uncertainty, there is a call from time to time for further induction based on wider groups of fact and on better insight into their nature.

[2] It is in this respect akin to the process of Interpretation as defined by Royce. Cf. *Problem of Christianity*, vol. ii, pp. 149 f.

[3] There is something inexorable about the truth; it is not what it is because of anyone's wishes. It is the Rock; and because of this, the primary need of the heart for finality, there is the recurrent appeal to Revelation and to its attribute, Authority. The Christian Church asserts this authority: it has the truth: *Sit ut est aut non sit.*

The difficulty has been to admit growth into what is final. We must have both. When any person or group adopts the position, insisting exclusively on finality, we immediately become conscious of the human element with all its trivialities and self-importances intruding upon the legitimate ideal. Whenever, on the other hand, the Modernist insists on the human element, with its implications of the possibilities of change and growth, the uneasy spectre of flabbiness, desertion of the central citadel of finality, appears. Neither profession alone is tolerable.

The solution lies in these experiences themselves. Something is final in what I have; but not all that I have is final. It is the drawing of this invisible line that is required. This cannot be done by geometry: it requires a process of distillation, repeated distillation, which gradually reveals the essence of unchangeable validity which from the beginning has been the strength of the mixture.

[4] It is peculiar to Christianity that in its view revelation is progressive and unfinished: this is one of the meanings of the doctrine of the Holy Spirit, the perpetual contemporaneousness, personalness, and novelty of the unfolding of the meaning of its truth. No one who declines to admit that form of change which means the arrival of new light – "He shall guide you into all truth" – has understood this doctrine.

The succession of such hypotheses – since each supplies a lack in the preceding – constitutes a consecutive argument, or development; it is the "dialectic" of religious insight in the legitimate meaning of that word. For "dialectic" may be defined as consecutive induction.[5]

In proportion as any religion grows in self-understanding through grasping its own essence, it grasps the essence of all religion, and gains in *power to interpret* its various forms.

To interpret is the best gift which one religion can bring to another. Power to interpret is the power to say more truly or in more understandable language what an idea or a usage "means"; to interpret is to give a voice to what is relatively inarticulate and defenceless. It is indeed to some extent to improve and alter, in so far as it separates the chaff from the wheat; but it does keep the wheat and bring it to market. The interpreter is able to save a great deal which the honest but rude excluder feels impelled to throw away.

In this sense, Reconception is the way of a *true conservatism*: it conserves as much as possible of what is worth conserving in other faiths; it provides a permanent frame for all those scattered "accents of the Holy Ghost" which, treasured in local traditions here and there, are robbed by their separateness of their due force.

There is, one feels, a certain *noblesse oblige* in the relations among religions; those who have travelled far in the path of self-understanding have an obligation to those less skilled in self-explanation. Instead of using this advantage to beat their opponents down, it becomes a matter of chivalry to express for them their meanings better than they themselves could express them. The joy of refutation is a poor and cheap-bought joy in comparison with the joy of lifting a struggling thought to a new level of self-understanding.

Thus, instead of attempting to shut other religions up in metaphysical compartments, and then destroying the compartments,

---

[5] This notion of the empirical dialectic is to be distinguished from the pseudo-deductive dialectic of Hegel, as well as from the experimental pragmatism of Dewey; it is, I suggest, the union of their valid elements.

it would certainly be fairer – not to say more honorable – if we were to attempt rather to anticipate for them what they mean, opening to them that larger room toward which they trend.

Let us suppose, for example, that the cult of ancestors in China leans too much toward a "worship" of the finite, and to a dependence on some magical exchange with them for family fortune. The point to which we have to attend is that the family bond is a normal part of religion in any community; that it has a reasonable place in ritual; that it need not be superstitious; that it requires to be made elastic and compatible with regard for the new national spirit; but that it ought on no account to be expunged.

Homer Ling, civil engineer in the Public Works Dept. of Amoy, a graduate of Massachusetts Institute of Technology, is a third generation Christian. He provided the city of Amoy and the International Settlement on an adjacent island with its new water supply, an admirable piece of engineering. His grandfather was obliged on becoming a Christian to destroy his ancestral tablets. He himself was planning (1932) to build in Amoy an ancestral hall for his clan, in the belief that the cult of ancestors is not inherently inconsistent with Christianity, and that China requires for its new life a renewed hold on the moral bonds of the family which the changing conditions tend to dissolve.

Or if the Buddhist doctrine of the Void appears to us what it literally professes to be, a worship of nothing at all, the most empty and meaningless, the most dehumanizing of all objects of faith, we are surely bound to look beyond the letter; and to interpret the baffling words in terms of the Ineffable of all mysticism, the "Gott ist ein lauter Nichts" of Silesius, or the "stille Wüste der Gottheit" of Eckhart – vehement rejections of the applicability of our qualities or our idea of "thing" to the being of the Absolute. For us, too, the real is no "thing".

The principle is that the ideas of others, like all living entities, must be given the benefit of their direction. They are presumably in partial error. If so, we always have the choice between two comments: either "You are on the wrong track"; or else "*This* is what you are trying for." The latter remark calls for a far severer labor of thought. It cannot be made solely on the basis of a dogma faithfully held. "Whom therefore ye ignorantly worship, him declare I unto you" is not the remark of a mind bringing forward a settled formula. It is the remark of one who has paid in terms of contemporary observation and new thinking the high cost of the power to interpret.

How does this method make for a world faith?

Evidently, if one and only one religion could succeed in absorbing into its own essence the meaning of all the others that religion would attract the free suffrage of mankind to itself. Any such result would necessarily be remote, since the essence cannot be taken by storm; light upon its nature will appear only gradually, and through the slow intimations of meaning as intuitive understanding of the expressions of other faiths is increased. The specific social and historical functions of the local religions could in their nature never be completely replaced by the essence of a universal religion; a truly universal religion would provide a place for such local functions.

But, as Synthesis is mutual, so is Reconception. All religions in contact with one another will be spurred to this kind of deepened self-understanding. At present, in the Far East, Buddhism, Christianity, Hinduism, driven by the intense cultural self-consciousness of the historical moment, are all attempting to restate their own essences, and so to state them as to include what they regard as significant in the others. This makes again for a growing resemblance among religions – that is, among the conceptions of the essence of Buddhism, Christianity, Hinduism, that emerge.[6] And there is certainly no immediate tendency to diminish the number of particular religions.

Nevertheless, the process *does tend to a decision*, not through a conflict of faiths or a campaign for world dominance, but through the unforced persuasiveness of relative success in this effort to become a better vehicle of truth.

[6] Rev. C. Burnell Olds, of Okayama, found that all groups consulted by him in Japan were prepared to agree that the essence of religion is love – love as the basis of the universe and as the root of human righteousness. In this formulation, however, the essence of *religion* is in the foreground, whereas our present concern is with the particular essences of the several religions – the essence of Christianity, etc.

The notion of competition among religions is intrinsically distasteful: competition to displace is precisely that element of discord which the statesman finds most repulsive in the religious scene. But there is an aspect of competition which is right and endurable – a competition to understand and include, a rivalry as to which religion can best express the meaning of the rest; which can save most of the religious treasury of the race – such a rivalry can hardly beget antagonism.

Nor could it be a misfortune for the race if the several living religions should find themselves spurred in one another's presence to such a rivalry. When all religions are losing their hold on multitudes no one can say that any of them is doing too well, through its human representatives, what a religion has to do for the soul of man! They are all wretched vessels. They are all wrapped in sanctimony, dusty-eyed with self-satisfaction, stiff-jointed with the rheum-rust of their creedal conceits, so timorous under the whips of conformity that only a few dare the perilous task of *thinking*, and the complacency-disturbing task of trying the spirit of other faiths. They wear the aspect of senility, while the world is crying to them to be young; they can no longer take a true creed on their lips, and have it carry the meaning of truth, since the blood, life, passion are gone out of it, and it has become a festoon of dried husks. Men are not unready for faith, even for concrete and particular faith, if they can find life in it. These are their questions:

Which religion, in its account of the need and lostness of the human heart, can get farthest beyond platitudes and mere general lament, into the region of the literal struggle of human life with evil, sordidness, and that blight of meaninglessness which besets human success no less than human failure. Which one most truly diagnoses the root of the malady? Which one provides a positive meaning for life without relying on a tinselled and sugared other-worldliness on one hand, nor falling, on the other, into the cant of "timeless values"?

Which religion does in fact most verifiably save men from greed, lust, and hatred, and without destroying their virility and effectiveness as members of race and social order? Which is most proof against hypocrisy, duplicity, and pretence?[7] Which confers most genuine zest for dangerous and principled living, releases positive moral power, abets a single-mindedness which can discount accident, hostility, and failure? Which one develops greatness without narrowness, and conviction without servility. Which one begets prophets who can get the ear of the godless, sophisticated, intelligent, sagacious, and critical, as well as the ear of the suggestible, dependent, sentimental, or committed?

Which religion is most fertile? Which best sustains that metaphysical urge which is the life of the arts, of great and new poetry, drama, architecture, music? A true religion invites cosmic courage, including the belief that the human mind is called upon to know its universe – not to find its equation, but by degrees to understand it. It is not cowed by the spectacle of infinity; it is freed to see meanings in things, to play with traditional ideas, as Dante, Milton, Bunyan played, setting other men free from literalism and the planetary provincialisms of the human outlook. The order of culture is religion, art, philosophy – religion being the fruitful center, when it is alive.

Which religion is most fertile in men? Which sends into the life of the state those convinced and solitary persons who give what no society could ever require of them or even define, and yet without which any society dies of anaemia?

And which religion, while thus serving the public life of its time, can best retain its own proud authority? Which best escapes being harnessed to nostrums and "movements", while evaluating them as they come and go? Which resists being drawn excitedly into the great social programme of the moment through a self-

---

[7] President Lim, Confucianist, knew that the deacons of a certain Christian church in Amoy were engaged in a lucrative trade of smuggling liquor into the Settlement. He confronted some of them with this knowledge, saying: "Why do you do this? If your own doctrines are true, you will go to Hell." And me he confronted with the question, "Why does Christianity not touch the conscience? Confucianism does!"

This was, I presume, partly by way of a *tu quoque*, in view of the usual western conception of Confucianism as a cult of external propriety without sincerity. But few of us realize to what an extent since the war of 1914 the feeling has spread in the Orient that Christianity is a religion recommended to others, not seriously entertained by its professors.

betraying dread that it may lose its "leadership"? Which refrains with greatest inner stability from crying up its wares when the world goes awry, as if its value suddenly rose with general panic and disaster? Which best retains, and confers, amid its ferments, incitements, and ovulations, the serenity of the eternal and the all-embracing peace of God?

When the religions realize that these are the questions which they must eventually meet, and that no charter from the Most High God will excuse them from meeting them, nor give them any dominion on the earth if they do not, the search for their own essence may become, as it is due to be, a grave and anxious search rather than any mere exercise of scholarly speculation.

This process needs a new institution. Though Reconception is always going on, wherever religious self-consciousness is alive, it requires in the present world-period for its favorable pursuit an institution widely different from the usual type of Protestant mission – not to supplant that mission but to supplement it.

The mission is set for teaching; the required institution must be set for learning as well. The mission is set for the announcement of doctrine; this institution must be set as well for conversation and conference. The mission is set for activity; this institution must be set also for leisure, contemplation, study. The mission is set for address to its own region; this institution must be set for give and take with the thought and feeling of a nation and a world.

The essential parts of such an institution are, beside the quarters for living and hospitality, the library, the facilities for conference, meditation, worship, the goodwill of the religious leadership of all groups in the region, access to natural solitude and to the life of city and country.

And prior to all this, or perhaps connected with it as a training place, a school for the higher study of the thought, art, and literature of the surrounding culture.

What is required is a watch-tower of thought and understanding, in which the chief activity is not the building of the Church but the activity of the reflective observer, qualified by a deep knowledge of the spiritual backgrounds of the life around him, prepared to meet its best thought on its own ground, and sensitive

to the movements of change always present in that life. For the
Protestant missions, this function, essential to any vital progress
in meeting the new Orient, is an almost vacant function. The
Roman Catholic missions are better provided.

At Kurseong, about eight miles southward of Darjeeling, there is
St. Mary's, a university for the final studies of Jesuit missionaries.
Every Jesuit who is to work in India goes first, after perhaps two
years of college study in his own country, to an institution in Southern
India, where he receives four years of "philosophical training". He
learns here something of the sciences and philosophies of the West,
but also something of the languages, literatures, and religions of
India. After this, he spends three years as apprentice to some existing mission, or makes his own studies among the Indian people. A
young friend of mine from St. Louis had spent these years on the
Indian road; with his bedding-roll on his back, he had gone through
the countryside, stopping in villages, eating, drinking, living with
villagers, incidentally taking some of their diseases, coming through
alive and with an intimate knowledge of some phases of Indian life,
as well as a command of one or two dialects. Following this appren-
ticeship, there are the final three or four years at St. Mary's, the
"theological training". This includes, beside study of theology and
philosophy of the West, further study of the religious classics of
India. The library is well stocked with these books. Not until these
ten to eleven years of training are finished can a Jesuit act as a
missionary in his own right. He is usually in his early thirties when
this course is completed. And with what result? This at least: that
wherever you meet a Jesuit missionary in India, you meet a man of
culture, of broad sympathy, who has taken the trouble to know the
deeper phases and sources of the life around him. While in Darjeeling, I wished to visit a Tibetan monastery. But I had no way of
access, nor could I gain any information about its personnel and
activities until I met a Father Wright, English Jesuit, who told me
about its library, the monks who were philosophically interested, with
whom I could converse. The men who come out from St. Mary's are
a group of strongly equipped spirits, reflecting competently on the
whole range of the cultural problems of India, and of its connections.
I think of them as a sort of wing over Asia, poised, unhurried, with
firm judgment and far vision, putting the strength of their insight at
the service of the work of the Church, and ready to converse with
the traveller who has similar concerns. In comparison with this, our
Protestant institutions are set for prompt delivery of partly prepared
men. It is as though the graduate level of adept preparation were out
of tune with our sense of haste and scantiness of means. Yet the

resources of the Protestant societies are in general beyond those of the Catholic societies; and certainly in the aggregate, far greater. The real lack, among Protestants, is a lack of perception; a certain triviality and crudity in the sense of the work to be done; a supposition that we already know enough, and that more thinking is a luxury that can be dispensed with. In my judgment, this pioneering shack-built conception of the mission has had its day; and whatever notable achievements lie before the mission of the future are to be the reward of depth of competence rather than of the attempt to *cover the ground* with a superficial propaganda.

In respect to the stern conditions of the work of understanding we have much to learn from such a foundation as St. Mary's. But there are as yet no institutions, Protestant or Catholic, which have the aim and amplitude of the institution here proposed.[8] Germs of such an enterprise do indeed exist here and there, which indicate that the need is making itself felt. And in time, I foresee a chain of such centers set around the world, hospitable to qualified enquirers, and contributing – as centers of art contribute to the life of art – to sustain the continuing enterprise of reconceiving religion through world culture, and world culture through religion.

[8] In its conception there is some analogy in the ashram of Tagore at Santiniketan, where Hindu, Christian, Moslem, Buddhist find themselves at home, and where creative work in several of the fine arts adds itself to scholarship, worship, social experiment, to bring to a single focus the new and the old life of Asia.

F

# 7

# TOLERANCE
## Arnold Toynbee

ANOTHER VERSION OF the liberal Christian attitude toward other religions appears in the voluminous writings of the English historian Arnold Toynbee (1889–    ). Raised in the Church of England and educated at Oxford, Toynbee worked for the British Foreign Office during the two World Wars and was a member of the British delegations to the peace conferences after both wars. He was professor of history at the University of London from 1919 until his retirement in 1955 and also director of studies at the Royal Institute of International Affairs during the latter part of this period. He has travelled widely and lectured often in the United States.

Toynbee is best known for his monumental twelve-volume work *The Study of History* (1934–61). His fundamental thesis is that civilizations rather than nations or periods are the most significant units of historical study, and he distinguishes twenty-six of them in the history of the world. The key to the rise and fall of civilizations is the theory of challenge and response. The successful or unsuccessful response to physical and moral challenges determines the coming into being, growth, breakdown, and disintegration of civilizations. All civilizations have decayed or perished except our Western civilization. Breakdown and disintegration, however, are not predetermined but are a matter of human freedom, especially on the part of creative minorities.

The unusual aspect of Toynbee's theory is the central place he gives to religion (see Vol. VII). Civilization is the handmaid of religion. The history of civilizations has a religious purpose, namely, the manifestation of the true religion and the salvation of mankind. A new religion usually appears during the period of decay of a civilization. Toynbee sees four higher religions or "universal churches" in the world today: Christianity, Islam, Mahayana Buddhism, and Hinduism. (In a later work he has expanded this to seven by including Judaism, Zoroastrianism, and Hinayana Buddhism.) Each of these religions offers salvation, that is, communion with the one true God, but in different ways. Toynbee calls the higher religions to distinguish the essentials which they hold in common from the non-essentials which divide them, and he looks forward to reconciliation and harmony among the religions.

The selection below is the last of the four Hewett Lectures which Toynbee delivered at three American theological schools in 1955 and which were published in 1957 under the title *Christianity Among the Religions of the World*. In the first chapter Toynbee investigates the criteria for comparisons between religions, and he concludes that these should be neither beliefs nor practice, but rather the attitude or spirit of a religion, such as its attitude toward man, evil, and suffering. Toynbee next discusses the characteristics of the contemporary world in which the religions find themselves, especially the spread of secular Western technology and the revival of man-worship in totalitarianism. The third chapter is an analysis of the relation of Christianity to the Western civilization which is unifying the world. Toynbee's point here is that while Christianity served as the midwife of western civilization, the latter contains many elements from other sources and is now independent of Christianity. In his final chapter Toynbee calls Christians to purge Christianity of its Western accessories, its claim to uniqueness, its exclusive-mindedness and intolerance, and to see the other religions as coming from God and as presenting some facet of God's truth. Then in peaceful competition the best religion will absorb into itself what is good in the other religions and will ultimately win the allegiance of the human race. (These points have received more extensive elaboration in the last two chapters of Toynbee's Gifford Lectures, *An*

*Historian's Approach to Religion* (1956).)

Toynbee's view of the relations among the religions seems to be a combination of the approaches described above as "Relativity" and "Essence". He continually quotes the famous saying of Symmachus to the effect that the different religions are merely different ways to the same goal. And he asserts that all religions embody in different ways and in varying degrees of fidelity the essence of true religion. Besides the problems with these views which have been discussed above, there is a further difficulty in Toynbee's approach. Sometimes he seems to treat the relations among the religions from the point of view of Christian faith, and sometimes he seems to speak from some platform which transcends all the religions, including Christianity (see Vol. XII, pp. 98 ff.). If the former, then we need to know more about the relation of the revelation of truth in other religions to that in Christianity. For example, are they identical or complementary or is the former fulfilled in the latter? On the other hand, if Toynbee speaks from a point of view which transcends all the religions, then we need to know what this point of view is and on what grounds he affirms it. Finally, it can be argued that the tolerance for which Toynbee calls should be understood primarily as an attitude of respect toward other persons, toward their integrity and freedom, rather than as an attitude toward their beliefs which tends toward relativism or indifferentism.

# What Should be the Christian Approach to the Contemporary Non-Christian Faiths?*

I HAVE SUGGESTED THAT, in the unified world that has been called into existence by the world-wide expansion of the post-Christian

* From Arnold Toynbee, *Christianity Among the Religions of the World* (New York: Charles Scribner's Sons, 1957 and London: OUP, 1958), pp. 83–112. Copyright 1957 by the Trustees, under the Will of Waterman T. Hewett.

modern Western civilization, all the living higher religions ought to subordinate their traditional rivalries and make a new approach toward one another in face of a fearful common adversary: a revival of the worship of collective human power, armed with new weapons, both material and spiritual. I have also suggested that we might consider whether this reconciliation can be achieved without abandoning convictions, because, without convictions, a religion has no spiritual power.

If the great religions of the world are to approach one another they must find common ground, and I believe that the necessary common ground exists. The most important piece of common ground is one that has always been there since mankind first came into existence. This permanent common ground is human nature, especially the self-centeredness which is the Original Sin in human nature. The call to wrestle with Original Sin is the challenge in response to which all the higher religions have arisen. The positive response to this challenge has been very different in each case, but all the religions are grappling with the same problem; and it can hardly be an accident that, as has been pointed out in recent years, the higher religions, as we know them today, all made their appearance in the world within a certain period of time, within something less than a thousand years of one another. They all made their appearance after Original Sin had shown its power by causing the downfall of one or two generations of secular civilizations. In other words, the higher religions appeared at a moment when mankind had received surprising and humiliating setbacks in its endeavors. These setbacks opened the way for humility, and humility opens the way for spiritual illumination.

For practical purposes, human nature can be taken as being uniform and permanent. It is, of course, true that every individual human soul is in one sense unique and different from every other. It is also true that, within the general framework of a psychological uniformity, a number of different psychological types have been identified by present-day schools of psychologists. But these psychological types seem to be distributed equally among all races, and the differences of individual character also cut across all differences of race. So, in a broad way, we may take human nature as being uniform, and we may also take it as being permanent. Theoretically, no doubt, human nature is in process of changing. If we believe that man was generated from some prehuman species of creature, it seems possible that he may be evolving into some other species of creature. But, if there has been any change since the rise of the first civilizations about five thousand years ago, this change has been so slight as to be imperceptible; and the period of time with which we are concerned in considering the living higher religions is even less than five thousand years. These religions entered the stage of history about two thousand years after the dawn of the earliest civilizations; and within these last two or three thousand years the change in human nature, if there has been any change at all, has been infinitesimal. The human nature with which we have to grapple in our own lives today is the same human nature that evoked the higher religions two or three thousand years ago. So the higher religions have common ground in the permanence and universality of human nature. They have a further piece of common ground in the present state of the world.

The unification of the world by the modern Western civilization has confronted all the living higher religions with a special set of common problems. We have reviewed them already, but it may be convenient to recapitulate them. First there is "the annihilation of distance" by modern Western technology. This has converted all local problems into world-wide problems. It is true that human nature has always been uniform. Original Sin has always been carried by mankind wherever mankind has spread. But, till recently, the consequences of Original Sin might work themselves out locally in one part of the world without affecting other parts. Today we are all of us one another's keepers in the sense that any effect produced by Original Sin in any one part of the world immediately affects the rest of the human race. This is a new situation that has been produced by "the annihilation of distance". Then the replacement of Christianity by technology, as Western man's foremost concern, has allowed the worship of collective human power to reassert itself, this time armed by technology and animated by Jewish and Christian fanaticism. And then, again, there are the effects of the emancipation movement that has been set in motion today all over the world by the diffusion of modern Western ideals.

All the higher religions are having to come to grips with this movement of emancipation; and, as I suggested in the second chapter, this notion of emancipation is an ambiguous one. There is a movement for the emancipation of power-combines which flows from the worship of collective human power; and there is also a movement for the emancipation of formerly penalized classes of individuals – women, industrial workers, peasants, "natives" – which flows from the worship of the pursuit of individual happiness. The emancipation of "Leviathan" is contrary to everything for which Christianity and the other higher religions stand. Higher religions and "Leviathan" cannot co-exist permanently. On the other hand, the movement for the emancipation of individuals could be redeemed by being reconsecrated. The worshippers of "Leviathan", whether they are Fascists, Nazis, or Communists, jeer at the liberal democratic worshippers of the pursuit of individual happiness. They jeer at them for putting their treasure in such a trivial aim as this; and in truth they have a case, if secular individual happiness is pursued as an end in itself. The attainment of a secular higher standard of living is always unsatisfying, even when this standard is not merely a material one, but includes non-religious spiritual values. But true individual happiness can be pursued and achieved if the aim is to liberate the individual for attaining the true end of man, which is to glorify God and to enjoy Him forever. To emancipate individual souls in this spiritual sense is the traditional common aim of all the higher religions; and they have all addressed themselves to all men. Each of them has preached a new way of individual salvation, not just to a privileged minority but to all mankind without distinction of sex or race or class. So it seems that the higher religions can come to terms with the present worldwide movement for the emancipation of individual souls. It is the higher religions, and they alone, that can give this movement significance and satisfaction by bringing it back to its true spiritual goal; and their greeting to it should be: "I will be your leader." It would be more accurate to say: "I will be your leader again", because this movement for the pursuit of happiness turns out, when one looks back to its historical beginnings, to have had a Christian origin. It has been set in motion by the post-Christian civilization of the modern West, and it is part of the modern West's heritage from its Christian past. Its ultimate inspiration comes from the Christian belief that individual souls have a supreme value for God.

Here there seems to be a possibility of harmonizing all the main movements in the contemporary world except the worship of "Leviathan" in its alternative Nationalist and Communist forms. In this connection, modern Western technology seems to have a constructive and beneficent part to play. It is true that a merely material raising of the standard of living is unsatisfying if pursued as an end in itself. At the same time, it is also true that the spiritual level cannot be raised for mankind in general unless the material standard is raised for "the depressed classes" – and, today, three-quarters of the human race are still depressed: they are still primitive peasants, living just above the starvation line and often falling below it. A higher level of spiritual life is not ultimately compatible with gross injustice; and the co-existence, in the past, of saintliness and injustice explains why, hitherto, a voluntary acceptance of poverty has always played so large a part in the experience and life of the saints of all the great religions.

The saints have embraced poverty for more than one reason: in order to share the common lot of the mass of mankind, and also in order to extricate themselves from the spiritually demoralizing effect of material welfare. This is obviously demoralizing when it is the monopoly of a privileged minority, as it always has been in the past. But let us imagine a future state of affairs in which material goods will be in such abundant supply that there will be enough for everyone in the world to have his fill. This picture of the future does not now seem utopian, when we view it in the light of our technological achievements. Yet the example of the medieval Western monasteries shows that, when

material wealth and efficiency and success increase out of proportion to the sublimation of the spiritual life, they tend to choke
and smother the spiritual life and would have the same tendency
even if their fruits were justly distributed. For all these reasons,
the saints in the past have embraced poverty, and the last-men-
tioned reason is a permanent reason for embracing poverty if
one is seeking the goal of spiritual perfection. In the past the
material resources of civilization were not sufficient to bring the
amenities of civilization within the reach of more than a small
minority of the members of society; and, in those past conditions,
social injustice was perhaps part of the price that had to be
paid for civilization. But in our time modern Western technology
is making social injustice avoidable, and is therefore making it
intolerable. The higher religions all believe in the consecration of
human personalities by bringing them into harmony with God or
absolute reality, greatly though they differ from one another in
their prescriptions for achieving this spiritual result. Social justice
– not as an end in itself, but as a means toward the end of
glorifying God and enjoying Him – is evidently in harmony with
the spiritual purpose of the higher religions. In fact, social justice
can be achieved only as a by-product of the achievement of this
spiritual purpose that reaches so far beyond it.

This brings us to the question: In the particular social circumstances in which we are living today, against the permanent and
universal background of human nature with its Original Sin,
what must Western Christians do, for their part, in order to meet
their brothers, the followers of the other higher religions, on the
ground that is common to all of us? This question is confronting
all of us today in a world that is rapidly coalescing. I dare say
the Congress of the Buddhist World, which recently has been
in session in Burma, has been discussing this very question. But,
for us in the West, it is more profitable to discuss it from our side.
We have to consider the action that *we* should take, the spirit in
which *we* should meet our non-Western fellow men.

My first suggestion would be that we in the West should try
to purge our Christianity of its Western accessories. Here an
admirable example has been set by the Western Christian mis-

sionaries in the earliest wave of Western missionary work in
modern times: the Jesuit missionaries in China and India in the
sixteenth and seventeenth centuries. The Jesuits were, of course,
highly cultivated men. They were masters of all the resources
of Western Christendom, which, by that time, was a highly
cultivated civilization. And when they came upon the civilizations
of China and India they were able to appreciate the fact that
here they were in the presence of great cultures, which, on the
secular side, were built upon different foundations from the
Western culture – upon different philosophies, for instance. The
Jesuits were not unmindful of the fact that, in the early centuries
of the life of the Christian Church in the Graeco-Roman World,
the fathers of the Church – especially the Alexandrian fathers,
Clement and Origen, in the second and early third centuries of
the Christian Era – had been aware of the same problem of having to express Christianity in terms familiar to the people to
whom they were addressing themselves. In that time and place,
Christianity had to be interpreted to people with a Greek philosophical education. The Jesuit missionaries realized that the
Greek terms in which Christianity had been expressed from the
time of the Roman Empire onwards were not the best terms for
making it acceptable to the minds and the hearts of Chinese and
Indians. So they deliberately set themselves to divest their Christianity of its Western and its Graeco-Roman accessories and to put
it to the Chinese and the Indians in their own terms.

This operation is one that is necessary at all times, because we
are always relapsing from the worship of God into the worship
of our tribe or of ourselves; and therefore we Christians, whether
we are Western Christians or Eastern Christians, tend to treat
Christianity as if it were the tribal religion of our particular
civilization. In the West we tend to treat it as something that is
inseparable from the West, and even as something that derives its
virtue not so much from being Christian as from being Western.
You may remember that, at the time of the negotiations of the
Vatican agreements between Mussolini and Pope Pius XI, only a
few weeks before the agreements were finally concluded, Mussolini made a characteristic speech in the Italian Senate in which

he sounded the praises of the Italian people and glorified their historical achievements. Just think, he said on this occasion, what our Italy has done for a wretched little oriental sect that started life far away in Palestine, in a remote corner of the Roman Empire where it had no prospects and no influential members. Left to itself, Christianity would have been bound to wither and die away. It was salvaged, thanks to being carried to Rome. There the Italian genius made its fortune, and now it has become the universal Roman Catholic Church of which Italy has the honor to be the center. A week or two later, the Pope addressed a letter to one of his cardinals in which he replied to Mussolini's speech. The scene of Christ's ministry, the Pope pointed out, was not Italy but Palestine; and the Church was universal already in the age of the Apostles when Palestine was still the field of their labors. It was universal in Saint Peter's hands when he was still in Palestine and before he went to Rome. The universality of the Christian Church was independent of its associations with Rome and with Italy. Coming from the mouth of the Pope, the bishop of Rome, this pronouncement was impressive and authoritative. It was a remarkable declaration of the universality of Christianity, and condemnation of any attempt to identify it with one's own city or country or tribe or civilization. Mussolini's account of the history of Christianity was indeed hstorically untrue, besides being spiritually wrong. In the preceding chapter I have contended that Christianity has always been a gospel not just for the West but for the whole human race, and that there have always been important non-Western churches. If we approach the followers of non-Western Christianity and of the non-Christian higher religions as Christians simply and not as Christian Westerners – if we can distinguish our religion from our civilization – we shall be more likely to succeed in getting on to terms with our neighbors and appealing to both their hearts and their minds.

My next suggestion is more controversial, because it raises a more crucial issue. We ought also, I should say, to try to purge our Christianity of the traditional Christian belief that Christianity is unique. This is not just a Western Christian belief; it is in-

trinsic to Christianity itself. All the same, I suggest that we have
to do this if we are to purge Christianity of the exclusive-mindedness and intolerance that follows from a belief in Christianity's
uniqueness.

Here I should like to draw a distinction which, I think, is all-
important, though also, no doubt, debatable. I should say that
one can be convinced of the essential truth and rightness and
value of what one believes to be the fundamental points in one's
own religion – and can believe that these tenets have been received by one as a revelation from God – and at the same time
not believe that *I, my* church, *my* people, have the sole and
unique revelation. If one accepts, and builds on, the Jewish and
Christian vision of God as being love, one would feel it unlikely,
no doubt, that I and my church and my people had not had
*some* revelation from God. If God loves mankind, He would have
made a revelation to us among other people. But, on the same
ground and in virtue of the same vision of what God's nature is,
it would also seem unlikely that He would not have made other
revelations to other people as well. And it would seem unlikely
that He would not have given His revelation in different forms,
with different facets, and to different degrees, according to the
difference in the nature of individual souls and in the nature of
the local tradition of civilization. I should say that this view is
a corollary of the Christian view of God as being love.

Nevertheless, to purge Christianity of its exclusive-mindedness
is a much harder task than to purge it of its Western accretions.
The vein of exclusiveness and intolerance in Christianity is not,
I should say, an especially Western deformation of Christianity;
it is a congenital feature which is part of Christianity's and also
part of Islam's heritage from Judaism. Just as the vision of God
as being love is a heritage from Judaism, so is the other vision of
God as being a jealous god, the god of *my* tribe as against the
gentiles *outside* my tribe or my church or whatever my community may be. Yet, however hard it may be to purge Christianity
of its exclusive-mindedness it seems imperative for Christians to
achieve this spiritual feat, and this for a number of reasons. The
paramount reason is that exclusive-mindedness is a sinful state

of mind. It is the sin of pride, and we know that the sin of pride is an arch sin, because it is a gateway for the entry of all the other sins, and a roadblock across the path of repentance. The sin of pride is insidious. Its first form is in the first person singular – *I* am self-centered and proud, *I* am egotistic about *my*self; but this is the less insidious of the two forms of the sin, because it is comparatively easy to see through oneself and to perceive that one is not the center of the Universe. The sin of pride becomes mortally dangerous when it is translated from the singular into the plural, from egoism into what, to coin a word, one might call "noism". I am told that, in Arabic, there is a word for the sin of pride in the collective first person plural. The Arabs call this "nahniyah" from the Arabic word "nahnu", meaning "we". When we are committing the sin of pride in the first person plural it is easy to persuade ourselves that we are not proud of *ourselves*; we are proud of our family, our people, our community, our church. We persuade ourselves that our feeling is not personal to ourselves; yet we do not escape the sin of pride by magnifying it from the singular into the plural. We increase its danger – in the first place because it is easier for us, in this case, to believe that we are not committing it, and in the second place because the sin of pride in the plural has far more material power behind it than the feeble power of any sinful individual.

This sin of pride, especially in the first person plural, is an expression of self-centeredness; and this is another reason for trying to cast it out. As an expression of self-centeredness it is incompatible with the Christian intuition that God is not self-centered but just the opposite: self-sacrificing. If God is self-sacrificing, if the Christian vision of God as being self-sacrificing is a true vision, as we believe it to be, then it follows that all we human beings who see that vision and believe it to be the truth should do our best to follow it to the extent of our feeble powers, and therefore should do our best to break out of self-centeredness in the plural as well as in the singular. That would be the only way of putting ourselves in harmony with a god who is not self-centered but is self-sacrificing. And then the historian, surveying the present scene with his eyes looking over his shoulder into the past, would say that in the past this arrogant, intolerant vein in Christianity has in fact led – and, you might even say, has rightly led – to the rejection of Christianity. In the seventeenth century, Christianity was rejected first by the Japanese, then by the Chinese, and finally by the intellectual leaders of the Western World in Western Christendom itself, and in every case for the same reason. The same Christian arrogance, if Christians fail to purge it out of Christianity now, will lead to the rejection of Christianity in the future. If Christianity is presented to people in that traditional arrogant spirit it will be rejected in the name of the sacredness of human personalities – a truth to which the whole human race is now awakening under the influence of the modern Western civilization, which originally learned that truth from the Christianity that modern Man has been rejecting. Christian arrogance is un-Christian and anti-Christian, and here we seem to be confronted again with the unresolved conflict – inherited by Christianity and Islam from Judaism – between two visions of the nature of God, two visions which, I believe, are mutually incompatible.

What, then, should be the attitude of contrite Christians toward the other higher religions and their followers? I think that it is possible for us, while holding that our own convictions are true and right, to recognize that, in some measure, all the higher religions are also revelations of what is true and right. They also come from God, and each presents some facet of God's truth. They may and do differ in the content and degree of the revelation that has been given to Mankind through them. They may also differ in the extent to which this revelation has been translated by their followers into practice, both individual practice and social practice. But we should recognize that they, too, are light radiating from the same source from which our own religion derives its spiritual light. This must be so if God is the god of all men and is also another name for love.

We have also to reckon with a point that was brought up in one of the discussions that I had the advantage of having, after one of the lectures on which this book is based, with members of my audience. When one makes comparisons between religions, the great difficulty is that one's relation to the religion in which one has been brought up is very much more intimate than one's relation to other religions which one has learned to know later in life, and therefore, to some extent, from outside. In comparing one's family religion or ancestral religion with other religions, one is comparing two things to which one's emotional relation is different; and therefore it is difficult to make an objective judgment between them. I think the great difference is that one's feelings about one's own religion, whether they are feelings of assent and love and loyalty or feelings of repudiation and hostility, are inevitably stronger than one's feelings about other religions, whether one's feelings about these other religions are friendly or hostile. When one tries to discount one's special emotional feeling for one's ancestral religion, one is in danger of leaning over backwards and going to the other extreme of rejecting one's own religion rather violently and admiring other religions rather uncritically just because of one's having no such intimate acquaintance with them. One knows one's ancestral religion from inside, for evil as well as for good. I myself am conscious of not feeling so indignant at the crimes committed by Muslim fanaticism as I feel at the crimes committed by Christian fanaticism; and I think this is because those Muslim misdeeds are not part of my own ancestral religious history, and so I do not feel the same responsibility for them that I feel for the misdeeds of the religion and the church in which I myself have been born and brought up.

Here, then, is an obstacle to intercourse between members of different religions. Yet this obstacle cannot be an insuperable one; for, long before the present annihilation of distance by modern Western means of communication, the members of different religions have had meetings and discussions, and there have been conversions from one religion to another. I think we can foresee that, if the world continues to grow together into a single family, objective judgments between different living religions will become in the course of time rather less difficult to make, as the unification of the world proceeds. I think one form that this unification will take will be a unification of our different cultural heritages. Christians and Muslims are already familiar with the fact that the Jewish cultural heritage was, from the beginning, a part of the Christian and Islamic cultural heritage. I think one can foresee a time when the heritages of Islam and Buddhism will also have become part of the Christian society's background. The heritage of Christianity always has been, to some extent, a part of the Islamic society's background. One might also foresee its becoming part of the Buddhist society's background. And in our time already we have seen how the Christian heritage did become part of the background of a great Hindu saint, the Mahatma Gandhi. We have seen how Gandhiji held the allegiance of the whole Hindu world, though his Hinduism was obviously tinged and blended with elements of Christianity which he himself did not disown. And we have seen the immense effect on the world of this two-fold religious inspiration harmonized in one great soul.

On a less exalted plane than Gandhi's we already see Christians of ordinary spiritual stature making individual choices in grown-up life between the Protestant and the Catholic versions of Western Christianity and between the Western and non-Western versions of Christianity. This exercise of free choice has given birth to Roman Catholic Uniate Churches composed of Christians who are ex-Eastern Orthodox or ex-Monophysite or ex-Nestorian; and the Protestant Western Churches, too, have their converts from non-Western Churches. Both the Protestant Western Churches and the Catholic Western Church also have converts from Hinduism and Buddhism and Confucianism, as well as from the primitive religions. It is true that converts to Christianity from Judaism are less common, and converts to Christianity from Islam are very rare indeed; but, on the whole, I think we can already see a tendency for people to pass by deliberate choice from one religion to another, in contrast to the traditional state of religious affairs in which, almost automatically, one remained for life in the religious communion into which one had been introduced by the accident of being born in a particular place at a particular time. I think this tendency toward making a free choice of religion in grown-up life is likely to increase as the world grows closer together.

In the light of history I should not expect to see mankind
converted to a "syncretistic" religion, constructed artificially out
of elements taken from all the existing religions. Such artificial
religions have been, and are being, manufactured; but I should
not expect to see any of them capture the imagination and the
feelings and the allegiance of mankind. I should not expect this
because such attempts are generally made only partly for religious
reasons and partly for utilitarian reasons which are other than
religious. I am thinking of attempts in the past like the Mughal
emperor Akbar's attempt in India, in the early years of the
seventeenth century, to create a new composite religion blending
elements of Islam and Hinduism and Zoroastrianism and Christianity; or the attempt of the Roman Emperor Julian to reverse
the triumph of Christianity in the Roman Empire by building
up artificially a pagan counter-church in which he tried to weld
together all the non-Christian religions in the Roman Empire.
It is notorious that such attempts have failed in the past, and I
think they are also likely to fail in the future, as far as the past is
any guide to the future. At the same time, when I find myself in
Chicago and when, travelling northwards out of the city, I pass
the Bahai temple there, I feel that in some sense this beautiful
building may be a portent of the future. I suppose the Chicagoan
Bahais are mostly converts from Christianity. It is true that one
can become a convert to Bahaism with a minimum of disturb-
ance of one's ancestral religious roots. Of all the Judaic religions,
Bahaism is the most tolerant. In its catholicity, it comes near to
Mahayanian Buddhism or to Hinduism. I would not say that
I expect to see a coalescence of the historic religions, but I think
it may be expected, and also may be hoped, that all religions,
while retaining their historic identities, will become more and
more open-minded, and (what is more important) open-hearted,
toward one another as the world's different cultural and spiritual
heritages become, in increasing measure, the common possession
of all mankind. I should say that, in learning more and more to
respect, reverence, admire, and love other faiths, we should be
making progress in the true practice of Christianity. And the
practice of the Christian virtue of charity need not prevent us

from holding fast to what we believe to be the essential truths and ideals in our own Christian faith.

Here we come to a point of capital importance which is also a high controversial one. I think we can and should continue to preach these truths and ideals to the non-Christian majority of our fellow human beings, and, when I say preach, I am using the word in the most inclusive sense, to include not merely expounding Christianity by word but also giving practical examples of it in action. One can see, from what has happened in the past, that, in winning people's assent and allegiance and devotion, action has always counted, and rightly counted, for far more than words. The death of one martyr will probably have more effect, illogical though this may seem, than volumes and volumes of the most competent theological exposition of the solitary martyr's faith. If we can express what we believe to be the essential truths and precepts of our own religion in action as well as in words, and if at the same time we can be receptive to the truths and ideals of the other faiths we shall be more likely to win the attention and goodwill of the followers of those other faiths. If we can learn to present Christianity in this spirit, we can perhaps manage to present it with conviction without at the same time relapsing into Christianity's traditional sin of arrogance and intolerance.

I have spoken of "essential elements" in Christianity and other religions, and this compels me to declare what I myself consider to be the essential elements in Christianity. One attempts this at one's peril, but in writing this book I should not be doing my duty if I did not make the attempt. So, with great diffidence, I will pick out three points in Christianity which seem to me to be essential. The first point is that Christianity has a vision of God as loving His creatures so greatly that He has sacrificed Himself for their salvation. The essence of this vision is conveyed in four verses of the second chapter of Saint Paul's Epistle to the Philippians. In the King James version at least one of the sentences in that passage has been mistranslated in a way that misrepresents the meaning. I should translate the passage like this:

"The spirit that you should have is the spirit that was in Christ

Jesus. There He was in the form of God, yet He did not take being on an equality with God as a prize to be clutched. No, He emptied Himself by assuming the form of a servant, taking on a human guise. But He did not only expose Himself in human shape; He humbled Himself by being submissive to the extent of submitting to die, and this by a death on the cross."

I feel that this passage sums up the first essential point in Christianity. The second essential point would be a conviction that human beings ought to follow the example that God has set them in His incarnation and crucifixion. And the third point would be not just to hold this conviction theoretically but to act on it as far as one is able. Here the gap between the Christian ideal and Christian performance has been, as we all recognize, enormous. But this *is* the Christian ideal; and it is impossible to profess Christianity without knowing that this is its ideal and without feeling a call from Christ to act on it in one's own life as far as one can. I should say that these three points are essential in Christianity, but I should not say that they are exclusively Christian. I think that they have non-Christian precedents in mankind's past, and also living non-Christian parallels.

Let us think first of the Christian vision of Almighty God as being self-sacrificing. Is not that a Christian heritage from nature-worship? Does it not come, at any rate historically speaking, from the vision of a vegetation god, a grain god, a Tammuz or Adonis or Osiris, who sacrifices himself in order to give Man the bread of life? The material bread of life, which those vegetation gods gave to Man at their own cost, is the image that has given us the vision of the spiritual bread of life. And then we have the Christian vision of Christ deliberately divesting Himself of His divine bliss in order to bring salvation to Man. This, I think, has a parallel in the "northern" or "late" or Mahayanian Buddhist vision of the being who in that version of Buddhism is called a Bodhisattva. It is an interesting point of the history of Buddhism that, between the birth of the earlier school of Buddhism and the birth of the later school, Buddhism seems, at any rate to an outside observer, to have changed its ideal. I have mentioned that the ideal of the earlier school of Buddhism was to liberate oneself from suffering. This was presented as the paramount aim toward which every sentient creature, human or non-human, should strive. In the later version of Buddhism that ideal has been replaced by one which seems to a Christian observer to have moved in a Christian direction. In this later Buddhism the ideal figure is not the Buddhist ascetic sage who has liberated himself from existence by fighting his way, through rough and strenuous spiritual exertions, into the peace of Nirvana. It is the Bodhisattva, a being of the highest spiritual nature known to Man who has fought his way to the threshold of Nirvana, and who then, like the Buddha himself during his forty years on earth after his enlightenment, has deliberately refrained from entering into his rest in order to remain in this world of suffering. The Bodhisattva has voluntarily postponed his self-release for ages and ages (the Buddhists and Hindus reckon in large numbers) in order to show the way of salvation to his fellow beings by helping them along the path on which he himself is refraining, out of love and compassion for them, from taking the last step.

You might perhaps comment: "Well, yes, that is a form of self-sacrifice, but it is a rather unheroic form, is it not, compared with the Christian vision of a god who, instead of just refraining from entering into bliss, deliberately steps out of bliss in order to suffer crucifixion." A comment on this comment might be that every great ideal has its price. When one compares the religions of the Indian school with the religions of the Palestinian school one might say: "Yes, it is true that the Indian religions are less heroic, but they have also been less atrocious." There have been persecutions and martyrdoms in Eastern Asia as well as in Western Asia and in the Western World, but on the whole the Chinese government was milder in its persecutions of Buddhism than the Roman government or the Protestant and Roman Catholic governments in the modern West have been in their persecutions of Christianity. The ordeals to which the Buddhist martyrs in China were put may have been less severe than those inflicted on the Christian martyrs in the Roman Empire; but then the temperature both of government and of religion has been lower in Eastern Asia both for evil and for good. So I

would come back to my point that, in the later Buddhist idea of
the Bodhisattva, we do have, independently of Christianity, the
vision of a self-sacrificing figure. It is not God, but it is a supreme
being – a being who has reached the highest point to which
sentient creatures can rise.

In the first chapter of the history of Christianity, while Christianity was fighting a spiritual war with man-worship in the form
of the worship of the Roman Empire, it was at the same time
competing peacefully with a number of religions of its own kind:
the worship of the goddess Isis, the worship of the goddess Cybele,
and Mithraism. In entering into a charitable competition with
another group of sister religions – the other living higher religions
of the contemporary world – Christians today can feel sure, in
advance, of two things. In a peaceful competition the best of the
competing religions will eventually win the allegiance of the
whole human race. If we believe that God is love we shall also
believe that the whole human race will eventually turn to whichever vision of God is the fullest vision and gives the greatest
means of grace. We can also forecast that the winning religion,
whichever it may be, will not eliminate the other religions that
it replaces. Even if it does replace them, it will achieve this by
absorbing into itself what is best in them. In winning the competition between the higher religions in the Roman Empire,
Christianity did not really eliminate Isis-worship or Cybele-worship or Mithraism. One of the means by which it won, and one
of the conditions on which it won, was that it should and did
absorb into itself what was valuable in those rival religions. In
the ideal of the church militant on earth one can see the abiding
imprint of Mithraism on Christianity. As for the influence of the
worships of Isis and Cybele, one sees this in the rather unhappy
difference of feeling and opinion and attitude, between Protestants
and Nestorians on the one side, and Roman Catholics and Eastern
Orthodox Christians on the other, over the cult of the Virgin
Mary. Now whether that cult is literally descended from Isis-
worship or Cybele-worship I do not know. But I think a psycholo-
gist would say that it is psychologically associated with their
replacement. I think he would say that the vision of the mother

goddess has so strong a hold on human nature that it cannot be banished permanently from any religion that is to last for long or is to command the allegiance of great numbers of people. So I imagine that, if I were a Roman Catholic, I should take with equanimity the Protestant strictures on the cult of the Virgin, shocking though in many ways that cult has been, and is, to Protestant feelings.

For these reasons, I believe that Christians today can face the future with confidence if they face it with charity and humility. The crucial point that I want to make is that we can have conviction without fanaticism, we can have belief and action without arrogance or self-centeredness or pride. At the end of the struggle in the Roman Empire between the victorious Christian Church and the local pre-Christian religion, there was a celebrated incident at the time when the Christian Roman imperial government was forcibly closing the pagan temples and suppressing pagan forms of worship in the western part of the Roman Empire. In the course of this campaign the government ordered the removal, from the senate house at Rome, of the statue and altar of Victory which had been placed there by Julius Caesar. The spokesman of the Senate at the time, Quintus Aurelius Symmachus, had a controversy with Saint Ambrose on the subject, and the documents have survived. Symmachus was beaten, not in argument, but by *force majeure*. The government simply closed the temples and removed the statues. But, in one of his last pleas, Symmachus has put on record these words: "It is impossible that so great a mystery should be approached by one road only." The mystery of which he is speaking is the mystery of the universe, the mystery of man's encounter with God, the mystery of God's relation to good and evil. Christianity has never answered Symmachus. To suppress a rival religion is not an answer. The question raised by Symmachus is still alive in the world today. I think we shall have to face it in our time.

# 8

# DIALOGUE
## Paul Tillich

MEDIATING BETWEEN THE dialectical theology of Barth and Brunner and the liberal point of view represented in Hocking and Toynbee is the work of Paul Tillich (1886–1965), who stands among the most creative and influential theologians of this century. The son of a Lutheran pastor in the German province of Brandenburg, Tillich was educated at the universities of Berlin, Tübingen, Halle, and Breslau. After service as a chaplain in World War I, he taught philosophy and theology at the universities of Berlin, Marburg, Dresden, Leipzig, and Frankfurt. The experience of the war and the influence of Kierkegaard led to Tillich's break with philosophical idealism and to his sharing many of the concerns of Barth in the early days of the dialectical theology. At this time he also held a position of leadership in the religious socialist movement in Germany.

Dismissed from his position at Frankfurt by the Nazis, Tillich came to teach at Union Theological Seminary in New York in 1933. In 1954 he went to Harvard as a University Professor, and in 1962 he became professor of theology at the Divinity School of the University of Chicago. In his thought and writings Tillich combines the insights of German idealism, existentialism, and depth psychology with the Christian tradition. One of his first public lectures and one of his last books were on the subject of the theology of culture. He developed his theological system as a series of correlations between existential questions arising out of the cultural situation and theological answers implied in the symbols of the Christian message. Besides his three-volume *Systematic Theology* (1951–1963), Tillich's major works include *The Religious Situation* (1926), *The Interpretation of History* (1936), *The Protestant Era* (1948), *The Courage to Be* (1950), *Love, Power, and Justice* (1954), and *The Dynamics of Faith* (1957), as well as three volumes of sermons.

The problem of the nature of religion and the significance of the world religions was always a fundamental concern for Tillich. His definition of religion as "ultimate concern" makes it a universal element in human life and thus includes such "quasi-religions" as fascism, communism, and liberal humanism. Tillich affirms a universal revelation of God which is the source of the religious experience, the myths, and the cults of the various religions, and which constitutes a preparation for the final revelation in Christ. He suggests that a typological analysis of the history of religions shows that the concreteness of man's ultimate concern drives him toward polytheistic structures, while the absolute element in his ultimate concern drives him toward monotheistic structures, and the need for a balance between these drives him toward trinitarian structures. Tillich believes that the history of religions should be a major source for Christian theology, and his *Systematic Theology* includes many references to other religions. His last public lecture was entitled "The Significance of the History of Religions for the Systematic Theologian", and in it he expressed the hope that Christian theology might in the future be developed in dialogue with the insights of other religions.

An extended visit to Japan in 1960 gave Tillich for the first time the opportunity for first-hand contact with living Eastern religions. His conversations with representatives of Japanese Shintoism and Buddhism at that time constitute the background for the selection below taken from the Bampton Lectures delivered at Columbia University in 1961. In the first lecture he asserts that the main characteristic of the present encounter of the world religions is their confrontation with the quasi-religions of our time, and he raises the question of the future of the religions in the face of the victory of secularism throughout the world. In the

second lecture Tillich is concerned to point out that Christianity
has not held an exclusively negative attitude toward other religions. Although there have been periods of exclusivism, the more
common attitude toward other religions has been a dialectical
union of acceptance and rejection. The third lecture and the conclusion of the fourth are reproduced below. The fourth and final
lecture is entitled "Christianity Judging Itself in the Light of
Its Encounters with the World Religions". Tillich gives
examples of the way in which Christianity has both judged other
religions and at the same time been influenced by them. This has
involved Christianity in a continuous struggle to criticize all its
religious elements in the light of the norm of Christ.

Tillich's approach to other religions involves elements of many
of the other views discussed in the Introduction and illustrated
in the selections, especially those designated "Essence", "Development–Fulfillment", and "Revelation–Sin". His interpretation of
other religions as based on revelation is close to that of Brunner,
although the influence of sin is played down. The final paragraph
in the selection below indicates his affinity with Hocking's theory
of Reconception.

# A Christian–Buddhist Conversation*

## I

IN THE FIRST chapter we drew a panorama of the present encounters of religions and quasi-religions in many areas. We did
it with a particular emphasis on the quasi-religions, their nature
and their superior historical dynamics. It was the encounter of
nationalism, communism, and liberal humanism with the religions
proper which was at the center of our interest, because it is
decisive for our present religious situation. In the second chapter
Christian principles of judging non-Christian religions were discussed and the universalism of Christian theology in most cen-

* From Paul Tillich, *Christianity and the Encounter of the World Religions* (New York: Columbia University Press, 1963), pp. 53–75, 94–97.

turies was shown. We illustrated with examples from the history of the Church the Christian belief that revelatory events underlie all religions and quasi-religions, but also the theological idea that the revelatory event on which Christianity is based has critical and transforming power for all religions.

On the basis of this judgment of the non-Christian religions and quasi-religions on the part of Christianity, I intend now to discuss a concrete encounter of Christianity with one of the greatest, strangest, and at the same time most competitive of the religions proper – Buddhism. The discussion of this encounter will not be merely descriptive; it will be presented in a systematic way as a dialogue about the basic principles of both religions. In order to do this it is first necessary to determine the systematic place of both Christianity and Buddhism within the whole of man's religious existence. Such an attempt is perhaps the most difficult one in the comparative study of religions, but if successful it is the most fruitful for the understanding of the seemingly incomprehensible jungle which the history of religion presents to the investigating mind. It is the attempt to erect signposts pointing to *types* of religions, their general characteristics, and their positions in relation to each other.

The establishment of types, however, is always a dubious enterprise. Types are logical ideals for the sake of a discerning understanding; they do not exist in time and space, and in reality we find only a mixture of types in every particular example. But it is not this fact alone which makes typologies questionable. It is, above all, the spatial character of typological thinking; types stand beside each other and seem to have no interrelation. They seem to be static, leaving the dynamics to the individual things, and the individual things, movements, situations, persons (e.g. each of us) resist the attempt to be subordinated to a definite type. Dialectical thought has discovered this and has shown the immense fertility of the dialectical description of tensions in seemingly static structures. The kind of dialectics which, I believe, is most adequate to typological enquiries is the description of contrasting poles within one structure. A polar relation is a relation of interdependent elements, each of which is necessary for the other one and for the whole, although it is in tension with the opposite element. The tension drives both to conflicts and beyond the conflicts to possible unions of the polar elements. Described in this way, types lose their static rigidity, and the individual things and persons can transcend the type to which they belong without losing their definite character. Such a dynamic typology has, at the same time, a decisive advantage over a one-directed dialectics like that of the Hegelian school, in that it does not push into the past what is dialectically left behind. For example, in the problem of the relation of Christianity and Buddhism, Hegelian dialectics considers Buddhism as an early stage of the religious development which is now totally abandoned by history. It still exists, but the World-Spirit is no longer creatively in it. In contrast, a dynamic typology considers Buddhism as a living religion, in which special polar elements are predominant, and which therefore stands in polar tension to other religions in which other elements are predominant. In terms of this method, for example, it would be impossible to call Christianity the absolute religion, as Hegel did, for Christianity is characterized in each historical period by the predominance of different elements out of the whole of elements and polarities which constitute the religious realm.

However, one may point to the fact that we distinguish between living and dead religions on the one hand, and between high and low religions on the other hand, and ask: Does this not mean that some religions *did* disappear completely after the rise of higher forms, and could not Buddhism be considered, as it is with Hegel and in neo-orthodox theology, as a religion which is, in principle, dead? If this were so, a serious dialogue would be impossible. But it is not so! While specific religions, as well as specific cultures, do grow and die, the forces which brought them into being, the type-determining elements, belong to the nature of the holy and with it to the nature of man, and with it to the nature of the universe and the revelatory self-manifestation of the divine. Therefore the decisive point in a dialogue between two religions is not the historically determined, contingent *embodiment* of the typological elements, but these elements themselves. Under the method of dynamic typology every dialogue between religions is accompanied by a silent dialogue *within* the representatives of each of the participating religions. If the Christian theologian discusses with the Buddhist priest the relation of the mystical and the ethical elements in both religions and, for instance, defends the priority of the ethical over the mystical, he discusses at the same time within himself the relationship of the two in Christianity. This produces (as I can witness) both seriousness and anxiety.

It would now seem in order to give a dynamic typology of the religions or, more precisely, of the typical elements which, in many variations, are the determining factors in every concrete religion. But this is a task which by far transcends the scope of this book, which may be considered as a small contribution to such a typology. The only statement possible at this moment is the determination of the polarities of which Christianity and Buddhism occupy the opposite poles. Like all religions, both grow out of a sacramental basis, out of the experience of the holy as present here and now, in this thing, this person, this event. But no higher religion remained on this sacramental basis; they transcended it, while still preserving it, for as long as there is religion the sacramental basis cannot disappear. It can, however, be broken and transcended. This has happened in two directions, the mystical and the ethical, according to the two elements of the experience of the holy – the experience of the holy as being and the experience of the holy as what ought to be. There is no holiness and therefore no living religion without both elements, but the predominance of the mystical element in all India-born religions is obvious, as well as the predominance of the social–ethical element in those born of Israel. This gives to the dialogue a preliminary place within the encounters of the religions proper. At the same time it gives an example of the encounter and conflict of the elements of the holy within every particular religion.

## II

Buddhism and Christianity have encountered each other since early times, but not much of a dialogue resulted from the encounter. Neither of the two religions plays a role in the classical literature of the other. Buddhism made its first noticeable impact on Western thought in the philosophy of Schopenhauer, who with some justification identified his metaphysics and psychology of "will" with Indian, and especially Buddhist, insights. A second influx of Indian, including Buddhist, ideas occurred in the beginning of our century when Buddhist sources were published in attractive translations, and men like Rudolf Otto, the Marburg theologian and author of the classical book, *The Idea of the Holy,* began a continuous and profound personal and literary dialogue between Christianity and the Indian religions. The discussion has been going on ever since, both in the East and the West – in the East not only from the side of Indian Hinduism but also from the side of Japanese Buddhism. This points to a third and more existential encounter, the missionary attack of Japanese Zen Buddhism on the Western educated classes, both Christian and humanist. (The reason for the success as well as the limits of this Buddhist invasion in the West will be discussed later.)

Is there a corresponding impact of Christianity on Buddhism? To answer this, one must distinguish, as with respect to all Asiatic religions, three ways in which Christianity could have influenced them – the direct missionary way, the indirect cultural way, and the personal dialogical way. Missionary work has had a very slight impact on the educated classes of the Asiatic nations, although the conversion of outstanding individuals proves at least a qualitative success of the missions. But in a nation like Japan, where superior civilizing forces have shaped almost all classes of society, missionary success is very limited. In Indian Hinduism the masses are more open to Christian missionary work, as the South Indian church shows, but in the upper classes it is rather a Christian humanism which has taken hold of important individuals. For in all Asiatic religions the indirect, civilizing influence of Christianity is, for the time being, decisive, and not its missionary work. There is a third way, the dialogical–personal, of making inroads into Buddhist spirituality. It is immeasurable, quantitatively as well as qualitatively, but it is a continuous reality and the basis of the dialogical material to be given here.

If we look at the mutual influences between Christianity and Buddhism as a whole we must conclude that they are extremely small – not comparable with the impact of Christianity on the Mediterranean and Germanic nations in the far past, and on many religiously primitive nations in the recent past, or with the impact Buddhism once had on the lower classes as well as the cultured groups of East Asia, for example in China and Japan. And, certainly, the mutual influence of the two religions cannot be compared with the tremendous influence the quasi-religions have had on both of them. So it may happen that the dialogue between them, in a not too distant future, will center on the common problems which arise with respect to the secularization of all mankind and the resulting attack of the powerful quasi-religions on all religions proper. But even so the interreligious dialogue must go on and should bear more fruits than it has up to now.

A dialogue between representatives of different religions has several presuppositions. It first presupposes that both partners acknowledge the value of the other's religious conviction (as based ultimately on a revelatory experience), so that they consider the dialogue worthwhile. Second, it presupposes that each of them is able to represent his own religious basis with conviction, so that the dialogue is a serious confrontation. Third, it presupposes a common ground which makes both dialogue and conflicts possible, and, fourth, the openness of both sides to criticisms directed against their own religious basis. If these presuppositions are realized – as I felt they were in my own dialogues with priestly and scholarly representatives of Buddhism in Japan – this way of encounter of two or more religions can be extremely fruitful and, if continuous, even of historical consequence.

One of the important points which is valid for all discussions between representatives of religions proper today is the unceasing reference to the quasi-religions and their secular background. In this way the dialogue loses the character of a discussion of dogmatic subtleties and becomes a common enquiry in the light of the world situation; and it may happen that the particular theological points become of secondary importance in view of the position of defense of all religions proper.

## III

The last remark leads immediately to the question to which all types of religions proper and of quasi-religions give an answer, whether they intend to do so or not. It is the question of the intrinsic aim of existence – in Greek the *telos* of all existing things. It is *here* that one should start every religious discussion, and not with a comparison of the contrasting concepts of God or man or history of salvation. They can all be understood in their particular character if the particular character of their concept of the telos has been understood. In the telos-formula of the Greek philosophers their whole vision of man and world was summed up, as when Plato called the telos of man ὁμοίωσις τῷ θεῷ κατὰ τὸ δυνατόν (becoming similar to the god as much as possible). In the dialogue between Christianity and Buddhism two telos-formulas can be used: in Christianity the telos of every-*one* and everything united in the Kingdom of God; in Buddhism the telos of every*thing* and everyone fulfilled in the Nirvana. These, of course, are abbreviations for an almost infinite number of presuppositions and consequences; but just for this reason they are useful for the beginning as well as for the end of a dialogue.

Both terms are symbols, and it is the different approach to reality implied in them which creates the theoretical as well as practical contrast between the two religions. The Kingdom of God is a social, political, and personalistic symbol. The symbolic material is taken from the ruler of a realm who establishes a reign of justice and peace. In contrast to it Nirvana is an ontological symbol. Its material is taken from the experience of finitude, separation, blindness, suffering, and, in answer to all this, the image of the blessed oneness of everything, beyond finitude and error, in the ultimate Ground of Being.

In spite of this profound contrast, a dialogue between the two is possible. Both are based on a negative valuation of existence: the Kingdom of God stands against the kingdoms of this world,

G

namely, the demonic power-structures which rule in history and personal life; Nirvana stands against the world of seeming reality as the true reality from which the individual things come and to which they are destined to return. But from this common basis decisive differences arise. In Christianity the world is seen as creation and therefore as essentially good; the great Christian assertion, *esse qua esse bonum est,* is the conceptualization of the Genesis story in which God sees everything he has created "and behold, it was very good". The negative judgment, therefore, in Christianity is directed against the world in its existence, not in its essence, against the fallen, not the created, world. In Buddhism the fact that there is a world is the result of an ontological Fall into finitude.

The consequences of this basic difference are immense. The Ultimate in Christianity is symbolized in personal categories, the Ultimate in Buddhism in transpersonal categories, for example, "absolute non-being". Man in Christianity is responsible for the Fall and is considered a sinner; man in Buddhism is a finite creature bound to the wheel of life with self-affirmation, blindness, and suffering.

## IV

It seems that here the dialogue would come to an end with a clear statement of incompatibility. But the dialogue goes on and the question is asked whether the nature of the holy has not forced both sides to include, at least by implication, elements which are predominant in the other side. The symbol "Kingdom of God" appears in a religious development in which the holiness of the "ought to be" is predominant over the holiness of the "is", and the "protesting" element of the holy is predominant over the "sacramental" one. The symbol appears in prophetic Judaism, in the synoptic type of early Christianity, in Calvinism, and in the social type of liberal Protestantism. But if we look at Christianity as a whole, including the types just mentioned, we find a large amount of mystical and sacramental elements, and consequently, ideas concerning God and man which approximate to Buddhist concepts. The *esse ipsum*, being itself, of the classical Christian doctrine of God, is a transpersonal category and enables the Christian disputant to understand the meaning of absolute nothingness in Buddhist thought. The term points to the unconditional and infinite character of the Ultimate and the impossibility of identifying it with anything particular that exists. Vice versa, it is obvious that in Mahajana Buddhism the Buddha-Spirit appears in many manifestations of a personal character, making a non-mystical, often very primitive relation to a divine figure possible. Such observations confirm the assumption that none of the various elements which constitute the meaning of the holy are ever completely lacking in any genuine experience of the holy, and, therefore, in any religion. But this does not mean that a fusion of the Christian and the Buddhist idea of God is possible, nor does it mean that one can produce a common denominator by depriving the conflicting symbols of their concreteness. A living religion comes to life only if a new revelatory experience appears.

This dialogue leads to the general question of whether the controlling symbols, Kingdom of God and Nirvana, are mutually exclusive. According to our derivation of all religious types from elements in the experience of the holy, this is unthinkable, and there are indications in the history of both symbols that converging tendencies exist. If in Paul the Kingdom of God is identified with the expectation of God being all *in* all (or *for* all), if it is replaced by the symbol of Eternal Life, or described as the eternal intuition and fruition of God, this has a strong affinity to the praise of Nirvana as the state of transtemporal blessedness, for blessedness presupposes – at least in symbolic language – a subject which experiences blessedness. But here also a warning against mixture or reduction of the concrete character of both religions must be given.

The dialogue can now turn to some ethical consequences in which the differences are more conspicuous. In discussing them it becomes obvious that two different ontological principles lie behind the conflicting symbols, Kingdom of God and Nirvana, namely, "participation" and "identity". One participates, as an individual being, in the Kingdom of God. One is identical with everything that is in Nirvana. This leads immediately to a different relation of man to nature. The principle of participation can be reduced in its application to such a degree that it leads to the attitude of technical control of nature which dominates the Western world. Nature, in all its forms, is a tool for human purposes. Under the principle of identity the development of this possibility is largely prevented. The sympathetic identification with nature is powerfully expressed in the Buddhist-inspired art in China and Korea and Japan. An analogous attitude in Hinduism, dependent also on the principle of identity, is the treatment of the higher animals, the prohibition to kill them, and the belief, connected with the Karma doctrine, that human souls in the process of migration can be embodied in animals. This is far removed from the Old Testament story in which Adam is assigned the task of ruling over all other creatures.

Nevertheless, the attitudes toward nature in Christianity and Buddhism are not totally exclusive. In the long history of Christian nature-mysticism the principle of participation can reach a degree in which it is often difficult to distinguish it from the principle of identity, as, for example, in Francis of Assisi. Luther's sacramental thinking produced a kind of nature-mysticism which influenced Protestant mystics and, in a secularized form, the German romantic movement. It is not Christianity as a whole, but Calvinistic Protestantism whose attitude toward nature contradicts almost completely the Buddhist attitude. In Buddhism the controlling attitude to nature increased with the migration of Buddhism from India through China to Japan, but it never conquered the principle of identity. Every Buddhist rock garden is a witness to its presence. The statement I heard that these expressively arranged rocks are both here and, at the same time, everywhere in the universe in a kind of mystical omnipresence, and that their particular existence here and now is not significant, was for me a quite conspicuous expression of the principle of identity.

But most important for the Buddhist-determined cultures is the significance of the principle of identity for the relation of man to man and to society. One can say, in considerably condensed form, that participation leads to agape, identity to compassion. In the New Testament the Greek word agape is used in a new sense for that kind of love that God has for man, the higher for the lower, and that all men should have for one another, whether they are friends or enemies, accepted or rejected, liked or disliked. Agape in this sense accepts the unacceptable and tries to transform it. It will raise the beloved beyond himself, but the success of this attempt is not the condition of agape; it may become its consequence. Agape accepts and tries to transform in the direction of what is meant by the "Kingdom of God".

Compassion is a state in which he who does not suffer under his own conditions may suffer by identification with another who suffers. He neither accepts the other one in terms of "in spite of", nor does he try to transform him, but he suffers his suffering through identification. This can be a very active way of love, and it can bring more immediate benefit to him who is loved than can a moralistically distorted commandment to exercise agape. But something is lacking: the will to transform the other one, either directly, or indirectly by transforming the sociological and psychological structures by which he is conditioned. There are great expressions of compassion in Buddhist religion and art, as well as – and here again I can witness – in personal relations with friends, but this is not agape. It differs in that it lacks the double characteristic of agape – the acceptance of the unacceptable, or the movement from the highest to the lowest, and, at the same time, the will to transform individual as well as social structures.

Now the problem of history comes into the foreground of the dialogue. Under the predominance of the symbol of the Kingdom of God, history is not only the scene in which the destiny of individuals is decided, but it is a movement in which the new is created and which runs ahead to the absolutely new, symbolized as "the new heaven and the new earth". This vision of history, this really historical interpretation, has many implications of which I want to mention the following. With respect to the mode of the future, it means that the symbol of the Kingdom of God has a revolutionary character. Christianity, in so far as it works in line with this symbol, shows a revolutionary force directed toward a radical transformation of society. The conservative tendencies in the official churches have never been able to suppress this element in the symbol of the Kingdom of God, and most of the revolutionary movements in the West – liberalism, democracy, and socialism – are dependent on it, whether they know it or not. There is no analogy to this Buddhism. Not transformation of reality but salvation from reality is the basic attitude. This need not lead to radical asceticism as in India; it can lead to an affirmation of the activities of daily life – as, for instance, in Zen Buddhism – but under the principle of ultimate detachment. In any case, no belief in the new in history, no impulse for transforming society, can be derived from the principle of Nirvana. If contemporary Buddhism shows an increased social interest, and if the sectarian "New Religions" in Japan (some of them of Buddhist origin) are extremely popular, this remains under the principle of compassion. No transformation of society as a whole, no aspiration for the radically new in history, can be observed in these movements. Again we must ask: Is this the end of the dialogue? And again I answer: Not necessarily. In spite of all the revolutionary dynamics in Christianity there is a strong, sometimes even predominant, experience of the vertical line, for instance in Christian mysticism, in the sacramental conservation of the Catholic churches, and in the religiously founded political conservatism of the Lutheran churches. In all these cases the revolutionary impetus of Christianity is repressed and the longing of all creatures for the "eternal rest in God, the Lord" approaches indifference toward history. In its relation to history Christianity includes more polar tensions than Buddhism, just because it has chosen the horizontal, historical line.

But this is not the end of the dialogue. For history itself has driven Buddhism to take history seriously, and this at a moment when in the Christian West a despair about history has taken hold of many people. Buddhist Japan wants democracy, and asks the question of its spiritual foundation. The leaders know that Buddhism is unable to furnish such a foundation, and they look for something which has appeared only in the context of Christianity, namely, the attitude toward every individual which sees in him a person, a being of infinite value and equal rights in view of the Ultimate. Christian conquerors forced democracy upon the Japanese; they accepted it, but then they asked: How can it work if the Christian estimation of every person has no roots either in Shintoism or in Buddhism?

The fact that it has no roots comes out in a dialogue like the following: The Buddhist priest asks the Christian philosopher, "Do you believe that every person has a substance of his own which gives him true individuality?" The Christian answers, "Certainly!" The Buddhist priest asks, "Do you believe that community between individuals is possible?" The Christian answers affirmatively. Then the Buddhist says, "Your two answers are incompatible; if every person has a substance, no community is possible." To which the Christian replies, "*Only* if each person has a substance of his own is community possible, for community pre-supposes separation. You, Buddhist friends, have identity, but not community." Then the observer asks: "Is a Japanese democracy possible under these principles? Can acceptance of a political system replace its spiritual foundations?" With these questions, which are valid for nations all over the non-Western world, the dialogue comes to a preliminary end. . . .

And now we have to ask: What is the consequence of this judgment of Christianity of itself for its dealing with the world religions? We have seen, first of all, that it is a mutual judging which opens the way for a fair valuation of the encountered religions and quasi-religions.

Such an attitude prevents contemporary Christianity from attempting to "convert" in the traditional and depreciated sense of this word. Many Christians feel that it is a questionable thing, for instance, to try to convert Jews. They have lived and spoken with their Jewish friends for decades. They have not converted them, but they have created a community of conversation which has changed both sides of the dialogue. Some day this ought to happen also with people of Islamic faith. Most attempts to convert them have failed, but we may try to reach them on the basis of their growing insecurity in face of the secular world, and they may come to self-criticism in analogy to our own self-criticism.

Finally, in relation to Hinduism, Buddhism, and Taoism, we should continue the dialogue which has already started and of which I tried to give an example in the third chapter. Not conversion, but dialogue. It would be a tremendous step forward if Christianity were to accept this! It would mean that Christianity would judge itself when it judges the others in the present encounter of the world religions.

But it would do even more. It would give a new valuation to secularism. The attack of secularism on all present-day religions would not appear as something merely negative. If Christianity denies itself as a religion, the secular development could be understood in a new sense, namely as the indirect way which historical destiny takes to unite mankind religiously, and this would mean, if we include the quasi-religions, also politically. When we look at the formerly pagan, now communist, peoples, we may venture the idea that the secularization of the main groups of present-day mankind may be the way to their religious transformation.

This leads to the last and most universal problem of our subject: Does our analysis demand either a mixture of religions or the victory of one religion, or the end of the religious age altogether? We answer: None of these alternatives! A mixture of religions destroys in each of them the concreteness which gives it its dynamic power. The victory of *one* religion would impose a particular religious answer on all other particular answers. The end of the religious age – one has already spoken of the end of the Christian or the Protestant age – is an impossible concept. The religious principle cannot come to an end. For the question of the ultimate meaning of life cannot be silenced as long as men are men. Religion cannot come to an end, and a particular religion will be lasting to the degree in which it negates itself as a religion. Thus Christianity will be a bearer of the religious answer as long as it breaks through its own particularity.

The way to achieve this is not to relinquish one's religious tradition for the sake of a universal concept which would be nothing but a concept. The way is to penetrate into the depth of one's own religion, in devotion, thought, and action. In the depth of every living religion there is a point at which the religion itself loses its importance, and that to which it points breaks through its particularity, elevating it to spiritual freedom and with it to a vision of the spiritual presence in other expressions of the ultimate meaning of man's existence.

This is what Christianity must see in the present encounter of the world religions.

# 9

# CATHOLICISM
## Hans Küng

THE ROMAN CATHOLIC attitude toward other religions since the
Middle Ages has involved a balance or dialectic between positive
and negative tendencies. On the one hand, Aquinas' doctrine of
the possibility of a natural knowledge of God together with such
doctrines as that of baptism of desire, implicit faith, invincible
ignorance, God's universal will to save, and the universality of
Christ's atonement, have tended toward a positive interpretation
of other religions. But when Jesuit and Dominican missionaries
in Asia in the sixteenth and seventeenth centuries developed
extreme attitudes of adaptation and accommodation toward other
religions they were condemned. Again in the later nineteenth
and early twentieth centuries extreme modernist attitudes toward
other religions were also condemned. On the other hand, when
the principle that there is no salvation outside the Church has
been interpreted literally or rigorously, as in the case of Father
Feeney of Boston, these interpretations have also been condemned.

The experience of the ecumenical movement and the increasing encounter with the other world religions since World War II
has produced in the Roman Catholic Church a growing concern
and a volume of theological writing on the attitude toward other
religions which now exceeds that in Protestant circles. This came
to a focus in the Second Vatican Council, which has produced
the first official declaration concerning other religions in the
history of the Church of Rome. The "Declaration on the Relation-

ship of the Church to Non-Christian Religions" originally dealt only with the Jews. But as a result of the objections of bishops from Africa and Asia it was expanded to include the other world religions. The Declaration affirms that "all peoples comprise a single community" which has its one origin and goal in God, whose saving design extends to all men. It declares that "the Catholic Church rejects nothing which is true and holy in these religions" and exhorts its members through dialogue and colla- boration with the adherents of the other religions to "acknow- ledge, preserve, and promote the spiritual and moral goods" found among them. After explicit mention of Hinduism, Budd- hism, and Islam, the Declaration concludes with a statement on the Church's common heritage with the Jews and rejects all forms of anti-Semitism.

One of the men named as an official theologian of the Vatican Council by Pope John XXIII was Hans Küng (1928–   ), pro- fessor of theology at the University of Tübingen. Born in Swit- zerland, Küng was educated at the Pontifical German College and the Gregorian University in Rome. He first became well known through his doctoral dissertation at the Sorbonne, which was published under the title *Justification: The Doctrine of Karl Barth with a Catholic Reflection* (1957) and in which he asserts a fundamental agreement between Barth and the Catholic tradi- tion on this doctrine. After a brief period of parish work in Lucerne and a year of teaching at the University of Münster, Küng joined the Catholic faculty of theology at Tübingen in 1960, where he is also director of the Institute of Ecumenical Studies. Küng's reputation as one of the leading "progressive" spokesmen for church reform and reunion was made with his book *The Council, Reform and Reunion* (1960), which was written specifi- cally with the Second Vatican Council in view. His other works include *Structures of the Church* (1962) and *The Council in Action* (1963).

The original title of the selection below was "The World Reli- gions in God's Plan of Salvation", and it was written for a con- ference on "Christian Revelation and Non-Christian Religions" which was held in Bombay in 1964, one week after the Vatican

Council had approved the Declaration on Non-Christian Religions mentioned above. It was published in a volume of essays by Küng entitled *Freedom Today*, which is the first volume in a series entitled *Theological Meditations* edited by Küng. The other essays concern the freedom of the individual, of the Church, of theology, and of "a Pope", namely, John XXIII, who, Küng believes, brought a new spirit of reform, openness, and freedom into the Roman Church. The final section of the essay on "The Freedom of Religions" has been omitted. It is entitled "The Church Free for the World Religions" and concerns the Church's service of the religions. The Church is not called to triumph over the religions but to serve them by understanding them, affirming solidarity with them, and by bearing witness to their common origin and goal in God. Küng's approach to other religions is a clear example of the one described above as "Salvation History". It seems to overlook the radically different views of salvation among the religions. A criticism of this approach from a conservative point of view is given in H. van Straelen's book, *The Catholic Encounter with World Religions* (Westminster, Md.: The Newman Press, and London: Burns and Oates, 1966).

# The Freedom of Religions*

## CHRISTIANITY AS MINORITY

IN HIS BOOK *Eastern Religions and Western Thought,* Sarvepalli Radhakrishnan makes use of a story which may well be taken as characteristic not only of Buddhism and Hinduism but of many other educated non-Christians in Asia:

> Once upon a time, Buddha relates, a certain king of Benares, desiring to divert himself, gathered together a number of beggars blind from birth, and offered a prize to the one who should give

* From Hans Küng, *Freedom Today* (New York: Sheed Ward, 1966), pp. 110–124, 132–145, 147–148, 159–160. Copyright by Sheed Ward, Inc., New York, 1966. Included in its original form as ch. I of *Christian Revelation and World Religions,* ed. Joseph Neuner, S.J. (London: Burns & Oates, 1967).

him the best account of an elephant. The first beggar who examined the elephant chanced to lay hold on a leg, and reported that an elephant was a tree-trunk; the second, laying hold of the tail, declared that an elephant was like a rope; another, who seized an ear, insisted that an elephant was like a palm-leaf; and so on. The beggars fell to quarrelling with one another, and the king was greatly amused. Ordinary teachers who have grasped this or that aspect of the truth quarrel with one another, while only a Buddha knows the whole. In theological discussions we are at best blind beggars fighting with one another. The complete vision is difficult and the Buddhas are rare. Asoka's dictum represents the Buddhist view. "He who does reverence to his own sect while disparaging the sects of others wholly from attachment to his own, with intent to enhance the splendour of his own sect, in reality, by such conduct inflicts the severest injury on his own sect."[1]

It is perhaps an open question whether Radhakrishnan's tolerance derives chiefly from the Vedanta or rather from Western idealism and nineteenth-century theological liberalism. The important point for us is precisely that this type of tolerance is characteristic of a large number of people of *both* East *and* West. How many Europeans and Americans are there who would, in one way or another, subscribe to these words of Gandhi's: "I believe in the Bible as I believe in the Gita. I regard all the great faiths of the world as equally true with my own. It hurts me to see any one of them caricatured as they are today by their own followers."[2]

But let us as believing Christians be realistic and not immediately start complaining of "relativism" and "indifferentism". Is it so easy for us to deny the large measure of breadth and depth that speaks through this view, the generosity and magnanimity, the compassion and human concern, radically opposed to all the vast mass of religious prejudices and misunderstandings, religious conflicts, and that real contradiction in terms, "wars of religion"? Does not this view perhaps rest upon a vision of God that is greater, more exalted, more reverent than the vision of those for whom God is allowed to be only the God of one party, one religious party?

[1] Sarvepalli Radhakrishnan, *Eastern Religions and Western Thought* (New York and London: OUP, 1940), pp. 308 ff.
[2] Quoted from Radhakrishnan, *op. cit.*, p. 313.

Are we not forced to think a little, when we set these Buddhist and Hindu testimonies side by side with a classic testimony of Catholicism, in the explicit form in which it was solemnly proclaimed to the world by Pope Boniface VIII eighteen hundred years after Buddha, and in which it is still to be read today in Denzinger's *Enchiridion*: "We are required by faith to believe and hold that there is one holy Catholic and apostolic Church; we firmly believe it and unreservedly profess it; outside it there is neither salvation nor remission of sins.... Further, we declare, say, define and proclaim that to submit to the Roman Pontiff, is, for every human creature, an utter necessity of salvation" (Denzinger, 468 f.). Again and again this "Outside the Church no salvation" has been repeated and re-emphasized. But the situation has grown more and more difficult: not only for the Catholic Church but also for the Protestant Churches, some of which take an even more exclusive stand in regard to the world religions – hence for the whole of Christendom. It is necessary at this point to recall to mind certain facts, all of them only too familiar to us, but the full combined force of which needs to be kept before our eyes if we are to be serious enough in our search for an answer. These, then, are the questions men are asking us today:

Outside the Church no salvation: Can you actually keep on saying this when you look with honesty at the *present time*, and consider that of the more than three billion present inhabitants of the earth only about 950 million are Christians, and that of these only about 584 million are Catholics? That in India only 2.4% are Christians and only 1.2% Catholics, while in China and Japan only about 0.5% are Christians? That even in Europe, both in the great cities and in many rural areas, only a fraction of those calling themselves Christians take any practical part in the Church? What have you to say about this salvation of these millions who live in the *present time* outside the Catholic Church and altogether outside Christianity?

Outside the Church no salvation: Can you keep on saying this when you look without prejudice at the *past*, and consider that the years of humanity's existence before Christ and without

Christ are not, as the Bible suggests, five thousand two hundred (a figure which already troubled the minds of the Fathers of the Church) but may amount to six hundred thousand or more; so that the question which the Church Fathers used to ask, "Why did Christ come so late?" has taken on a sharpness of an entirely new kind? What have you to say about the salvation of the countless millions who have lived in the *past* outside the Catholic Church and altogether outside Christianity?

Outside the Church no salvation: Can you keep on saying this when you look realistically at the *future*, and consider that statistics show that numerically the non-Christian nations of Asia and Africa are going to outstrip by far the Christian nations of the West? That merely to preserve the present numerical relationship there would have to be, not the half-million converts to the Catholic Church which there are each year, but six and a half million? That it has been calculated that by the year 2000, China alone may number seventeen hundred million people, four hundred million more than the present population of Europe, the Soviet Union, North and South America, and Africa combined? What have you to say about the innumerable millions and billions who are going to live in the *future* outside the Catholic Church and altogether outside Christianity?

Now, we are all aware of these facts. But do we not need to come to terms in a new way *theologically* with the fact that, in face of past, present, and future, in face of human history on *all* continents and in *all* epochs, we, the Catholic Church and Christendom generally, are clearly a *small, insignificant minority*. Looked at in this way, the problem is by no means only one for the churches of the missions, but equally for the churches at home. Yet it remains a special problem for the missionary churches for this reason: that it would seem that the age of mass missionary achievements, in Asia at any rate, is over as far as the foreseeable future is concerned. To get the whole problem clear, we need at this point to refer to two other aspects of it, both of them again well known:

1. In our day a period of world history is coming finally to an end; the one which is called in Europe "the modern age" and

which began four hundred years ago with the discovery of what were to us new continents. The peoples of Asia and Africa are enthusiastically adopting western science, technology, and industrialization, and thus a world-economy and a world-civilization are taking shape. But at the same time something else has become an accomplished fact in a few years: the age of the political, economic, and cultural expansion of the white peoples, of exclusive western domination of the world, and of all that goes by the name of colonialism, is over. We all know that the situation of the Christian missions, excessively linked as they have been with that age and its political, cultural, and social system, is not being made any easier by this change. They are no longer borne along by the current but have to swim against it. They are being forced in a new way to justify their work, which is very difficult. And we can sense that "No salvation outside" is not good enough an answer. As for our problem, in any case, we have to realize that today evangelization is directed less and less toward "poor heathens", but rather toward modern men in industrialized states with great and ancient cultures.

2. It is not only politically and socially, not only economically and technologically, that the peoples of Asia and Africa are entering upon a new period of world history, but religiously as well. What many Christians expected has not taken place: the old religions, confronted by European culture and hence by the Christian religion, have not slowly but surely withered away. True, religious indifferentism is growing apace in the countries of Asia and Africa as elsewhere, but the great non-Christian world religions, Hinduism, Buddhism, Mohammedanism, not only are not withering away but are developing with fresh vigor. The four hundred years of the Christian missions were for them – as the Indian writer K. M. Panikkar, for instance, emphasizes in *Asia and Western Dominance* [3] – merely a transition stage during a period when the peoples of Asia were politically and culturally weak. In their eyes, the age of the Christian missions is, as a whole, over and done with. The non-Christian world religions have to a great extent passed over from the defensive

[3] New York: John Day & Co. and London: Allen & Unwin, 1959.

to the offensive. Along with the rest of the great and ancient history of its peoples, Asia is reflecting on the great tradition of its ancient religions. In Hinduism, indeed, this process of reflection has long been in operation, precisely because of the pressure of Christianity. On the one hand, this renaissance of the world religions leads to an assimilation of the heritage of western thought (as witness Radhakrishnan), and, on the other, to the development of a not inconsiderable missionary drive, threatening a reversal on the religious front. We become all the more aware that "no salvation outside" is not a good enough answer in this new, direct competition with the great world religions. For the purposes of our problem we need to realize that the theological question facing us today is not merely that of the individual person outside the Church and Christianity but of these *religions themselves* outside the Church and Christianity.

An answer of some sort must be given. Is the minority to be prohibited from enquiring about the fate of the majority: is it not rather obliged to do so? The questions arising are so urgent, for the churches both at home and in the missions, that we are absolutely required to face the problem. We cannot, as theologians sometimes do, solve it by recourse to a "dialectical theology" employing an *a priori*, negative, polemical concept of "religion": the idea that in the world religions "religion" means simply a projection of psychological need and an attempt at self-help, that it is a work of human autonomy, a taking care of oneself and asserting of oneself in the face of God, that it is an expression of fear and falsehood and, ultimately, of unbelief and godlessness. It is quite illegitimate for Christians to assume or assert this idea as self-evident; it would need to be established, with all the necessary distinctions and nuances, as true of the present situation. But as soon as we try to do this, we come up against the real ambivalence in the term "religion", which prevents any concept of it from being purely negative.

Nor can we, faced with all the questions arising from the mass of mankind outside Christianity, content ourselves with a polite theological "ignoramus". The European finds it only too easy to compensate for his lack of knowledge about world religions by passing arrogant judgment on that which he does not know. If we cannot give an adequate answer to these questions we must not be surprised if the men of today either content themselves with enlightened indifferentism, like Lessing with his fable of the three rings, each claimed as genuine and none in fact the father's real ring, or else follow Voltaire in pouring scorn on the arrogance of "salvation monopolists". After two thousand years of Christian history and missionary effort, the plurality of religions still persists. This, even more than the distressing plurality of the various Christian confessions, makes questionable a claim to be absolute on the part of that faith which, more than, and in a different sense from, any other world religion, claims the support of a uniquely valid revelation of God. A theologian has got to enquire seriously whether, to someone whose Christianity is not a matter of mere repetition but of reflection, the revelation of Christ does not have something positive to say on these questions concerning the salvation of pagans (that is, the "unevangelized"), ancient and modern.

We shall in the first instance try to reach toward an answer by the closer examination of the axiom "No salvation outside". This introduces us to what may be called an ecclesiocentric view of the problem. We shall see later on that another view of it is also possible.

## OUTSIDE THE CHURCH NO SALVATION?

The axiom "extra Ecclesiam nulla salus" goes back to the image of the Ark of Noah, used in 1 Peter 3. 20 to portray salvation through baptism. But we note that while this text does indeed state positively that there is "salvation inside the ark", it makes no simple assertion that there is "no salvation outside the ark". Rather, the text says that Christ, who "died for sins once for all, the righteous for the unrighteous, that he might bring us to God" (3. 18), preached the good news after his death to "the spirits" (the fallen angels or the godless generation of the time of the flood, or both) "who formerly did not obey" (3. 19–20), and hence were not inside the ark. The text would then mean that even the worst of sinners, even after this life, is not excluded from Christ's call to salvation. So what we have here is in fact an assertion of "salvation outside the ark", with the presupposition of "no salvation outside *Christ*".[4]

The axiom itself began to be worked out by Ignatius of Antioch, Irenaeus, Clement of Alexandria and others, receiving from Origen its first complete formulation, now cast in negative terms: Outside this house, that is, the Church, no one is saved (*In Jesu nave* 3, 5, *PG* 12, 841). The axiom was applied by Cyprian with fully consistent juridical exclusiveness (*De unitate Ecclesiae* 6: *CSEL* III/1, 214 f.). And here at once we encounter something that has been constantly verified on later occasions: whenever this axiom in its negative formulation has been taken in the precise literal sense of the words, it has led to heresy. Thus Cyprian – consistently, as it might surely seem – concluded from it that baptism administered by heretics outside the Church was invalid, and that martyrdom outside the Church was valueless. Cyprian's position was rejected by the Church. Although, unlike Cyprian, Augustine distinguishes between more and less grave cases of heresy, he, too, could see no possibility of salvation even for the less grave cases. The strict literal sense in which the axiom was taken is shown in this sentence from Augustine's disciple, Fulgentius of Ruspe: "Hold fast as most certain and have no manner of doubt that not only all heathens but also all Jews and all heretics and schismatics who die outside this present Catholic Church will go into that everlasting fire which was prepared for the devil and his angels."

Medieval scholasticism is entirely in line with Augustine. Here again the axiom led to errors which have since been rejected by the Church, as, for instance, that priests separated from the Catholic Church lose the power to consecrate. And the very Pope who produced the most rigid formulation of "Outside the papal Church no salvation" was the one who brought the papacy to the very brink of disaster (the taking prisoner of Boniface VIII and the Great Western Schism with three Popes all excommuni-

[4] For the history of the axiom, see the references in my essay in *Festschrift G. C. Berkouwer*, 1965.

cating each other); the rigorous doctrine of the bull *Unam Sanctam* was not maintained by subsequent popes.

But what was needed to effect a break-through was the tremendous historical event of the discovery of whole new continents with civilized and morally good inhabitants. Now it was not merely *known* that there were lands and peoples outside the Church (this fact was *known* in the Middle Ages); now it became unavoidable to take a positive *interest* in them. After the assimilation of this lesson of history it was now taught not only by theologians like Bellarmine and Suarez but by the Council of Trent as well (Denzinger, 796) that baptism could be received not only, as by Christians, *in re* (baptism of water) but also *in voto* (baptism of desire). Against the rigorism of the Jansenists, the proposition was condemned that "Outside the Church there is no grace" (Denzinger, 1379). Finally, Pius IX so interpreted the meaning of "outside" – in reference not only to unbaptized pagans but also to Christians separated, as they had now been for many long years, from the Catholic Church – that he was able at the same time to affirm explicitly: "... it must equally be held as certain that those who labor under ignorance of the true religion, if this ignorance be invincible, are not held guilty in this respect in the Lord's eyes. But now, who would be so arrogant as to lay down the limits of such ignorance, considering the nature and variety of peoples, religions, intelligence and so many other things?" (Denzinger, 1647). And when the encyclical *Mystici Corporis* once more gave a somewhat rigorous formulation of the axiom, and Fr. Feeney with a group of Catholics in Boston tried to take the words of the encyclical quite literally, declaring, like the early Fathers of the Church, that everyone outside the Catholic Church was damned, the Holy Office had to intervene, to protest against this statement[5] and finally, by excommunication, to declare *extra Ecclesiam* a person who stated that no one could be saved outside the Church. Fr. Feeney has so far not made his submission.

Now, what had in fact been happening here, in these inter-

[5] See the Letter to Archbishop Cushing of Boston, published in the *American Ecclesiastical Review*, 77 (1952), pp. 307–311.

pretations extending from Trent to Pius XII? What had in fact been done was to state perfectly clearly, even while formally maintaining the "no salvation outside" axiom, that there is salvation even outside the Church, outside the visible Catholic Church (which is how the word had always been understood in Catholic tradition). But this ambiguous mode of expression has been a source of confusion to a great many Catholics. Today they do not know how they are supposed to take the statement that there is "no salvation outside the Church", since, on the one hand, they have to say that outside the Church there is *no* salvation, and on the other, they are supposed to admit that outside the Church there *is* salvation. Is there salvation outside the Church or not? An honest answer to the question has to be "Yes" or "No", not "Yes *and* No".

In order to arrive at a clarification, which needs to be something more than a clarification of idiom and linguistic usage, I should like to contribute a few propositions to the discussion by which even those who are not specialists in theology may be helped in understanding their faith and explaining it to non-Christians. The following seem to me to be important points:

1. The fact that men can be saved outside the Catholic Church is no longer disputed by anybody. The Second Vatican Council has explicitly affirmed this in the new Constitution on the Church (November 21, 1964); "But if some men do not know the Father of our Lord Jesus Christ, yet acknowledge the Creator, or seek the unknown God in shadows and images, then God himself is not far from such men, since he gives life and inspiration to all (cf. Acts 17. 25-28), and the Saviour wills that all men should be saved (cf. 1 Tim. 2. 4). Those who, while guiltlessly ignorant of Christ's Gospel and of his Church, sincerely seek God and are brought by the influence of grace to perform his will as known by the dictates of conscience, can achieve eternal salvation. Nor does divine Providence deny the assistance necessary to salvation to those who, without having attained, through no fault of their own, to an explicit knowledge of God, are striving, not without divine grace, to lead a good life" (*De Ecclesia* II, 16).

2. But precisely because it is possible for people to be saved

outside the Church, this axiom, in its negative, exclusive formulation, continues time after time, no matter what efforts are made to explain it, to occasion innumerable misunderstandings both inside and outside the Catholic Church. While it may have helped the Church and her mission:

(*a*) Such a concept of the Church contradicts the way in which the Church is understood in the New Testament and in Christian tradition as derived from it.

(*b*) As has already been said, such a concept of the Church is in no way necessary in order to see the possibility of the salvation of non-Christians.

(*c*) Such a concept of the Church makes it unnecessarily difficult for missionaries to preach to non-Christians about joining the community of the Church, since they would have to preach at the same time that all men of good will are already in the Church.

(*d*) Such a concept of the Church is rightly rejected by thinking non-Christians as a piece of pure theological construction and speculation; they feel that it is a somewhat impudent notion in us Christians, when they explicitly and of their own full volition do not choose to be members of the Church of Christ, to incorporate them tacitly in the Church against their will and their express choice, as though this were something that could be done over their heads.

The problem of the salvation of non-Christians is not to be solved by a theological construct.

3. The basic *theological* solution, to which we must next turn our attention, is to be found in a positive assessment of the significance of the world religions in relation to God's universal plan of salvation, and hence in a consideration, proceeding from the New Testament, of the place and task of the Church in that world which is not the Church. This involves, in contrast to the statement that "Outside the Church there is no salvation", the working out not of the Church's claims upon the world and dominion over it but her service of the world. In other words, the Church is to be understood not as a closed society of those in possession but an open community of those who serve and help.

We shall return to this in a moment.

4. As a preliminary practical solution of how to handle the axiom itself, the following suggest themselves to me:

(a) In *dogmatic* teaching, the statement is to be preserved as an expression of Catholic tradition and at the same time exhibited in all its limitations and liability to misunderstanding. It should be emphasized that the crucial point is that salvation is given to us in Christ and in him alone, whether a person of goodwill ultimately finds himself inside or outside the visible communion of those who believe in and confess Christ.

(b) In *preaching,* this statement should be as far as possible set aside and not used, because it causes more misunderstanding than understanding. The history of the ecumenical Councils teaches us that this kind of thing has often happened. The Council of Nicaea worked on the supposition that there is only one hypostasis in God. Later ecumenical Councils abandoned this formula, because it gave rise to misunderstanding, and spoke of one physis and three hypostases. As in the doctrine of the Trinity, so in Christology: The Council of Chalcedon deliberately avoided the use of certain Christological formulae which had been used at the Council of Ephesus under the influence of Cyril of Alexandria. Thus, even at that date the Church distinguished – to quote John XXIII – between the content of faith and the form in which it is clothed. The dress can change, the faith remains the same. We believe in salvation through Christ in the Church. But the formula "Outside the Church no salvation", easy to misunderstand and damaging to the Church's mission, should, for the sake of this very faith, no longer be used.

This somewhat negatively critical look at the ecclesiocentric view has prepared the ground for a positive and constructive presentation of the theocentric view.

## GOD'S FREE AND ALL-EMBRACING GRACE

How does the destiny of non-Christian mankind appear if we look, not primarily at the Church, but at God; if we consider non-Christian mankind not from the point of view of the Church's system but from that of God's will and plan for salvation; if, we proceed not from *intra* to *extra* but from *extra* to *intra*?

Non-Christians often accuse the Bible of intolerance. The God of the Bible is said to be exclusive, the God only of Jews and Christians. Is this true? It cannot, most certainly, be disputed that the Old and New Testaments are far removed from any kind of superficial indifferentism. They are totally focused on conversion to, and faith in, the one God of Abraham, Isaac, and Jacob, the God and Father of Jesus Christ. But does this mean that the God of the Bible is the God of a part of mankind only, a superior sort of tribal god? Let us take a closer look. What judgment is passed upon pagans by the Old Testament, by Jesus himself, and finally by apostolic preaching? . . .

1. In the light of the universalist testimonies that pervade the Old and New Testaments it is quite impossible to maintain that the Bible takes a purely negative attitude of exclusive intolerance toward other religions.

2. It is perfectly clear that the God of the Bible is not only the God of Jews and Christians but the God of all men.

3. The *negative* statements concerning the error, darkness, lies, and sin of the pagan world refer to paganism in so far as it sets itself against the saving will of God. These negative statements are to be understood not as a definitive sentence of damnation but as a call to conversion addressed to the pagans of the present day. The fate of earlier pagans, or those not confronted with the revelation of Christ, is of only indirect interest to the Bible.

4. The *positive* statements about the pagan world show that there exists a primitive, original communication of God to the whole of mankind. This is something asserted explicitly by individual witnesses, and assumed throughout the Bible: the Gentiles can know the God of grace. This knowledge of God is not simply a self-sufficient human activity of "natural theology", but a response to the basic revelation of the God of grace in creation, of which man is himself, in the first instance, a part. Thus even before their encounter with the Gospel of Christ, there is already a history of God's presence to the pagan peoples, a history in which decisions are taken. There is no explicit answer

in the Bible to the question of who, among those pagans un-
touched by the Gospel, are saved. But it is certain that even in
the darkness of paganism God is near to every human being,
is indeed necessary for his very life.

The Second Vatican Council has Scripture as its support when
it affirms:

> One is the community of all peoples, one their origin, for God
> made the whole human race to live over the face of the earth. One
> also is their final goal, God. His providence, His manifestations of
> goodness, His saving design extend to all men, until that time when
> the elect will be united in the Holy City, the city ablaze with the
> glory of God, where the nations will walk in His light.[6]

Such, then, is the perspective of this problem when the starting-
point is not the Church but God's will and plan for salvation, as
it is made known to us, and so far as it is made known to us, in
Scripture. The question of what lies outside the Church is one
which can be asked but, as we have seen, is difficult to answer.
As to what lies outside *God* and his plan of salvation, this is
not a real question at all. If we look at God's plan of salvation,
then there is no *extra*, only an *intra*; no outside, only an inside,
for "God desires *all* men to be saved and to come to the knowledge of the truth. For there is *one* God, and there is *one* mediator
between God and men, the man Christ Jesus, who gave himself
as a ransom for *all*" (1 Tim. 2. 4–6).

Within this great and gracious, all-embracing *intra*, this inside,
it is now possible to give a positive account of the relationship of
the world religions to the Church and of the Church to the world
religions.

## CHRISTIAN UNIVERSALISM

We are taking the concept of "religion" as widely as possible.
We include in it not only the theistic religions, which acknowledge a God or several gods, but also the non-theistic religions,
which ascribe divine attributes to a supreme principle or an all-
pervading power or energy. Indirectly and analogously we even

[6] Second Vatican Council's *Declaration on the Relation of the Church
to Non-Christian Religions*, 1.

include what Paul Tillich called "quasi-religions", in which it is perfectly possible for men of good will to be gripped by something which is for them an ultimate concern (or "idea"), to which all other concerns are subordinate and which gives to the lives of such people their ultimate meaning: e.g. national concern in nationalism; social concern in Communism; liberal-humane concern in liberal humanism with its faith in science. These "quasi-religions" can also be called "substitute religions", thus drawing attention to their underlying deficiency. But the term is not to be taken as involving any automatic disqualification of the honest intentions and good faith of those who serve such an "idea", often with utter commitment.

It is impossible to overlook the fact that, on the one hand, these quasi-religions, turning to their own account the secularization and religious indifference which go with technology and industrialization, constitute a greater threat to Christianity than the real religions, theistic or non-theistic, and that, on the other hand, the quasi-religions are also at present a greater threat to the non-Christian religions than are the Christian missions. From this point of view, too, a dialogue between the Church and the real religions would seem to be called for. But this threat must not cause us to overlook the fact that even the quasi-religions, because of their positive elements and concerns, can have a religious character for men of good will. Hence, while they will not be dealt with directly in our consideration of world religions (the problem they present being in other respects very different from that of the real religions), yet they must be at least indirectly included. What, fundamentally, then, have we, as Christians, to say of the world religions?

1. We confess right from the start that we are trying to answer this question from the *Christian* standpoint. And no one has a right to describe this, in advance, as intolerant and exclusive. It may indeed be described as a "dogmatic" standpoint. On this, it should simply be said that in this sense the non-Christian religions, too, proceed from a "dogmatic" or "absolute" standpoint. If we set aside early primitive religions and religious experiences, and the religions of myth, achieving a general view of

reality, which succeeded them, and confine ourselves to religions which have in some way broken out of myth, we can then distinguish, phenomenologically, three types in the development of religions. They *all* have a "dogmatic" starting-point.[7]

It is a *dogmatic* type of religion, first appearing in Greece but particularly successful in modern times in the form of the *Enlightenment,* which discards myth as a pre-scientific form of knowledge while erecting *rational, "scientific" knowledge* into an absolute and subordinating everything in the religious field to it.

But the religions at the opposite pole to this are also dogmatic: those taking the form of "mysticism", to which the myths are mere symbols – perhaps to be seen through as illusory, perhaps to be preserved – while it is the *inner, formless, mystical experience of the divine* which is made into an absolute. When, for instance, Radhakrishnan, whose religious mysticism includes a number of characteristics belonging rather to the Enlightenment, affirms that there is in the endless multiplicity of religions, in their forms and languages, an underlying identity which makes possible a profound spiritual communion between the various religions, this is entirely unobjectionable. But when he simplifies this identity to the point of asserting that all articulate religious statements, all revelations and confessions of faith, all authorities and rites are relative, and the *only* thing that has any ultimate validity is that inner spiritual experience of the absolute which appears in different forms in all religions and can never be adequately expressed, then he is taking up a dogmatic standpoint. It is only possible to make all religions *equal* if the underlying, formless, mystical experience is being set up as an *absolute.* We Christians are reproached with preaching to non-Christians the absoluteness of the revelation made in Jesus Christ. But do we have to feel that it is any more tolerant, are we not bound to feel it almost as a declaration of war on all forms of faith which are historical in their way of thinking, when someone seeks to

---

[7] Cf. J. Ratzinger, "Der christliche Glaube und die Weltreligionen", in *Gott in Welt. Festschrift Karl Rahner* (Freiburg-Basel-Vienna, 1964), vol. 2, pp. 287–305.

impose upon us the absolute of an ultimate, exclusively valid mystical experience, with no room for anything superior to it?

Ultimately, it has to be a decision of faith – and we Christians hold that we have sufficient grounds for the one we make – which of the two is to be regarded as decisive: the mystic's *experience of identity*, striving to be immersed in the monist All-and-One, described both as "nothing" and as "all", or the *otherness* of the God who calls us, as experienced by the prophet not in absorption by him but in obedience to his call. And hence whether we understand God, as in the religions of mysticism, as the purely *passive*, in relation to whom man is active (through absorption, immersion, ascent, union), or whether we understand God, whom the very purest among us cannot, of himself, discover, as the truly *active*, who acts upon man and so brings him to activity. And hence again whether one accords preference to the "great religious personalities" and ascetics who have achieved perfect interiority, or to the simple ministers of the Word, whose desire is to be obedient in faith to the revealing Word. Whether, then, one ultimately reduces the person to the *impersonal* or, as we do, the impersonal to the *person*; whether one ultimately takes the non-historical way of dissolving all history in the identity of eternal recurrence, or, as we do, seeks to understand history truly *historically* as progress toward a goal.

As against the religions of enlightenment and the religions of mysticism, then, Christianity, considered simply in terms of a phenomenology of religion, appears as a way whose starting-point is neither more nor less "dogmatic" than that of other religions. If even the sceptic – which Radhakrishnan is not – claims to be able to assert his scepticism and to contradict those who question its validity, then the Christian may also claim to be able to defend the reality of God's call in Christ and to contradict those who dispute it. The Christian way, as Ratzinger rightly describes it, is the mature version of something that arose in Israel and was taken up again in the post-Christian era by Mohammedanism: "revolutionary monotheism", which regards as the absolute neither rational scientific knowledge nor ineffable religious experience, but the divine summons made in the prophet: but which does not – like other, evolutionary forms of monotheism – tend toward an equation of God with the gods, belief in one god with belief in many gods, but, by hearing God's summons, has achieved a revolutionary smashing of myth and overthrowing of the gods of myth.

I am not concerned here to make an apologetical defense of our faith, for which there seem to be many interior grounds, but simply to demonstrate that our particular starting-point is not to be regarded in advance as illegitimate. The non-Christian peoples of Asia, who have adopted Western science, technology, political democracy, and thus – whether they like it or not – a whole series of secularized Christian ideas, will be able to see for themselves whether, through what they have thus taken over, a certain correction of their religious convictions in a Christian direction is imposing itself: a correction, for instance, of cosmic pessimism and of anti-historical cosmic cyclism; the setting of a higher value on the visible world, on the individual and concrete, on the individual person, on the equality of all men; the positive evaluation of a non-cyclic, progressive historical process, of the necessity of reforming the world, of practical social love of neighbor, of history as having a goal, etc.

2. Now, given the legitimacy of the Christian starting-point, what has the Christian faith to say of the world religions? The Old and New Testaments do indeed treat of the peoples, but not of the religions as such. Nevertheless, the biblical material on the evaluation of paganism, which we have tried to elucidate a little, gives us a good foundation on which to summarize our conception in thesis form.

(a) *Despite whatever truth they have concerning the true God, the world religions are in error.* We do not need to go over what the Old and New Testaments say of the error, lies, sin, and darkness of the pagan world. Nor do we need to bring together, from the material supplied by comparative religion, the appalling evidence which supports this negative judgment. All this is an expression of estrangement from God and from him whom the gracious God has sent, and who is not only light but *the* Light, not only truth but *the* Truth. Hence the Gospel of Jesus Christ demands not the fulfillment of the world religions but a metanoia, a conversion and return from false gods to the true God in Jesus Christ.

(*b*) *The world religions do, though in error, proclaim the truth of the true God.* Though they are far from God, God is not far from them. Though they flee from the true God, they are yet graciously held by him who is their God too. By him they are made able, in the midst of all their errors, to speak truly of him. The grace of the true God can witness to itself even through false gods, and can trace the image of the true God even through its misplaced and dissociated features. The grace of the true God is able to transform the mere service of idols into concealed worship of God, and mere erroneous, confused, and superstitious belief or unbelief into hidden faith. Hence in its summons to conversion the Gospel of Jesus Christ does not require the renunciation of whatever in the world religions "is true, whatever is honorable, whatever is just, whatever is pure, whatever is lovely, whatever is gracious" (Phil. 4. 8).

(*c*) *As against the "extraordinary" way of salvation which is the Church, the world religions can be called the "ordinary" way of salvation for non-Christian humanity.* God is the Lord not only of the special salvation history of the Church but also of that other salvation history: the universal salvation history of all mankind. This universal salvation history is bound up with special salvation history in a common origin, meaning, and goal, and is subject to the same grace of God. *Every* historical situation, outside the Church as well as inside it, is thus included in advance within his grace. Since, as a matter of Christian faith, the true God seriously and effectively wills that *all* men should be saved and none lost unless by his own fault, every man is intended to find his salvation within his *own* historical condition. "Within his own historical condition", means here, within his particular individual and social environment, from which he cannot simply escape; it means, finally, within the religion socially imposed on him from which, equally, he cannot normally simply escape. Man's religion, as the religion of a social being who is essentially social, is never merely an individualist, subjectivist activity in a purely private interior zone, but always an activity in a particular social embodiment, i.e. in the form of a particular religion, a concrete religious community.

But since God seriously and effectively wills the universal salvation history of the whole of mankind, although he does not, indeed, legitimize every element (some being erroneous and depraved) in these religions (even the Old Covenant was not perfect!), yet he does sanction the *religions as such* – as social structures. These, although in different senses and degrees, are in their own way "legitimate religions".[8] A man is to be saved within the religion that is made available to him in his historical situation, which, for the man in question, is not merely an external framework but, if it is *genuine*, forms a part of himself. Hence it is his right and his duty to seek God within that religion in which the hidden God has already found him. All this until such time as he is confronted in an existential way with the revelation of Jesus Christ. The religions with their forms of belief and cult, their categories and values, their symbols and ordinances, their religious and ethical experience, thus have a "relative validity"[9] and a "relative providential right to existence".[10] Through the grace of the one God they can be – though they need not necessarily be – the way *of salvation* within universal salvation history. When, and where, and how they actually are, this does not come within the scope of our judgment. But through the grace of the one God they can be the way of salvation. Considering the incomparably greater number of people in the world religions, compared with which Christendom is a small minority, we can speak of these religions as the general, the "ordinary", way of salvation, beside which the way of salvation in the Church appears as something altogether special and extraordinary: the way of the

---

[8] See K. Rahner, "Das Christentum und die nichtchristlichen Religionen", *Schriften zur Theologie* 5 (Einsiedeln-Zürich-Cologne, 1962), pp. 147–154. [E.T., "Christianity and the Non-Christian Religions", *Theological Investigations*, V (Baltimore: Helicon Press, 1966), pp. 125–131.]

[9] Cf. J. Neuner, "Missionstheologische Probleme in Indien", in *Gott in Welt. Festschrift Karl Rahner* (Freiburg-Basel-Vienna, 1964), 2, 401 f.

[10] H. R. Schlette, *Die Religionen als Thema der Theolgie* (Freiburg-Basel-Vienna, 1963), p. 39. [E.T., *Towards a Theology of Religions* (New York: Herder and Herder and London: Burns and Oates, 1966), p. 37.]

Church can be seen as the high and excellent and "extraordinary" way of salvation! It is thus that we today, on the basis of our clearer insight into mankind's historical situation and into the universalist perspective of the Christian message, can adapt our former theological terminology (though the question is not primarily one of terminology): the way of salvation for mankind outside the Church can be described as the "ordinary" way, that within the Church as the "extraordinary" way of salvation.[11]

(d) *The world religions teach truth about the Gospel of Christ, which, in their error, they do not know as that which it really is: the Truth.*

1. Despite their errors the religions teach the truth of Christ when, in a multitude of insights, they recognize *man's need of salvation*; when they discern the loneliness, the helpless and forlorn state of man in this world, his abysmal fear and distress, his evil behavior and false pride; when they see the cruelty, perdition, and nothingness of this world, and the meaning and meaninglessness of death; when, because of this, they look for something new, and long for a transformation, a rebirth, and a redemption of man and his world.

2. Despite their errors, the religions teach the truth of Christ when they recognize God's *graciousness*: when, that is, they know that the Godhead, for all its nearness, is far off and hidden, that it is the divine itself which must grant us its nearness, presence, and accessibility; when they know, then, that man cannot draw near to it by himself, relying on his own innocence, but that he needs to be purified and reconciled that he can only arrive at life through death, that sacrifice is needed for the purging of guilt; more, that man cannot redeem himself but is dependent on the loving mercy of God.

3. Despite all their error, the religions are teaching the truth of Christ when they listen to the *voice of their prophets*: when they thus, through their prophets, receive courage and strength for a new break-through into a revival and renewal of religion as it has been handed down.

Thus, the world religions make a constant claim on the

[11] *Ibid.*, p. 85. [E.T., p. 81.]

H

Church's thoughtful attention: confronted by the manifold *falsity* in the world religions, the Church can reach a new and thankful awareness of the grace of her special election; but confronted by the manifold truth in the world religions, she must become humbly aware of her own numerous betrayals and constant falling-short of the message of her Lord.

*(e) It is the Gospel of Jesus Christ that is able to liberate the truth of the world religions from their entanglement in error and sin.* Though the religions do in many ways proclaim the truth of Christ, yet they do not know him whose truth they proclaim; in all their proclamation of truth they fail to recognize him who, as the Father's Word, is *the* Truth. It is this which, despite the light which they shed at very many different points, constitutes their basic darkness, in which they themselves cannot see, and which can be illuminated only by him who is *the* Light.

1. The religions are structures which, because of God's gracious revelation of himself in creation, are light, and at the same time, because of man's failure to recognize the true God in Christ, are darkness. Thus they are *not* "natural theology", "natural piety", "natural morality", but are sharply ambiguous: on the one hand, embraced, upheld, and penetrated by God's grace, and yet, on the other hand, in the bonds and oppression of man's betrayal and wickedness. It is only necessary to look at the history of religion in the concrete to see all the appalling error and moral weakness, to see how little these religions know of the true nature of God and the true nature of man, how constantly they fall either into an abrupt dualistic separation or an overweening monistic union with him. How often, for instance, in Hinduism is the reality of the free and living God either exaggerated in its transcendence into the impersonal absolute of esoteric philosophers or reduced, in its encounter with man, to the anthropomorphic, materialized object of a ritualistic and magical popular piety! Similar things could be said of the Hindu understanding of sin and redemption, of law and of providence.[12] However inappropriate that arrogant lack of understanding may be which rejects

---

[12] Cf. Neuner, *op. cit.,* pp. 405–409; also *Hinduismus und Christentum. Eine Einführung,* ed. J. Neuner (Vienna-Freiburg-Basel, 1962).

the world religions as simply false, it is no less inappropriate to idealize them in utopian fashion as uniformly perfect objectivizations of man's religious experience. Within every true message uttered by the world religions there always lingers the illusion of myth; in all their yearning for God there remains a denial and flight from God; in all their hope for God's grace, a concealed self-redemption; in all their genuine conversion, an inadvertent turning-away. The world religions all stand in need of demythologizing and the casting out of devils, of interiorizing and humanizing. As non-Christian religions, though they are certainly not simply un-Christian, yet they are pre-Christian, directed toward Christ. And again, it is better not to call these pre-Christian religions "anonymously Christian", because it is precisely they *themselves* who do not know their own Christian character, though Christ does not deny his presence to them. The men of the world religions are not Christians by profession, but by designation, by vocation, and in some sense already by their affirmative response.

2. Only the preaching of the Gospel of Jesus Christ is able in this situation to bring light and to dissipate darkness, to liberate the truth, which is here to a large extent oppressed and held in bondage. The Gospel of Jesus Christ lights up the point of man's deepest need, and shows where his real salvation is to be found, what God really means for men and what man really has to be in the sight of God, what the real communion is between God and man. That is what, at bottom, the world religions cannot know. They do not believe in and confess him who alone can give them this knowledge in faith. The world religions are only religions; they are not churches, for this means a community of those who believe in Christ and confess him. But the individual people in the world religions are called upon existentially by the Church of Christ to make the decision of faith in Christ only at that point in time when they are reached not only by some report or information about the Gospel of Jesus Christ but by the preaching of that Gospel itself. Much non-belief is not an unbelieving rejection of the message of salvation but merely an inadequate encounter with a message not possessing, for this

particular man, the inviting and demanding force of revelation. ...

*(f) Christian faith represents radical universalism, but one grounded and made concrete in, and centered upon, Jesus Christ.* This *radical universalism* means, as has already been said:

1. *Every* human being is under God's grace and can be saved: whether he be of this or that nation or race, of this or that caste or class, free or slave, man or woman, or even inside or outside the Church of Christ. Every human being can be saved, and we may hope that everyone is.

2. Every world religion is under God's grace and can be a way of salvation: whether it is primitive or highly evolved, mythological or enlightened, mystical or rational, theistic or non-theistic, a real or only a quasi-religion. Every religion can be a way of salvation, and we may hope that every one is.

But we Christians in the Church of Christ believe this not on the basis of an indefinable, unaccountable mystical experience, which can in fact be a form of myth. We believe it on the basis of the message and history of Jesus Christ which has been testified to us. It is in Jesus Christ, in whom God himself has spoken and acted for all men in a unique way, that our radical universalism is grounded, centered, and made concrete. Hence *Christian* universalism is equally far removed from a narrow, limited, exclusive particularism and from an enfeebling, disintegrating, agnostic, relativistic indifferentism. Hence we have nothing to say for the totalitarian *domination* of *one* religion, which suppresses *freedom.* But neither have we anything to say for a syncretist *mingling* of all religions, which suppresses *truth.* What we believe in is *service* of the religions of the world by the Church of Jesus Christ, in love, which unites truth and freedom.

From this aspect one must also see the relationship to the religion of Israel, which will always remain a very special one, since the Church of Jesus Christ stems from it. What sins Christians have committed against Jews over the centuries have been in effect sins against the Gospel of Jesus Christ. They can only be judged, and judged severely, and we must therefore pray for forgiveness. The anti-Semitism of the National Socialists and their unparalleled crimes would have been impossible without the latent and too often vicious anti-Semitism of the Catholic and other Christian churches. Today we must, with all our energy, seek a new, positive relationship precisely with the Jews, both in theology and practice....

What, then, is the Church's task among the world religions? The Church is not a privileged, exclusive club for those who have got salvation as opposed to those who have not got it. She is not the "exclusive community of those awaiting salvation" but "the historically visible vanguard, ... the explicit embodiment, historically and socially constituted, of something which the Christian hopes is also given as a hidden reality outside the visibility of the church".[13] She is, as Israel was, the *pars pro toto,* the minority there to serve the majority, "the small number which represents the whole". She is – to make use of an expression of the first Vatican Council – the *signum levatum in nationes* (Denziger, 1794), the sign of the last times lifted up among the nations of the world, the sign of the fulfillment of all things which is the work of God, and which is already visibly initiated in her.

So as the vanguard of humanity, as the sign to the peoples, the Church is the community of believers, who are witnesses of Christ, confessing him in word and deed. They believe and confess that which is already a reality for the people of the world religions too, even though they do not wish to acknowledge it. As this community of believers and witnesses confessing Christ in word and deed, the Church is a living invitation, a joyful challenge to the people of the world religions, calling on them to unite with her in faith and to witness with her to the great things which God the Lord has done not only for her but for all; to join in offering praise and thanks, in listening ever anew to the word of God, and celebrating ever again the banquet of love, in witnessing to Christ in daily life as people who love not only each other, but all others as well. The Church is this sign of invitation to the peoples so that from Christians *de jure* they may become Christians *de facto*; from Christians *in spe*, Christians *in re*; that from being Christians by designation and vocation they may become Christians by profession and witness....

[13] Rahner, *op. cit.*, p. 156. [E.T., p. 133.]

# IO

## PRESENCE
## M. A. C. Warren, John Taylor

So FAR WE have explored the attitudes toward other religions on the part of scholars: theologians, philosophers, and historians, whose knowledge of other religions is primarily academic. In the following selection we meet one approach of men who are Christian missionaries and who thus have had daily contact with people of other religions.

The "Christian presence" approach to other religions has been described in some detail in the Introduction. The term "presence" in this context was brought into current usage by the Roman Catholic worker-priests in France after World War II. They were attempting to find a new approach to the working classes who had become almost completely estranged from the Church. Instead of preaching and teaching while living apart from the people, they decided that they must first become deeply involved in their lives by living among them and working beside them, by being present with them. The term has now passed into general political usage and we find references to the "United Nations presence" in the Middle East or the "federal presence" in Mississippi.

In 1964 the World Student Christian Federation adopted the idea of "Christian presence" in a policy statement which defined the phrase as follows:

As an expression of our faith, it points to the incarnation: God became man like us and lived among us. The man Jesus uncovers life for us. His identification with man, his humility, his form as a

servant, his freedom, his interest in those who were cast out of
society for either good or bad reasons, his forgiveness and judgment,
and his death are so like ours, and yet so unlike ours, that they
never cease to fascinate us. His presence has shown God to us. And
after his death he is present, we are told, and goes his quiet way
through history.... (The word "presence") tries to describe the
adventure of being there in the name of Christ, often anonymously,
listening before we speak, hoping that men will recognize Jesus for
what he is and stay where they are, involved in the fierce fight against
all that dehumanizes.... (*Student World*, Vol. LVIII (1965), pp.
233 f.)

This attitude toward other religions has been elaborated most
fully in a series of volumes under this title which deals with the
"Christian presence amid" each of the world religions. The
editor of this series is M. A. C. Warren (1904–   ), and the first part
of the selection below is his general introduction to the series in
the volume by John Taylor. Warren was educated at Cambridge
University, and after working as a missionary in Northern Nigeria
he returned to parish work in England for ten years. As General
Secretary of the Church Missionary Society of the Church of
England from 1942 to 1963, Warren became one of the most
distinguished missionary leaders of this century. The CMS,
which was founded in 1799, is one of the oldest and largest of
the English missionary societies and has traditionally been associated with the evangelical or "low church" wing of the Church of
England. Warren's many writings include *The Christian Mission*
(1951), *The Christian Imperative* (1955), *Challenge and Response*
(1959), and *Perspective in Mission* (1964). He is now Canon and
Sub-Dean of Westminster.

The second part of the selection below is taken from the
volume of the *Christian Presence Series* by John V. Taylor
(1914–   ) entitled *The Primal Vision: Christian Presence Amid
African Religion* (1963). After study at Cambridge and Oxford
and a few years in parish work Taylor spent several years as a
CMS missionary in Uganda. He was a member of the International Missionary Council for fifteen years and Africa Secretary
of the CMS from 1959 to 1963. In that year he succeeded
Warren as General Secretary of the CMS. His other writings in-

clude *The Growth of the Church in Buganda* (1958), and with D. Lehmann, *Christians of the Copperbelt* (1961).

Taylor's book deals with various aspects of African traditional religion and of that way of looking at man and the world which persists as an inarticulate philosophy long after the old religion has been discarded. In recognition of the fact that so many of the features of African religion occur elsewhere in the world, he calls this the "primal vision" and suggests that it involves universal elements in man's understanding of reality. Taylor discusses the mythical and allusive character of African language, the view of the self as extending beyond the confines of the body, and the sense of cosmic oneness or the mystical awareness of the affinity of all things. Man is understood essentially as a member of a family or tribe which includes the ancestors. Sin is understood as that which tends to destroy the life-force of another person or the family group. There is a certain ambivalence between the attitude toward the distant High God and that toward the hero-gods and the pervasive divine power. Taylor concludes with an investigation of the place of leader-mediator figures and mediums or diviners in African religion. At various points in the book he offers suggestions as to how various elements of Christian faith make contact with African religion. The selection by Taylor includes the final chapter of the book, entitled *The Practice of the Presence*, plus two earlier passages.

It has been noted in the Introduction that the "Christian presence" approach to other religions is a particular attitude rather than an interpretation of the significance of the other religions. As a matter of fact it could be combined with any one of the other approaches outlined in the Introduction except perhaps for that designated "Truth-Falsehood". The "Christian presence" view represents the openness of the missionary to the concrete reality of the other person's religion and an unwillingness to prejudge it by some framework which may distort it.

# Christian Presence Amid African Religion*

## GENERAL INTRODUCTION

CHRISTIANS ARE BEING presented by the contemporary world with what is, in many ways, a unique opportunity of demonstrating the Gospel. Scarcely less unique is the opportunity being offered to them of discovering in a new and deeper way what that Gospel is. Those are large claims. Can they be justified?

What is this unique opportunity? At the very least it is the opportunity presented to Christians to demonstrate the fundamental truth of the Gospel that it is a universal message, whose relevance is not limited to any one culture, to any one system of thought, to any one pattern of activity. That is by no means the truism that it may appear to be. For more than four centuries the expansion of the Christian Church has coincided with the economic, political, and cultural expansion of Western Europe. Viewed from the standpoint of the peoples of Asia, and to a growing extent from that of the peoples of Africa, this expansion has been an aggressive attack on their own way of life. Quite inevitably the Christian Faith has for many in these lands been inextricably bound up with this Western aggression. But it has also to be admitted quite frankly that during these centuries the missionaries of the Christian Church have commonly assumed that Western civilization and Christianity were two aspects of the same gift which they were commissioned to offer to the rest of mankind.

This assumption was sometimes quite conscious and was explicitly stated. More often it was quite unconscious and would have been indignantly denied. But in neither case are we called upon to judge our fathers. Their sincerity can hardly be disputed. Their self-sacrificing devotion finds its monument today in the world-wide diffusion of the Christian Faith, the existence, in almost every country of the world, of a community of Christians

* From John V. Taylor, *The Primal Vision: Christian Presence Amid African Religion* (Philadelphia: Fortress Press and London: SCM Press Ltd, 1963), pp. 5–12, 34–36, 113–114, 196–205.

recognizably part of the Universal Church.

What we are called upon to recognize is that in the world of our time there is a widespread revolt against any form of domination by the West. Nations whose political independence was only achieved "yesterday" or is only about to be achieved "tomorrow" can be excused for having their own interpretation of the past, an interpretation unlikely to coincide with that which is prevalent in the West. This very waning of Western influence is in part our Christian opportunity. We are freer today than we have ever been to serve the Gospel without the risk of confusion between that Gospel and the "power" of the West.

But that is not all. The peoples of Asia and Africa, in their revolt against domination by the West, are presenting a specific challenge to the Christian Faith. In what does this consist?

There are three main ingredients in this challenge.

*First* there is a critical evaluation of the Christian religion which rejects it as something inherently Western, as something which fails to correspond to the *felt* needs of Asia and Africa. Christianity is, in such judgment, altogether too Western in its character and in the form which it assumes in its local manifestations. This rejection is the more serious in that Asian and African peoples are themselves, like us in the West, confronted by the bewildering demands of the modern world. All the old landmarks are disappearing. Everywhere there is a desperate search for some inner basis of security, some inner assurance which can enable men and women to face the storm. In the sequel, particularly in Asia, but not only there, the peoples of these countries are seeking to find this psychic security by digging deep into their own past. This is at once an expression of their revolt against the West and one explanation of the renaissance of the great ethnic religions. Further to this it is noted that in a new way these ancient religions are becoming themselves missionary. No longer content to be on the defensive, they are offering themselves as answers to the questionings of mankind.

Here is a situation which is new. Only once before, and then in its earliest centuries, has the Christian Church had to face a comparable challenge to its claim to meet the deepest needs of man's heart and mind. The devotees of Mithras, the mystery cults of the Mediterranean world, the Gnostics in that earlier day were serious competitors with the message of the Gospel. Their appeal failed. There followed the long thousand years during which Europe was isolated from the rest of mankind and built for itself its own peculiar civilization. Then suddenly, drawing on its inner dynamism, a dynamism closely related to its faith, the European world overflowed its narrow boundaries and began its great expansion. For a time it appeared as if nothing could arrest this expansion. It is of some importance to recognize that it is by no means certain that anything can! The scientific view of the world, with all its implications about human survival, is Western in origin. Communism and nationalism are Western concepts. It may well be doubted if anything can arrest the advance of all mankind toward something like a common civilization – if common destruction is avoided. Nevertheless, there is, at the moment, a significant pause in the impetus of Western expansion in its Christian expression. The challenge to Christians is precisely this, that the ethnic religions as well as secularist philosophies of life are offering themselves as the basis of the new world civilization. Both deny the relevance of Christianity.

The *second* challenge follows from the first. Can the Christian Faith not only prove its ability to meet the deep human needs of our time but also make peoples of different cultural backgrounds feel at home in the new world? This is a more complex task than would appear. For it is part of our paradoxical situation that, at a moment when the world is becoming so obviously interdependent, every nation in it is seeking to assert its own independence. And religion and culture are the means by which independence is asserted. Has the Christian Church got a Gospel to meet this situation? We may put the question this way – can the Christians of the West accept the fact that the expression which Christianity will receive in its Asian and African forms may well be, almost certainly will be, in many respects very different indeed from what we know in the West? That again could be worded as follows – are we of the West prepared to trust the Holy Spirit to lead the Christians of Asia and Africa or must a controlling Western hand be permanently resting on the Ark of God? Let no one imagine that those questions will find an easy or unanimous response from Western Christians.

There remains a *third* challenge. The Christian Church has not yet seriously faced the theological problem of "co-existence" with other religions. The very term seems to imply the acceptance of some limitation of the universal relevance of the Gospel. Can that be accepted? It can hardly be doubted that the answer must be "no". Are we then shut up to the alternatives of what in some disguise or other must be an aggressive attack on the deeply held convictions of those who live by other Faiths than our own?

This book, originally one in the *Christian Presence Series,* has been designed to express a deliberate recognition of the challenge outlined above and to suggest that there is a way in which they can be met without any betrayal of the Gospel – indeed, in deeper loyalty to that Gospel's real content.

*First* of the demands presented to us by this understanding of the contemporary world is a *glad* acceptance of the new situation in which the Christian Faith can everywhere be distinguished from its past historical association with Western political, economic, and cultural aggression. Here is the "great new fact of our time", every whit as great a fact as the existence of the Church in every land. Here is our great new opportunity, even though it may well be an opportunity to witness through suffering. The Cross, after all, was not a symbol of imperial domination but of the *imperium* of sacrifice. The Christian Faith has nothing to lose by suffering. In and through suffering it can perhaps speak home to the hearts and minds of suffering mankind better than in any other way.

*Second* of the demands upon us, to march with our gladness, is a deep humility, by which we remember that God has not left himself without witness in any nation at any time. When we approach the man of another faith than our own it will be in a spirit of expectancy to find how God has been speaking to him and what new understandings of the grace and love of God we may ourselves discover in this encounter.

Our first task in approaching another people, another culture, another religion, is to take off our shoes, for the place we are approaching is holy. Else we may find ourselves treading on men's dreams. More seriously still, we may forget that God was here before our arrival. We have, then, to ask what is the authentic religious content in the experience of the Muslim, the Hindu, the Buddhist, or whoever he may be. We may, if we have asked humbly and respectfully, still reach the conclusion that our brothers have started from a false premiss and reached a faulty conclusion. But we must not arrive at our judgment from outside their religious situation. We have to try to sit where they sit, to enter sympathetically into the pains and griefs and joys of their history and see how those pains and griefs and joys have determined the premisses of their argument. We have, in a word, to be "present" with them.

The present volume essays the ambitious task of offering some clues to what is happening in that spiritual conflict which is modern Africa. For spiritual conflict it is and that in its essence. The very cry of "*uhuru*", "freedom", is only in a derived sense a word of political or economic significance. It is by accident, tragic no less for being an accident, that it has racial overtones. The cry is wrung from the heart of what Laurens van der Post has described as "a battle about being and non-being; about having a soul of one's own or not having a soul at all". The cry may not even be directed against foreign dominion because it may just as well spring straight from the heart of an African who is the citizen of a politically independent country. It is important for us to understand this or we shall fail to understand that Africa of tomorrow, when all Africa will still be seeking "uhuru".

The spiritual conflict in Africa is a striving to re-establish that primal unity of man with both the material and the spiritual universe which African man instinctively feels to be true "being", and which hardly exists anywhere in Africa today. Believing this, the author seeks to establish first of all the essentially African way of feeling the truth about things, a "feeling after the truth", which finds expression in an illimitable anthology of proverbial sayings rather than in any systematic philosophy. To get at this feeling one has to be present with the African, living with him and entering into his world of thought. This Mr Taylor has done in a way not given to many and it is out of his own intimate knowledge of Africa and of rich friendships with many Africans in different parts of the continent that this book is written.

Africa is a vast continent, and all generalizations about Africa and Africans must be suspect. But we can find tracks into the forest, the enchanted forest of Africa, a world which the West only enters in its dreams. This book charts some of these tracks. One African translation of John 1. 16 in a literal rendering into English would read, "We have all received grace following hard upon grace": and the picture is of a procession of people threading their way single file along a bush or forest track. Certainly along the tracks marked here there is evidence that the grace of our Lord Jesus Christ is to be found at the heart of Africa's primal vision.

> Lift the stone and you will find me
> Cleave the wood and I am there.

That is not pantheism but the claim of the Omnipresent, full of grace and truth, in the fellowship of whose service is "uhuru" . . .

## The Language of Myth

To put the matter in its extremest form, leaving out of account neo-Africanism and the residuum of old ideas in the Church, as the Christian meets the pagan and attempts to proclaim Christ, is it a simple case of either-or? Westermann, whose opinion cannot lightly be ignored, said yes.

However anxious a missionary may be to appreciate and to retain indigenous social and moral values, in the case of religion he has to be ruthless ... he has to admit and even to emphasize that the religion he teaches is opposed to the existing one and the one has to cede to the other.[1]

Ruthlessness has had a long run in Africa, and so long as the missionary encounter is conceived of as a duologue one will have to "cede to the other". But may it not be truer to see it as a meeting of three, in which Christ has drawn together the witness who

[1] D. Westermann, *Africa and Christianity*, p. 94.

proclaims him and the other who does not know his name, so that in their slow discovery of one another each may discover more of him? It is even possible that the one who, as busy Martha, prays that her sister may be roused up to serve the Lord like herself, may learn to her surprise that that same sister has been drinking in words of his that she herself has never heard. Christ is incomparably unique. As a man in Christ the Christian shares that uniqueness; but as a man with another religion he stands in the same quest and under the same judgment as the pagan.

His desire and longing, therefore, must be to enter, sensitively and appreciatively, into that other man's world, not, first, in order to *talk* more effectively about his Lord but in order to *see* what the Lord of that world is like. Those who have not shared the terrors of a half-sinking ship at the height of a storm can never see the glory that comes walking on the waves at midnight. Only from within the nightmare world of the possessed can one know what he who casts out demons looks like, only from within the tomb can one hear the voice that summoned Lazarus, only from a cross see the dying robber's king. As Western Christians we have seen Christ coming, thank God, into our individualized lives, redeeming our particular situation, delivering us from our own type of temptation. But until our vision is aligned to the African way of looking at things, until we have felt our individuality vanishing and our pulses beating to communal rhythms and communal fears, how can we guess what that Lord looks like who is the Saviour of the African world? The motive of this approach, as Walter Freytag so often reminded us,

... is much more than providing information. It is trying to understand. There is a great difference between them. The mere possession of information may involve no change at all. But understanding involves a two-way traffic. For you do not "understand" anything until you have been touched (affected) yourself, until you get a new insight into who you are yourself. In the study of other religions you can amass information about their scriptures and doctrines. But you have not understood them until you have been compelled to interpret your own Gospel in entirely new terms. You have not really understood another religion.... There is no understanding of other religions which does not yield new biblical insights. What is more, such understanding also yields new insights as to the nature of the Church . . .[2]

It is the lordship of Christ which is in question. Either he is the Lord of all possible worlds and of all human cultures or he is Lord of one world and one culture only. Either we must think of the Christian Mission in terms of bringing the Muslim, the Hindu, the Animist into Christendom, or we must go with Christ as he stands in the midst of Islam, of Hinduism, of the primal world-view, and watch with him, fearfully and wonderingly, as he becomes – dare we say it – Muslim or Hindu or Animist, as once he became man, and a Jew. Once, led by the Spirit, the Church made its choice in this matter at the Council of Jerusalem and dared to win the Gentiles by becoming Gentile. Paul and those who followed him did not wait for history to reduce the Graeco-Roman world to chaos and drive its derelicts into the arms of the Church. They claimed that world in its strength and reformulated the Gospel in the terms of its wisdom. So Christ in his Church answered the call of the Greeks; he came where they were and became what they were. From within their own culture he challenged their strength and judged their wisdom. He turned their world upside down, just as he had turned Judaism upside down – just as, indeed, if he enters our Churches today, he turns our Christianity upside down. So would he challenge and judge and revolutionize the African world-view; but he must do it from the inside. . . .

## THE PRACTICE OF THE PRESENCE

This, like other books in the same series, is an attempt to explore an approach to men of another faith and culture which is reverent and attentive, and which consists essentially not of assertion, nor even of action, but of presence. If the preceding chapters have had any validity they point to the peculiar rightness of such an approach in Africa. The core of Africa's wisdom is that she knows the difference between existence and presence. "Europeans", they say, "are people who do not greet one another

[2] W. Freytag, quoted by M. A. C. Warren in *Basileia*, Evang. Missions-verlag, Stuttgart 1959, p. 164.

in the street." It is easy to excuse ourselves by pointing at the congestion in Oxford Street, but that is only to endorse their critique of such a civilization. For we ourselves know what it means, as a stranger passes us on the pavement, to catch a fleeting, spontaneous smile and to know we are recognized not by name but simply for our humanity. For a moment our presence to one another, eye to eye and face to face, dispels the isolation and lifts our hearts.

Africans believe that presence is the debt they owe to one another. That is why Nantume the schoolgirl came to sit silently as I ironed my clothes that day, and ended her visit as all such visits are closed, with the words, "I have seen you." Not to be seen, not to be recognized, to become invisible and anonymous, is the burden that subverts the integrity of all those whom the city swallows.

The primal vision is of a world of presences, of face-to-face meeting not only with the living but just as vividly with the dead and with the whole totality of nature. It is a universe of I and Thou. Let us not sentimentalize. Africa does not achieve this sensitive receptivity toward the other person all the time. There are many dull and blind and callous, and the range of their awareness is limited, as we have seen. But the vision is there and the longing is everywhere alive – which is more than we of the West can say.

The Christian, whoever he may be, who stands in that world in the name of Christ, has nothing to offer unless he offers to be present, really and totally present, really and totally *in* the present. The failure of so many "professional" Christians has been that they are "not all there"!

In the first place this means simply friendship, unassuming and undemanding, offered to the other man. "We come into his presence, not he into ours. He will feel the same way. If we strain to show off before him, we shall miss him. If we try to control him, he will fade away. No matter how familiar and good to us, presence is elusive. Its spontaneity rebuffs all forced intimacy." [3] If one offers such friendship in Africa, in spite of all the rising

[3] Ralph Harper, *The Sleeping Beauty*, Harvill, 1956, p. 122.

barriers of disillusionment and mistrust, it is likely to be met with
the same response that Saint-Exupéry expressed in his *Letter to a
Hostage*, which is so extraordinarily relevant to relationships in
Africa at the present time.

My friend, I need your friendship. I am weary of all these con-
troversies, of all these refusals to listen to the other man, of all the
fanaticisms! I can go to you without dressing up in a uniform, or
having to listen to the recitation of any Koran, or having to give up
any part of what is inside me. When I am with you there is no need
for me to be for ever defending my ideas or my conduct, no need to
plead my case, no need to prove I am right; I find peace.... Over
and beyond my clumsy expressions and the arguments with which
I may be deceiving myself, you merely consider the man in me. You
respect me as the exponent of certain beliefs, customs, loves and
loyalties, and my difference from you, far from diminishing you,
gives you increase. Your questions are those one puts to a traveller.[4]

A humble reverence that never desires to manipulate or possess
or use the other is always a feature of the face-to-face encounter
of true presence, and therefore it flourishes in silence. Ralph
Harper, whose exquisite book, *The Sleeping Beauty*, has done so
much to illumine the world of presence, has this to say:

Each order of experience has its own atmosphere. The atmosphere
of presence, of giving, of wholeness, is silence. We know that serious
things have to be done in silence, because we do not have words to
measure the immeasurable. In silence men love, pray, listen, compose,
paint, write, think, suffer. These experiences are all occasions of giving
and receiving, of some encounter with forces that are inexhaustible
and independent of us. These are easily distinguishable from our
routines and possessiveness as silence is distinct from noise.[5]

In contrast to the silence of God how much of the mission of
his Church seems to be contrived in "routines and possessiveness". As Harper goes on to say, "All men choose either compassion or jabbering. The more we chatter, the busier we seem,
but the farther from God's silence and God's Word." Those who
have lost the capacity for listening, who cannot be there for others,
are unable even to be truly present to themselves. In their busy
self-assertion they never meet themselves; they are distracted,

[4] Quoted in *Iesus Caritas*, Association Charles de Jésus, Paris, 1958,
p. 97.
[5] Ralph Harper, *op. cit.*, p. 111.

strained, dispersed. Only the silence, only the practice of the presence of God, in sacrament and meditation, in a steady painful flowering of sensitivity to all presences, can restore and integrate so that given-ness can be maintained.

"Compassion" is the final operative word to define what the way of presence really means. It sums up the listening, responsive, agonizing receptivity of the prophet and the poet. For it is impossible to be open and sensitive in one direction without being open to all. If a man would open his heart toward his fellow he must keep it open to all other comers – to the stranger, to the dead, to the enchanting and awful presences of nature, to powers of beauty and terror, to the pain and anxiety of men, to the menace and catastrophe of our time, and to the overwhelming presence of God. So many of our Eucharists fall short of the glory of God because, while purporting to concentrate on the Real Presence of Christ, they seem to be oblivious to the real presence of men, either in the worshipping family or in the world around. To present oneself to God means to expose oneself, in an intense and vulnerable awareness, not only to him but to all that is. And this is what, apart from Christ, we dare not do. Presence is too much for us to face.

In Dahomey a married man with children of his own is forbidden to use the same gateway to the homestead as his father, lest they meet face to face, life-force against life-force. By the same precaution, to avoid a direct encounter, man has tried to relegate God to a separate realm of existence. This is the truth that seems to emerge undeniably from a study of the primal vision. The celestial God whose divinity consists in kingly authority raised to an Olympian degree of remoteness is a man-made God, and in Africa we have actually seen the process taking place. And the more remote God is made to appear, the greater is the need for magic. If his hand is not there to protect and heal, if his eyes are indifferent to the mustering forces of darkness, then charms and spells and curses must be enlisted against them. Some see in the story of the coming of the magi to Bethlehem the representative magicians of that ancient world surrendering the instruments of their craft to the incarnate God.

Only Immanuel – God himself involved in every contingency – can render magic unnecessary.

The God whom, all along, Africa has guessed at and dreamed of, is One who is always and wholly present for every part of his creation. His trancendence has been too spatially conceived. It must be looked for in the quality of his love, and love, as Brunner has said, is "being there for others". In his sovereign will he created the universe by committing himself to it. The absolute difference between himself and all other is that his very nature is to give himself totally while remaining inexhaustibly himself. The bush burning but not consumed, the widow's cruse of oil, the loaves and fishes, the Eucharistic Bread and Wine – these are the true symbols of his relationship to the created world.

In Africa, as elsewhere, speculation about the existence of God may be less true than the sense of the presence of God, that Presence which mysteriously takes the initiative and, under many forms, suddenly confronts man on the road. "For," says Irenaeus, "as they who see the light are within the light and perceive its brilliancy, so they who see God are within God as they behold his splendour." [6]

Something of this is implicit, as we have seen, in the Bushman's story of *Dxui*. It is echoed, also, in the astonishing answer given by a Tswana to David Livingstone's question, What is holiness (*boitsepho*)?

When copious showers have descended during the night, and all the earth and leaves and cattle are washed clean and the sun rising shows a drop of dew on every blade of grass, and the air breathes fresh, that is holiness. [7]

Many of the fathers of Eastern and Celtic monasticism might have said the same. So also would at least one of the great Jewish rabbinic schools.

A heathen asked Rabbi Joshua ben Karka, Why did God speak to Moses from the thorn bush? Rabbi Joshua replied, If he had spoken from a carob tree or from a sycamore you would have asked me the same question! But so as not to dismiss you without an answer, God

[6] Irenaeus, *Adv. Haer.*, iv, 20. 7.

[7] D. Livingstone, *Expedition to the Zambesi*, Murray, 1865, p. 64.

spoke from the thorn bush to teach you that there is no place where the Shekinah is not, not even a thorn bush.[8]

Yet he might have said that a bush of thorns is the very place where one should most expect to see the full glory of the givenness of God. For the Cross is the measure of his self-commitment to the creation. It is the price of his patient, unpossessive friendship toward mankind. Its three hours of silence summed up all the long aeons of his watch for man's return; its loneliness was the desolation of a presence endlessly rebuffed, unrecognized, anonymous; its agony contained his eternal compassion toward the bent world. Middleton Murry, in his commentary on the letters of Keats, speaks of this attitude of enduring presence toward the mystery and paradox of existence.

"For this other kind of forgiveness," he says, "a forgiveness which forgives not only man, but life itself, not only the pains which men inflict but the pains which are knit up with the very nature of existence, we have no word. Let it be called ... Acceptance." [9] One would add that the Cross affirms that the divine acceptance is not complacency; it is acceptance of final involvement and responsibility.

Yet, intense as is his divine receptivity toward every sin and every pain in every creature, he is present also with vivid awareness toward all beauty, all faith, all achievement. For the joy that is set before him he endures, and his presence is vibrant with triumph and resurrection.

That is the tremendous Presence in the midst of the world from which our first parents hid themselves and from which Cain went forth into loneliness. That is the Presence which Moses knew, eye to eye and face to face, without which the building of the Chosen Community had no significance or attraction. That is the Presence which is promised unto the end of the world to those who go to disciple all the nations. And this alone is their warrant for believing that the way of presence is not merely a new missionary method, but God's own way of drawing Adam into

[8] C. G. Montefiore and H. Loewe, *A Rabbinic Anthology*, Macmillan, 1938, p. 13.

[9] Quoted by "Nicodemus", *Renascence*, Faber, 1943, p. 60.

his embrace and lifting the despoiled and threatened Creation up into his peace.

There have been a few moments in the history of the Church since the writing of the epistles to the Ephesians and the Colossians when men have built their faith upon this understanding of God. Irenaeus was one such, and the great Celtic saints followed in the same path. The eighth-century writer of the famous "Deer's Cry", which we know as St. Patrick's Breastplate, invoked in one prayer all the presences that met him with grace in the world of sense and of spirit. It sums up and contains all the spiritual awareness of the primal vision and lifts it into the fulness of Christ. Would that it were translated and sung in every tongue of Africa!

> I arise today
> Through a mighty strength, the invocation of the Trinity
> Through belief in the threeness
> Through confession of the oneness
> Of the Creator of Creation.
>
> I arise today
> Through the strength of Christ's birth with His baptism,
> Through the strength of His crucifixion with His burial,
> Through the strength of His resurrection with His ascension,
> Through the strength of his coming down for Judgment.
>
> I arise today
> Through the strength of the love of Cherubim,
> In obedience of angels,
> In the service of archangels,
> In prayers of ancestors,
> In predictions of prophets,
> In preachings of apostles,
> In faith of confessors,
> In deeds of righteous men.
>
> I arise today
> Through the strength of heaven; –
> Light of sun,
> Radiance of moon,
> Splendour of fire,
> Speed of lightning,
> Swiftness of wind,
> Depth of sea,

Stability of earth,
Firmness of rock.

I arise today
Through God's strength to pilot me,
God's might to uphold me,
God's wisdom to guide me,
God's hand to guard me,
God's shield to protect me,
God's host to save me,
From snares of devils,
From temptations of vices,
From all who shall wish me ill,
Afar and near,
Alone and in multitude.

I summon today all these powers between me and those evils,
Against every cruel merciless power that may oppose my body
    and soul,
Against incantations of false prophets,
Against black laws of pagandom,
Against spells of witches,
Against every knowledge that corrupts man's body and soul.

Christ to shield me this day
So that there come to me abundance of reward.
Christ with me, Christ before me, Christ behind me,
Christ in me, Christ beneath me, Christ above me,
Christ when I lie down, Christ when I sit, Christ when I arise,
Christ in the heart of every man who thinks of me,
Christ in the mouth of everyone who speaks of me,
Christ in every eye that sees me,
Christ in every ear that hears me.[10]

[10] Translation by Kuno Meyer, *Selections from Ancient Irish Poetry*
(2nd ed.), Constable 1913, p. 25.